THE ETHICS EDGE

SECOND EDITION

Edited by Jonathan P. West
and Evan M. Berman

D1315062

PRESS

ICMA is the premier local government leadership and management organization. Its mission is to create excellence in local governance by developing and advocating professional management of local government worldwide. ICMA provides member support; publications, data, and information; peer and results-oriented assistance; and training and professional development to more than 8,200 city, town, and county experts and other individuals throughout the world.

Library of Congress Cataloging-in-Publication Data

The ethics edge / edited by Jonathan P. West, Evan M. Berman. -- 2nd ed.
    p. cm.
  Includes bibliographical references.
  ISBN 0-87326-710-9
  1. Political ethics. 2. Business ethics. 3. Professional ethics. 4. Social values.
  I. West, Jonathan P. (Jonathan Page), 1941- II. Berman, Evan M.
  JA79.E8236 2006
  172--dc22

                                        2006030014

Copyright © 2006 by the International City/County Management Association, 777 North Capitol Street, N.E., Suite 500, Washington, D.C. 20002. All rights reserved, including rights of reproduction and use in any form or by any means, including the making of copies by any photographic process, or by any electrical or mechanical device, printed, written, or oral or recording for sound or visual reproduction, or for use in any knowledge or retrieval system or device, unless permission in writing is obtained from the copyright proprietor.

Printed in the United States of America

2013 2012 2011 2010 2009 2008 2007 2006

5 4 3 2 1

Foreword

A series of highly publicized scandals and ethics violations by both public- and private-sector officials has brought with it a renewed interest in ethics at all levels of government. At a time when many citizens have become cynical and distrustful of their elected and appointed leaders, local government professionals and scholars are focusing new attention on ethics research, education, and leadership.

This second edition of ICMA's book *The Ethics Edge* brings together the best and most current contributions to the field of ethics in government, continuing the organization's long-standing commitment to providing standards and guidance for its members and other professionals. In reviewing the literature, the editors cast a wide net—selecting local government examples when they existed and drawing in relevant articles with a private-sector or state/federal focus to flesh out the coverage.

The book is intended to help readers gain new insights into enduring values and principles, meet contemporary challenges such as those posed by new technologies, and institutionalize ethical norms, values, and behavior in their organizations through state-of-the-art ethics management practices.

A new feature of this edition is the inclusion of case examples drawn from real-life ethics dilemmas facing public officials. Each case presents a scenario, the perspectives of the players involved, the ethical principles at stake, and questions for discussion. The cases enhance the book's usefulness in public administration courses and provide professional managers with food for thought.

ICMA is grateful to Jonathan P. West and Evan M. Berman, who edited the volume; to ICMA member Stephen J. Bonczek and ICMA deputy director Elizabeth K. Kellar for contributing case examples; and to the publishers and authors who granted ICMA permission to reprint materials for inclusion. Other staff members who helped bring the volume to fruition were Ann I. Mahoney, director of publishing; Barbara H. Moore, editor; and Nedra M. James, publications assistant.

Robert J. O'Neill, Jr.
Executive Director
ICMA

About the Editors and Authors

Following are the affiliations of the editors and authors at the time of writing.

Editors

Jonathan P. West is Professor of Political Science and Director of the Graduate Public Administration Program at the University of Miami. For the past two decades he has taught a graduate course on ethics in the public sector. His research interests include public administration, human resource management, productivity, and ethics. Professor West has published nearly 100 articles and book chapters. His most recent books are *American Public Service: Radical Reform and the Merit System* (Auerbach, 2007) co-edited with Bowman; *Human Resource Management: Paradoxes, Processes and Problems* (2nd ed., Sage, 2006) and *The Professional Edge* (M. E. Sharpe, 2004), both co-authored with Berman, Bowman, and Van Wart; and *American Politics and the Environment* (Longman, 2002), co-authored with Sussman and Daynes. He is the managing editor of *Public Integrity*. He taught previously at the University of Houston and the University of Arizona and served as a management analyst in the U.S. Surgeon General's Office, Department of the Army, Washington, D.C.

Evan M. Berman is Professor in the Department of Public Administration at Louisiana State University. He has previously taught at the University of Miami and the University of Central Florida. Dr. Berman also served as a policy analyst for the National Science Foundation and as a consultant to the U.S. Congress. Dr. Berman has published nearly 100 articles and book chapters. His recent books include *Essential Statistics for Public Managers and Policy Analysts* (2nd ed., CQ Press, 2007), *Performance and Productivity in Public and Nonprofit Organizations* (2nd ed., M. E. Sharpe, 2006), *Human Resource Management: Paradoxes, Processes and Problems* (2nd ed., Sage, 2006), and *The Professional Edge* (M. E. Sharpe, 2004), the last two co-authored with Bowman, West, and Van Wart. He is managing editor of *Public Performance & Management Review*. He has published widely on the topics of ethics and productivity improvement in local government, and frequently assists local governments in conducting citizen surveys and community-based planning.

Article authors

Scott Avelino, Director, KPMG's forensic practice, Washington, D.C.

James S. Bowman, Professor, Department of Public Administration, Florida State University.

Stephen Covey, Founder and Chair of the Board, Covey Leadership Institute.

J. Patrick Dobel, Associate Dean, Graduate School of Public Affairs, University of Washington.

Gregory D. Foster, Professor, Industrial College of the Armed Forces, National Defense University, Washington, D.C.

H. George Frederickson, Edwin O. Stene Distinguished Professor, University of Kansas, Lawrence, Kansas.

David W. Haines, Associate Professor of Anthropology, George Mason University.

Leo Huberts, Professor of Public Administration and Public Integrity, Department of Public Administration and Organization Science, Free University of Amsterdam, Netherlands.

Michael Josephson, Author and Founder, Josephson Institute of Ethics.

Muel Kaptein, Professor of Business Ethics and Integrity Management, Department of Business-Society Management, Erasmus University Rotterdam, Netherlands, and KPMG integrity consultant and auditor.

Elizabeth K. Kellar, Deputy Executive Director, International City/County Management Association, and former member and chair, Montgomery County (Maryland) Ethics Commission.

Karin Lasthuizen, Senior Researcher on Integrity of Governance, Department of Public Administration and Organization Science, Free University of Amsterdam, Netherlands.

Wendell C. Lawther, Associate Professor of Public Administration, University of Central Florida.

Michael W. Manske, Associate Professor, Department of Criminal Justice, Washburn University, Topeka, Kansas.

Donald Menzel, Professor Emeritus, Division of Public Administration, Northern Illinois University.

Peter G. Northouse, Professor of Communication, University of Western Michigan.

Dennis F. Thompson, Alfred North Whitehead Professor of Political Philosophy, Harvard University.

Neal Trautman, Director, National Institute of Ethics, Longwood, Florida.

Montgomery Van Wart, Professor and Chair, Department of Public Administration, University of Central Florida.

Craig M. Wheeland, Associate Professor of Political Science, Villanova University.

Case authors

Stephen J. Bonczek is pursuing a career in financial services as a Financial Advisor. He has 30 years of local government management experience, including six manager/administrator positions in cities and townships.

Stuart C. Gilman, Director, Global Programme Against Corruption, United Nations Office on Drugs and Crime (UNODC).

Elizabeth K. Kellar, Deputy Executive Director, International City/County Management Association, and former member and chair, Montgomery County (Maryland) Ethics Commission.

Carol W. Lewis, Professor, Department of Political Science, University of Connecticut.

Contents

Introduction ix
Jonathan P. West and Evan M. Berman

Part 1 Foundations
Ethics: Time to Revisit the Basics 3
Gregory D. Foster

The Six Pillars of Character 11
Michael Josephson

Moral Compassing 18
Stephen Covey

The Ethical Professional: Cultivating Scruples 24
James S. Bowman

Part 2 Implementation: Ethical Leadership
An Ethics-Based Approach to Leadership 39
Montgomery Van Wart

Leadership Ethics 46
Peter G. Northouse

Political Prudence and the Ethics of Leadership 55
J. Patrick Dobel

Demonstrating Ethical Leadership by Measuring Ethics:
A Survey of U.S. Public Servants 69
Muel Kaptein, Leo Huberts, Scott Avelino, and Karin Lasthuizen

Part 3 Implementation: Ethics Management
The Corruption Continuum:
How Law Enforcement Organizations Become Corrupt 83
Neal Trautman

Fatal Choices: The Routinization of Deceit, Incompetence, and Corruption 89
David W. Haines

Building a Strong Local Government Ethics Program 101
Michael W. Manske and H. George Frederickson

Ethics Management in Cities and Counties 108
Donald Menzel

Partisan Politics, Ethics, and the Home Rule Charter:
A Township Manager's Ethical Dilemma 116
Craig M. Wheeland

Ethics Training in U.S. Cities: Content, Pedagogy, and Impact. 125
Jonathan P. West and Evan M. Berman

Part 4 Ethical Challenges

Ethical Challenges in Privatizing Government Services. 145
Wendell C. Lawther

Private Life and Public Office 156
Dennis F. Thompson

Public Cynicism: Manifestations and Responses. 167
Evan M. Berman

Current Ethics Issues for Local Government Managers 175
Elizabeth K. Kellar

Appendix A: Ethics Cases. 187

Appendix B: Techno Quiz: Ethics in the Age of Cybertechnology 201

Appendix C: ICMA Code of Ethics with Guidelines 205

Appendix D: For Further Reading 211

Introduction

Jonathan P. West and Evan M. Berman

The second edition of this book, *The Ethics Edge*, brings together up-to-date articles that provide new insights on values in government and the public administration profession. It highlights state-of-the-art ethics management practices and challenging ethical issues.

Clearly, ethics shape and define the nature of public professions. Managers and employees who are informed by ethics have an added "edge" because they are more likely to know the right thing to do, to undertake those actions, to justify actions on the basis of professional and moral criteria, and to protect themselves against being blindsided by allegations of ethical impropriety. These competencies are critical in today's management environment; ethics mold the aspirations and roles that managers fulfill in their organizations and jurisdictions and help define core values and beliefs that direct managerial action. By contrast, managers who act with inadequate regard to core values and professional ethics take an increased risk of jeopardizing their careers, the reputations of their jurisdictions, and the public interest.

The past decade has witnessed a resurgent interest in ethics in the wake of numerous scandals and ethics violations involving both elected and appointed officials. These scandals have left government with a public trust deficit and a profession besieged by voices that favor scaling back the role and size of government. The causes of these events, conditions, and attacks are varied and include public backlash against perceived growth of government, revelations of unethical and illegal conduct in the private and nonprofit sectors, and unscrupulous actions by a few high-profile public officials.

Two-track response

As a result of these developments, new efforts are underway in many jurisdictions and among professional organizations to rebuild public trust and respond to vitriolic attacks on the character and competence of public managers. Responses to ethics lapses often follow two separate, parallel tracks—one legal and the other behavioral. Laws and codes are adopted to define and forbid wrongdoing, and training efforts are undertaken to help employees and managers do the right thing.

The legal response to ethical concerns has been the passage of laws and policies defining and prohibiting unethical activities such as sexual harassment, discrimination, and invasion of privacy and mandating ethical behaviors regarding conflict of interest, financial disclosure, and post-service employment with contractors. Governments at all levels have adopted such laws and policies, and the laws have helped to highlight the need for proper conduct in many important situations and undoubtedly have had a deterrent effect on those who might engage in wrongdoing. Yet this track also has some limitations. Legal standards do not exist for all ethics-related areas of professional activity, and ethics laws are seldom sufficient to deal with a growing number of poorly defined situations. Laws cannot govern every foreseeable circumstance in which an ethics question is likely to arise. Moreover, employees and managers may not always be aware of the many provisions of ethics laws, and they may be unclear about how these laws apply to their situation. In fact, the extent of the deterrent effect is largely unknown. An interesting unintended consequence of vigorous prosecution has been to sharpen public distrust in government, as more corruption and other unethical acts are exposed. Thus, while the legal response continues to be important, it is increasingly regarded as insufficient for ensuring a proper ethical climate.

For these reasons, a second behavioral track has grown in importance. Training and information are employed to help managers and employees recognize the positive ideals of public service that are the hallmark of ethics. Training helps employees apply these aspirational concepts to their real-life work situations and identify strategies for dealing with ethical dilemmas. Through training and feedback, organizations further shape expectations about ethical conduct. Initially, many strategies centered on developing codes of ethics. Although codes have little impact when they merely "hang on the wall" or "collect dust on the shelf," they can be a first step in helping individuals and groups to think through their values and aspirations. But in the last five to ten years, training efforts have become more specific, using a broader range of scenarios and strategies shaping and defining ethical responsibility for specific workplace situations. ICMA contributed to those efforts by publishing *Ethical Insight, Ethical Action* (1988), a then state-of-the-art collection of articles. *The Ethics Factor* (1988) was an ICMA training package for local government managers and employees that provided cases, exercises, and guidance in developing codes. ICMA also published *Ethos* (1994), a multimedia CD-ROM that contains forty-two cases for ethical decision making. In the late 1990s, ICMA updated these earlier publications by publishing the first edition of *The Ethics Edge* (1998) and a new two-volume ethics training package, *Ethics in Action* (1999).

The dual legal and behavioral developments during the last decade now call for a new volume on ethics. Following these advances, the second edition of *The Ethics Edge* includes articles at the frontier of ethical thinking, applied to new, emerging areas, and takes stock of lessons and insights that have been learned. This second edition includes new selections about effective approaches in ethics management and the challenges public officials must confront. Many of these issues are confronted by managers in the private and nonprofit sectors as well. The book also includes articles about the ethics of managing information technology, rebuilding public trust, maintaining dual-career families, reconciling private life and public office, and addressing public cynicism. These new arenas for ethical action demand our concern. Some new articles deal with fundamental ethical virtues such as integrity, honesty, and prudence and present case examples of ethical dilemmas that encourage analysis from multiple perspectives. Together the selections examine ethics in new ways that have practical use for managers.

Fostering ethics in the organization

How is ethical behavior shaped and maintained in organizations? While consensus on this point among professionals and scholars is still evolving, it is now possible to identify a system with the following elements: (1) executive and managerial leadership that sets the tone of ethics in organizations; (2) codes of ethics that specify core values and norms; (3) human resource management (HRM) strategies that implement these values and norms through mechanisms such as hiring, promotion, performance appraisal, training, and termination; (4) daily management activities that sharpen ethical insight by discussing priorities, emphasizing the role of ethics, and giving feedback to employees about their behavior; and (5) the development of ethical insight and action by helping individuals to internalize ethics and hone their skills in exercising ethical judgment.

It is important that different aspects of the system work together in a mutually reinforcing way. Managerial leadership is crucial because others often look to their leaders to model exemplary moral conduct. Yet leadership is far more effective when it is buttressed by processes that promote ethics and values throughout the organization. One way to do this is to get people engaged in conversations about what it means to do the ethically right thing and how it can be done. The development of ethics codes is an appropriate starting point for discussion and for eventual agreement about core values and conduct. However, codes of ethics alone are not enough. The values must be implemented.

Human resource management provides many formal opportunities for implementation and increased accountability (e.g., emphasizing ethics in hiring and promotion). When people know that ethics is a criterion in promotion, it can shape behavior. Such formal strategies can be even more effective when supported by everyday discourse. What gets said or avoided on a daily basis by managers can sustain ethical expectations or undermine them. The missed opportunity to point out questionable ethics practices is not always without cost. When dialogue and feedback occur, they can help individuals shape and sharpen their moral judgment. But while individual judgment is key to ethical action, it requires a supportive environment of formal and informal practices. In short, organizational ethics is a system.

The selections in this volume highlight the interconnectedness of the ethics system. Some selections examine specific strategies used in cities and counties. Many jurisdictions do more than just adopt codes of ethics; their leaders provide examples of ethical conduct and foster discussion of ethics issues. In addition, cities offer training that deals with particularly vexing ethical matters. Some local governments make ethics a criterion in hiring, or they have ethics counselors to whom employees can go when they have questions. Where ethics codes exist, their content may be aspirational, prohibitive, or a combination of the two. Aspirational codes specify norms of appropriate behavior (e.g., responsibility, public service) that go beyond legal requirements. Prohibitive codes specify illegal or unethical conduct (e.g., conflict of interest, inappropriate acceptance of gifts) and consequences for violations. Hybrid codes combine elements of both. Codes are necessary to help shape ethical conduct, but they are most effective when combined with other pieces in the ethics system.

Leaders need to take inventory of their organization's ethical environment. One useful framework, the four-part pyramid, is offered by Driscoll and Hoffman (1997). Briefly, the four parts of the pyramid are

- Assessment of the ethical awareness of managers and employees: Are they adept at detecting ethical problems at work, or do they fail to recognize these as relevant issues? Effective use of hypothetical scenarios in training sessions can help to assess competencies in this area.

- Assessment of ethical reasoning: Can people in the organization reason through ethics problems and find solutions? Training in ethical reasoning may be needed if issues are framed exclusively in legal terms with insufficient attention to their ethical implications.

- Ethical action: Action is required near the top of the pyramid once ethical problems have been detected and reasoned through to solution. Failure to move from ethical insight and critical thinking to ethical action requires strategic intervention to ensure that ethics become effectively institutionalized.

- Ethical leadership: Finally, at the peak of the pyramid, is ethical leadership by top officials and everyone in the organization. Ethical leadership requires the moral judgment that is aided by a self-calibrated ethical compass as a guide to action.

This edition of *The Ethics Edge* includes selections that address ethics as both an individual challenge and an organizational one. It includes material that emphasizes the importance of leadership behavior, the development of ethics codes, and principled approaches to ethics. An entire section is devoted to ethical leadership in cultivating, maintaining, and expanding an organization's ethical environment.

Enduring concerns

Enduring values are fundamental to the study of ethics, and their examination ensures continuity with the past. Clearly, the concept of professional ethics is not new. The ancient Greeks (Socrates, Aristotle) had much to say about moral imperatives and civic and political responsibilities. The philosophic writings of Immanuel Kant (the categorical imperative), Herbert Spencer (social Darwinism), Jeremy Bentham (utilitarianism), and others continue to provide insight and valuable guidance to today's public managers. American writings and political developments in recent years have also emphasized wholeness of character and professional responsibilities, albeit primarily in the context of industrial society. Professional associations, including ICMA, adopted codes of ethics, declarations of ideals, and more. The content of these codes has not changed greatly over the years, although the contexts have changed and professional organizations have routinely revisited their codes. The codes emphasize professionalism, personal honesty and integrity, support for employees and others, and respect for democratic processes. These enduring values are often mentioned in the codes of corporate and nonprofit organizations as well.

The current upswing in ethical awareness implies that at some point these values must have been partially lost, deemphasized, or called into question. Mired in domestic strife, economic restructuring, and the development of international interdependencies, a new generation rejected traditional values in search of new paradigms. Today, as a new generation has come to assume positions of power and influence in government, managers are finding worth in the traditional, time-tested values. The buzz-words of today—responsiveness, inclusion, transparency, integrity, and empowerment—are ethical values and orientations. Indeed, the role of ethics as a personal, team, and organizational orientation is increasingly acknowledged.

Functioning in an era of fuzzy moral distinctions and ethical ambiguity leaves some managers and employees with a blurry moral compass, and efforts to determine the right thing to do can be confusing. This book provides grist for the mill of ethical reflection on core values that is empowering. For example, performance improvement efforts must be driven by values of responsiveness (improvement for whom?) and openness (e.g., consultation with stakeholders about intentions, options, and consequences) if they are to be effective. Managers must follow up their intentions with actions (i.e., exhibit prudence and integrity). Performance improvement must be more than a set of technical procedures if it is to have lasting impact: it must be ethically inspired. The articles presented in this edition of *The Ethics Edge* encourage leaders and managers to evaluate their ethical beliefs and analyze the ethical implications of their decisions. Understanding and acting on clearly articulated values is a powerful way for managers and employees to help foster more ethically sensitive organizations.

Selection of materials

This volume was designed to offer the best and most current literature on ethics in government. All but three of the eighteen selections were published after 2000, and most were published in 2003 or later. Three selections were retained from the first edition with no changes, and one other was updated. One of the six cases in Appendix A was commissioned to fill a gap in the available literature, and another was reprinted from a book on ethics in public service. Four cases were developed by ICMA. To obtain the best material available, it was necessary in a few instances to select an article with more of a business than a public administration slant or more of a state/federal government focus than a local one. However, the emphasis is mainly on local government applications. ICMA is a co-sponsor of *Public Integrity* journal, the source of six of the articles in this edition.

In addition to the substantially updated content, the second edition differs from the first in two important ways: First, new attention in this edition is given to the importance of ethical leadership, which has become especially important because of highly publicized scandals in the public, private, and nonprofit sectors in recent years. Second, case examples are included in the articles themselves as well as in the appendix. This allows readers to apply some of the theoretical and conceptual material to the real-world ethical dilemmas confronting local government decision makers.

For readers who search this book for specific information, the "matrix of coverage" at the end of this introduction lists some important topics and keys them to the corresponding selections and cases.

Contents

The articles in this volume are grouped into four parts: "Foundations," "Implementation: Ethical Leadership," "Implementation: Ethics Management," and "Ethical Challenges." Part 1 discusses terminology, virtues, values, principles, dilemmas, theories, and paradoxes and provides important background for those who are new to the subject of ethics in government. Parts 2 and 3 encourage readers to move from ideas to the world of action, where concepts are put into practice by leaders and managers. Part 4 explores specific issues at the forefront of ethics in the public sector. Readers may approach the material either selectively or sequentially. Those who read selectively will identify and peruse the articles that appeal to their interests, viewing each article independently from the others. Those who read sequentially will read the articles that set the foundations before proceeding to those that deal with specific implementation and will conclude with the critical ethical issues facing government.

Part 1: Foundations

Part 1 begins with Gregory Foster's article "Ethics: Time to Revisit the Basics." Foster's analysis helps to clarify what ethics is all about: right and wrong, good and bad, virtue and vice, benefit and harm, propriety and impropriety. It also clarifies what ethics involves: ethical reasoning, ethical choice, and ethical conduct. The author stresses that truth and justice provide the basis for trust. The next two articles are popular selections reprinted from the first edition. Michael Josephson defines and clarifies the "six pillars" of character: trustworthiness, respect, responsibility, fairness, caring, and citizenship. These pillars guide and improve the quality of ethical decisions. Josephson stresses the interdependence of these core values and principles and shows how each relates to the others. Stephen Covey then discusses principles that provide a "moral compass." He distinguishes principles and values and highlights the differences between management by maps (values) and leadership by compass (principles), offering practical examples of the latter.

The fourth selection builds on concepts in the first three selections by focusing on the challenge of cultivating scruples in the ethical professional. In an excerpt from his co-authored book *The Professional Edge* (Armonk, NY: M. E. Sharpe, 2004) James Bowman discusses professional and individual as well as organizational ethics. He demonstrates, among other things, the utility of James Svara's "ethics triangle," a tool that incorporates three different approaches to administrative ethics—virtue and intuition (integrity), rules or principles (justice/fairness), and results (utilitarianism).

Part 2: Implementation: ethical leadership

Part 2 is all new for this edition. It stresses the need for ethical leadership to improve and institutionalize ethical behavior in public organizations. Montgomery Van Wart's contribution, drawn from his book *Dynamics of Leadership in Public Service* (Armonk, NY: M. E. Sharpe, 2005), contrasts the power-based approach to leadership with the ethics-based approach; compares unethical, ethically neutral, and ethical leadership styles; and presents a model of ethical and exemplary leadership. Further in-depth examination of this subject is found in "Leadership Ethics" by Peter Northouse from his book *Leadership: Theory and Practice* (Thousand Oaks, CA: Sage, 2004). Northouse examines ethical theories based on self-interest versus interest for others, compares and contrasts different perspectives on ethical leadership, and isolates five principles that provide a foundation for the development of sound ethical leadership.

J. Patrick Dobel examines leadership from yet another perspective, arguing that political prudence is a vital moral resource for leaders to bridge the gap between ethics and political leadership. Also, he finds that prudence is a necessary but not sufficient condition for ethical leadership. Finally, Muel Kaptein and colleagues argue that periodic ethics surveys can reveal the extent and possible consequences of unethical behavior in organizations and illuminate the characteristics of ethical leadership.

Part 3: Implementation: ethics management

Part 3 presents new material that describes important operational concerns in implementing ethical principles in organizational settings. Neal Trautman examines corruption in law enforcement organizations, explaining how ethics scandals begin and evolve and proposing some solutions to the corruption problem. Trautman provides the backdrop for David Haines's contribution, which uses case material from federal and state agencies to show how minor instances of deceit, incompetence, and corruption can be tolerated or justified by organizations and how that can adversely affect organizational performance. Given the ethics problems mentioned by Trautman and Haines, it is necessary to consider managerial strategies and solutions to address these issues in local government. Michael Manske and George Frederickson describe the four pillars of a comprehensive ethics program established in Wyandotte County and Kansas City, Kansas, and share the lessons learned from the experience.

Next, Donald Menzel outlines the salient characteristics of ethics management in four local governments: Tampa, Florida; Chicago, Illinois; King County, Washington; and Salt Lake County, Utah. His article provides brief information on ethics codes, ethics commissions, investigation and enforcement actions, ethics training, and ombudspersons. In "Partisan Politics, Ethics, and the Home Rule Charter," Craig Wheeland provides a case from Goodnow, Pennsylvania, that shows how a low-level ethics violation can blossom into a highly publicized scandal adversely affecting the careers of elected and appointed officials. As a guide for analysis, he provides questions that are useful for ethics training. Finally, Jonathan West and Evan Berman report results of a national survey of local governments regarding the nature, extent, and delivery of ethics training as well as the reasons for using ethics training and its content, duration, and pedagogy. The authors present a model of the impact of ethics training and ethics management strategies on organizational culture, labor-management relations, and performance.

Part 4: Ethical challenges

Part 4 deals with vexing ethical issues confronting managers in the public service. In "Ethical Challenges in Privatizing Government Services," Wendell Lawther discusses fairness issues that occur when public employees compete against private or nonprofit contractors. He calls attention to the potential for cozy politics and the need to adopt innovative procurement practices as well as to invest in contract administration capabilities. Dennis Thompson examines the issue of "Private Life and Public Office," a challenge unique to those in government. Thompson considers how adverse publicity about the private lives of public officials can harm the democratic process by distracting citizens from important government policy and performance issues.

Evan Berman's selection, reprinted from the first edition, presents a theory of citizen cynicism concerning government, examines the extent of cynicism, and considers the ways that public officials can reduce the level of cynicism. In the final article Elizabeth

Kellar updates her selection from the first edition and examines current and emerging issues confronting local government administrators, including matters dealing with political neutrality, policy advocacy, fundraising, employment commitment, conflict of interest, procurement, investments, endorsements, and personnel and diversity issues.

Conclusion

This book of readings provides an orientation to ethics in government. It summarizes the key concepts and strategies that individuals and organizations use to deal with ethical dilemmas. It also highlights contemporary challenges and issues that face today's leaders and managers as they seek to build and maintain an ethical climate in a public sector setting. The salience of ethics issues at all levels of government has increased in recent years. While ethics in government is not a new topic, the types of ethical challenges confronting managers in this new millennium are different. New technologies, government reform strategies, rising cynicism, reconciling private life and public office, and privatization are all ethical challenges that need to be addressed. More enduring problems—conflict of interest, illegal actions, the appearance of impropriety, reneging on promises, partisan political pressures, and embellishing claims—all accentuate the need for strategic thinking and assertive leadership about ethics by public managers. This book discusses a host of practical tools and organizational initiatives that will aid administrators in this strategic thought process. It is our intent that the articles included here will assist in resolving specific ethical dilemmas that managers and employees will confront as well as in designing ethics management policies and programs to meet the needs of particular jurisdictions.

Matrix of coverage.

Chapters		Virtues	Values	Principles	Codes	Training/education	Cases	Leadership	Moral reasoning	Consequences	Accountability	Public interest	Resistance/corruption	Dilemmas/conflict of interests	Law/justice	Democracy	Organizational culture	Public relations/media	Theories	Responsibility/obligations	Enforcement/responses	Professionalism	Partnerships	Case 1	Case 2	Case 3	Case 4	Case 5	Case 6	Techno Quiz
1	Ethics: Time to Revisit the Basics	X	X	X					X					X	X									X						
2	The Six Pillars of Character	X	X	X											X			X												
3	Moral Compassing	X	X				X										X									X		X		
4	The Ethical Professional	X	X		X		X		X							X	X	X		X					X		X	X	X	X
5	Ethics-Based Approach to Leadership	X		X				X	X									X							X		X			X
6	Leadership Ethics	X	X	X				X		X					X				X	X					X		X			X
7	Political Prudence	X						X	X		X			X						X					X		X			X
8	Demonstrating Ethical Leadership				X	X		X		X			X				X							X	X					
9	The Corruption Continuum				X			X			X	X			X		X				X									
10	Fatal Choices					X	X	X				X					X			X				X			X			X
11	Building a Local Ethics Program				X	X			X	X	X									X										
12	Ethics Management				X	X	X							X	X					X	X	X						X		
13	Partisan Politics, Ethics, Home Rule				X			X		X	X			X		X	X	X	X	X					X		X			
14	Ethics Training in U.S. Cities					X			X								X			X										X
15	Ethical Challenges in Privatizing								X			X	X	X	X					X	X						X			
16	Private Life and Public Office	X						X		X	X	X		X			X	X		X					X		X	X	X	
17	Public Cynicism								X			X	X				X	X	X											
18	Current Ethics Issues				X	X									X		X	X	X	X					X		X			
19	Case 1					X	X	X	X						X									▨	▨	▨	▨	▨	▨	
20	Case 2			X	X		X			X					X	X								▨	▨	▨	▨	▨	▨	
21	Case 3			X		X						X			X	X		X				X	X	▨	▨	▨	▨	▨	▨	
22	Case 4			X	X		X								X					X	X	X		▨	▨	▨	▨	▨	▨	
23	Case 5			X	X	X	X					X	X	X			X			X				▨	▨	▨	▨	▨	▨	
24	Case 6		X	X										X	X	X				X				▨	▨	▨	▨	▨	▨	
25	Techno Quiz		X												X			X		X	X									
Total		8	7	9	9	5	9	10	5	9	5	9	6	12	11	6	6	6	5	8	8	8	3	3	8	2	7	4	3	6

Part 1

Foundations

Ethics

Time to revisit the basics

Gregory D. Foster

Ethics could be said to be very much like the weather in the sense that everybody talks about it but nobody does much about it.

Nearly all of us acknowledge the importance of ethics. Most of us hope for and expect ethical behavior and treatment from particular segments of society. Some of us pay close attention to the subject and seek to engage others in discussing (and practicing) it. But regrettably few of us really understand ethics as well as we think we do or as well as we should.

When people discuss ethics, there is a widespread tendency to gloss over the fundamental nature of the subject—as if it is so widely and well understood as to obviate the need for frustrating, time-consuming exegesis. The thinking is that it is better to immerse ourselves in real-world applications. After all, hasn't all that can be said on the subject already been said?

Yet, as with so many ostensibly well-understood concepts that provide continuing sources of disagreement, too much is left to assumption. Otherwise why do so many of us hedge our bets in daily discourse by consistently invoking the semantic couplet of "ethics and morality," much as we do in referring to "training and education" or "order and stability"? We aren't sure if there is a meaningful distinction between the two terms, but we don't want to sound stupid if there is, so we rarely mention the one without the other.

Why, similarly, do we so frequently conflate ethics and the law or morality and religion? Is complying with the law necessarily ethical and breaking the law unethical? Can a person be morally upright only by conforming to the dictates of religion? Conversely, does religiosity equate with ethical conduct?

And why, if we understand ethics so well, can't we reach readier agreement on what issues are ethical ones and thereby deserve to be treated as such? Pick an issue; the possibilities are endless: abortion; globalization; capital punishment; defense spending; gun control; genetic engineering; church-state relations; drugs; foreign aid; poverty, economic inequality, and welfare; intelligence gathering; affirmative action; covert operations;

From *The Humanist*, vol. 63, no. 2 (March/April 2003): 30-37. Reprinted with permission.

corporate performance and responsibility; democracy; military intervention; environmental degradation; government secrecy; privacy and transparency; health care; campaign financing; law enforcement and criminal justice; literacy and education; trade; immigration; propaganda; unemployment; homeland security.

Such matters, even if they are predominantly political, economic, social, or military in nature, nonetheless have demonstrable ethical dimensions or ramifications. If we fail to recognize this fact, if we fail more fundamentally to understand ethics itself, we do the issues and those affected by them a serious disservice.

Ethics can't be dealt with as Justice Potter Stewart famously dealt with the inherent complexity of pornography. We can't, in other words, avoid defining pornography and say we know it when we see it because it isn't clear that we do. Ethics can be meaningfully discussed and applied only when it is fully understood. Such understanding requires that we periodically revisit the basics.

What ethics is about

So for starters, what is ethics actually all about? Ethics is about right and wrong:

"No man is prejudiced in favor of a thing knowing it to be wrong. He is attached to it on the belief of its being right."— Thomas Paine, *The Rights of Man.*

"We do not call anything wrong, unless we mean to imply that a person ought to be punished in some way or other for doing it; if not by law, by the opinion of his fellow creatures; if not by opinion, by the reproaches of his own conscience. This seems the real turning point of the distinction between morality and simple expediency."— John Stuart Mill, *Utilitarianism.*

Ethics is about good and bad, or good and evil.

"Things then are good or evil, only in reference to pleasure and pain. That we call good, which is apt to cause or increase pleasure, or diminish pain in us; or else to procure or preserve us the possession of any other good or absence of any evil. And, on the contrary, we name that evil which is apt to produce or increase any pain, or diminish any pleasure in us: or else to procure us any evil, or deprive us of any good."— John Locke, *Concerning Human Understanding.*

"Moral philosophy is nothing else but the science of what is good and evil in the conversation and society of mankind. *Good* and *evil* are names that signify our appetites and aversions, which in different tempers, customs, and doctrines of men are different: and diverse men differ not only in their judgment on the senses of what is pleasant and unpleasant to the taste, smell, hearing, touch, and sight; but also of what is conformable or disagreeable to reason in the actions of common life....So long as a man is in the condition of mere nature, which is a condition of war, private appetite is the measure of good and evil: and consequently all men agree on this, that peace is good, and therefore also the way or means of peace, which...are *justice, gratitude, modesty, equity, mercy,* and the rest of the laws of nature, are good; that is to say, moral virtues; and their contrary vices, evil."— Thomas Hobbes, *Leviathan.*

Ethics is about virtue and vice.

"It seems to me that virtue is something other and nobler than the inclinations toward goodness that are born in us. Souls naturally regulated and well-born follow the same path, and show the same countenance in their actions, as virtuous ones. But virtue means something greater and more active than letting oneself, by a happy disposition, be led gently and peacefully in the footsteps of reason. He who through a natural mildness and easygoingness should despise injuries received would do a very fine and praiseworthy thing; but he who, outraged and stung to the quick by an injury, should arm himself with the arms of reason against this furious appetite for vengeance, and after a great conflict should finally master it, would without doubt do much more. The former would do well, and the other virtuously; one action might be called goodness, the other virtue. For it seems that the name of virtue presupposes difficulty and contrast, and that it cannot be exercised without opposition."— Michel de Montaigne, *Essays*.

"Vice, the opposite of virtue, shows us more clearly what virtue is. Justice becomes more obvious when we have injustice to compare it to. Many such things are proved by their contraries."— Quintilian, *Institutio Oratoria*.

Ethics is about benefit and harm.

"A man can confer the greatest of benefits by a right use of [such things as strength, health, wealth, generalship] and inflict the greatest of injuries by using them wrongly." — Aristotle, *Rhetoric*.

"The two essential ingredients in the sentiment of justice are the desire to punish a person who has done harm, and the knowledge or belief that there is some definite individual or individuals to whom harm has been done."— John Stuart Mill, *Utilitarianism*.

Ethics is about propriety and impropriety.

"*Socrates.* And will not the temperate man do what is proper, both in relation to the gods and to men—for he would not be temperate if he did not? Certainly he will do what is proper. In his relation to other men he will do what is just; and in his relation to the gods he will do what is holy."— Plato, *Gorgias*.

"Without an acquaintance with the rules of propriety, it is impossible for the character to be established."— Confucius, *The Analects*.

But ethics isn't simply about all these things—right and wrong, good and bad, virtue and vice, benefit and harm, propriety and impropriety. So too is it about principle—fixed, universal rules of right conduct that are contingent on neither time nor culture nor circumstance:

"If habit is not a result of resolute and firm principles ever more and more purified, then, like any other mechanism of technically practical reason, it is neither armed for all eventualities nor adequately secured against changes that may be brought about by new allurements."— Immanuel Kant, *Introduction to the Metaphysical Elements of Ethics*.

So too is it about character—the traits, qualities, and established reputation that define who one is and what one stands for in the eyes of others.

"Nothing can possibly be conceived in the world, or even out of it, which can be called good, without qualification, except a good will. Intelligence, wit, judgment, and the other *talents* of the mind, however they may be named, or courage, resolution, perseverance, as qualities of temperament, are undoubtedly good and desirable in many respects; but these gifts of nature may also become extremely bad and mischievous if the will which is to make use of them, and which, therefore, constitutes what is called *character,* is not good."— Immanuel Kant, *Fundamental Principles of the Metaphysics of Morals*.

So too is it about example—an established pattern of conduct worthy of emulation.

"When thou wishest to delight thyself, think of the virtues of those who live with thee; for instance, the activity of one, and the modesty of another, and the liberality of a third, and some other good quality of a fourth. For nothing delights so much as the examples of

the virtues, when they are exhibited in the morals of those who live with us and present themselves in abundance, as far as is possible. Wherefore we must keep them before
us."— Marcus Aurelius, *Meditations.*

And so too is it about conscience—"the voice of the soul," "the pulse of reason," "that
inner tribunal," "the muzzle of the will," "the compass of the unknown," "a thousand
witnesses."

"The moral sense follows, firstly, from the enduring and ever-present nature of the
social instincts; secondly, from man's appreciation of the approbation and disapproba-
tion of his fellows; and thirdly, from the high activity of his mental faculties, with past
impressions extremely vivid; and in these latter respects he differs from the lower animals.
Owing to this condition of mind, man cannot avoid looking both backwards and forwards,
and comparing past impressions. Hence after some temporary desire or passion has mas-
tered his social instincts, he reflects and compares the now weakened impression of such
past impulses with the ever-present social instincts; and he then feels that sense of dis-
satisfaction which all unsatisfied instincts leave behind them, he therefore resolves to act
differently for the future—and this is conscience."— Charles Darwin, *Descent of Man.*

What ethics involves

There is more to ethics, of course, than just knowing what it is about. As important to
understanding its nature is what it involves. Is there something about the process of ethical reflection and choice that distinguishes it from other modes of thought? Some years
ago Clarence Walton, former president of Catholic University, suggested the following:
"Ethics involves critical analysis of human acts to determine their rightness or wrongness
in terms of two major criteria: truth and justice."

Walton would have us understand, first, that ethics has virtually everything to do
with the quality—even more than the content—of our thinking. How we think may
not guarantee a right or best answer but it dramatically improves the prospects of finding one in sound, defensible fashion. As Pascal observed: "All our dignity consists...in
thought....Let us strive then to think well; that is the foundation of all morality."

To think well is to think critically. Critical thinking—the conscious use of reason—
stands clearly apart from other ways of grasping truth or confronting choice: impulse,
habit, faith, and intuition.

Impulse is nothing more than unreflective spontaneity—the sudden whim of a mind
on cruise control or autopilot. Given the magnifying and accelerating effects of the media,
impulsiveness is much more likely than deliberation in characterizing the response of
today's policy practitioners to the manifold crises that define contemporary political
affairs.

Habit is programmed repetition, the routinization of thought by which we remove
presumably mundane matters to our subconscious so they can be dealt with more efficiently or conveniently without the attendant need to constantly revisit first principles. For
example this is what we do when we standardize, generalize, or stereotype.

Faith, in the words of Walter Kaufman, "means intense, usually confident, belief that
is not based on evidence sufficient to command assent from every reasonable person."
Intensity of feeling and insufficiency of evidence are the operative features here. The
dictionary might tell us that faith is belief—in an idea, a person, an institution—without

need of certain proof. For the true believer, though, it isn't just the certainty of proof that is unnecessary; evidence itself is superfluous, especially evidence that contradicts an established belief system, worldview, or doctrine. This is what cognitive dissonance is all about—the prevalent human tendency to ignore or reject events or data that run counter to one's preconceptions or predispositions. Though faith and trust may go hand in hand, blind faith typifies a deadening of the intellect that may just as readily produce intolerance, disrespect, and distrust. The nineteenth-century Swiss philosopher Henri Frederic Amiel noted: "Action and faith enslave thought, both of them in order not to be troubled or inconvenienced by reflection, criticism and doubt."

Intuition is what we colloquially refer to as gut feeling or sixth sense—a way of speculative "knowing" based more on experience (lived or vicarious) than on reason, more on our overall sensory apparatus than on the workings of the mind. It is in this sense that a superficial impression of what appears to be—traits, behaviors, tendencies—so often gives birth to deep-seated pseudo-knowledge of what is. Intuition is neither entirely conscious nor entirely rational. In the words of George Santayana: "Intuition represents the free life of the mind, the poetry native to it...; but this is the subjective or ideal element in thought which we must discount if we are anxious to possess true knowledge."

What distinguishes these various forms of "unreason" from critical thinking is the systematic, investigative nature of the latter. "If you wish to strive for peace of soul and pleasure," said Heinrich Heine, "then believe; if you wish to be a devotee of truth, then enquire." Thinking critically is a disciplined pattern of thought or mode of inquiry that requires three things: first, questioning—assertions, opinions, and givens—rather than accepting them at face value; second, seeking and weighing evidence on all sides of an issue, not just evidence that affirms one's beliefs; and third, employing rigorous logic to reach defensible conclusions.

The object of critical thinking is to achieve a measure of objectivity to counteract or diminish the subjective bias that experience and socialization bestow on us all. Why should this be necessary? Because when we are dealing with matters of ethical concern, the well-being of someone or something beyond ourselves is always at stake. In the extreme, the lives of others may literally depend on the choices we make or don't make— whether we are jurors in a court of law judging the guilt or innocence of an accused, or policy-makers committing the blood and treasure of society to a foreign venture. The quality of our thinking, then, is a measure of the investment we are willing to make in an issue or situation. As Spinoza said, "If we live according to the guidance of reason, we shall desire for others the good which we seek for ourselves."

What is it, then, that we should think critically about? Human acts, suggests Walton— human rather than nonhuman—rather than thoughts. We focus on things human for two reasons. First, humans presumably possess abilities—predominantly intellectual—that other living species do not: the ability to make moral judgments, to deal with abstract concepts, to extrapolate from one set of circumstances to another, to exercise free will that surpasses conditioned response. "It is characteristic of man," said Aristotle, "that he alone has any sense of good and evil, of just and unjust, and the like."

Accordingly, a second reason we focus on humans is that we expect more of them than we do of other species. We don't expect the dog or cat, or even the dolphin or chimpanzee, to contemplate the propriety of its actions, to refrain from harming others, or to display empathy. We do expect such things from humans. But we also have grown to expect humanity's imperfections to outweigh its potential with disturbing frequency. Thus Mark Twain was moved to observe, with cynical accuracy: "The fact that man knows right from wrong proves his *intellectual* superiority to other creatures; but the fact that he can *do* wrong proves his *moral* inferiority to any creature that cannot."

We focus on human acts because acts have demonstrable effects on others. "The great end of life," said T. H. Huxley, "is not knowledge but action." To know is merely to possess the truth. To act is to do, to make something happen, to get some-thing done. Thoughts, in and of themselves, have tangible effects only if they are translated into acts. This assumes that thoughts and actions are separable, that one can act without thinking or think without acting, that it is possible to harbor hatred or prejudice, understanding or good will, in one's heart (or mind or soul) without actually putting such feelings into effect. It isn't always clear, of course, what constitutes action, and therein lies much moral ambiguity. Is speech an act? If I say I am homosexual, call someone a disparaging name, or advocate the overthrow of government, am I acting? Should I be held responsible for such thoughts? By the same token, is inaction action? If I do nothing—like possessing (but not using) nuclear weapons, ignoring genocide, or declining to pay United Nations dues—am I actually doing something?

Why do we critically analyze human acts? To determine their rightness or wrongness. There are any number of bases for making such determinations.

We might rely on some principle, precept, or rule: a law, executive order, or regulation, for example, that mandates or prohibits something (such as full financial disclosure or political assassination or the mishandling of classified information); or more abstract guidelines for behavior, such as the Golden Rule, the Ten Commandments, or an honor code that proscribes lying, cheating, and stealing.

We might be guided by the anticipated consequences or effects of our actions. Who benefits, and who is harmed? Who benefits most or what is the greatest benefit? Who is harmed least or what is the least harm? What consequences matter—physical ones only or also psychological and emotional ones? Temporally and spatially proximate ones only or also more distant ones?

We might concern ourselves with the intentions or motives behind one's acts. Does it matter why we do (or fail to do) something—or are results all that count? Do intentions outweigh effects or not? If I unintentionally inflict harm (or do good), should I be held culpable (or receive credit)?

We might focus on the rights of those involved in, affected by, or having a stake in our choices. Who deserves or doesn't deserve what—conditionally or unconditionally? Are there fundamental, natural rights that all persons deserve to enjoy merely by virtue of being human? Do rights reflect underlying needs that all humans recognizably have? Whose rights and which rights take precedence over others?

Conversely, we might emphasize obligations, the flip side of rights. Do those with a stake in our choices bear certain obligations toward others? Do the powerful or those in authority have special obligations, for example? Does the possession of rights impose attendant obligations?

Or we might be guided by values—traits, behaviors, or qualities to which we ascribe some worth or importance. The question in every case, of course, is which values—which normative values (or virtues)—should we seek, and which should we consider more important than others. Zeno, the Greek Stoic philosopher, spoke of wisdom, courage, justice, and temperance as primary virtues. Aristotle spoke more expansively of justice, courage, temperance, magnificence, magnanimity, liberality, gentleness, prudence, and wisdom, in that order. But there are yet other salutary values that seem no less worthy of attention: compassion, competence, decisiveness, empathy, honesty, integrity, loyalty, reliability, tolerance, and vision—to name but a few. The most nettlesome and difficult moral dilemmas we face often revolve around value conflicts in which two or more positive values are at stake in a given situation: duty verses friendship, for example, or honesty verses compassion, or loyalty to subordinates verses loyalty to superiors.

When we seek to determine the rightness or wrongness of something, we should do so with two major criteria in mind: truth and justice. Ralph Waldo Emerson made the monumentally insightful observation that "truth is the summit of being; justice is the application of it [truth] to affairs." The two go hand in hand. Ethics—ethical reasoning, ethical choice, ethical conduct—requires that we seek the truth, the pinnacle of life, in order to have a proper basis—the only legitimate basis—for achieving justice. Justice served is ethics realized.

Truth is what *is*—conditions, occurrences, statements whose existence and nature are there to be confirmed or verified by observation or reason. To possess truth is to have knowledge, the expected outcome of critical reasoning. If we possessed the truth, we would know what is ethical. But therein lies the rub. Truth is inherently elusive, and our ability to grasp it is tenuous at best, even illusory. Take any truth claim that passes for a statement of fact by those who believe it. To cite just one example: in the matter of whether women should be permitted to serve in combat, these are among the commonly asserted "truths" that drive discussion of the issue and ultimately determine whether justice is served or denied:

- Women are incapable of performing in combat.
- Women are less aggressive and less courageous than men. Combat requires aggressiveness and courage.
- Women destroy unit cohesion.
- The presence of women creates sexual tensions that otherwise wouldn't exist.
- Women require more protection than men. Women bring out natural protective tendencies in men.
- A woman's place is in the home.
- A minimally qualified man is preferable to a better qualified woman.
- A woman has less of an obligation to serve than a man does.
- The American people deserve the best defense the military can provide them.

Such claims pass for self-evident truth among those who are already thus predisposed. But such so-called truths are rarely anything more conclusive and unequivocal than arguable propositions that cry out for supporting evidence.

There is an old saying: "A man with a watch knows what time it is; a man with two watches isn't so sure." This aphorism suggests a number of things about certainty and doubt, fact and opinion, objectivity and subjectivity, perception, bias, conviction, and socialization. Truth, like beauty, may lie as much in the eye of the beholder as in the thing observed; there may be multiple claimants, all more or less equal in standing, to the same truth; two or more parties can observe the same thing but see something completely different, or even that the same party can observe the same thing over time but see something different each time. Believing something intensely, even if that belief is shared by others, doesn't necessarily make it true in some objective sense.

Truth—perhaps precisely because it is so difficult to grasp or discern—is the essential precondition for justice. If justice is to be served, other than by accident, it must be predicated on the truth. Of course in any given situation there may be multiple truths that we would like to have—or that we knowingly or unknowingly need.

Let us say the question at hand is how to respond—justly and justifiably—to the September 11, 2001, terrorist attacks on the United States. We would like to have the truth of what actually happened (however seemingly self-evident). We would want to know the truth of who did it, how it happened, why it happened, what its effects have been, and what the effects of particular responses will be (for example, will punishment deter future such incidents and enhance U.S. credibility?).

Or take global warming. If we are to respond to it appropriately (in a timely, conclusive, affordable manner that doesn't create or exacerbate harm for those affected), we clearly want to know the truth of whether it actually exists; whether it is temporary or permanent, natural or human-made, recurrent or not, widespread or confined; and what its causes, effects, and implications are.

Justice is about receiving one's due or getting what one deserves—whether we are talking about one's standing or status, one's access to valuable resources, or one's treatment at the hands of others. This could mean obtaining a proper (fair) share of humanity's or society's goods (wealth, perquisites, esteem, and basic necessities), or receiving appropriate rewards or punishments for what one has or hasn't done (from bonuses or promotions to criminal conviction or military retaliation). Why would (or should) we care, for example, if 5 percent of the population controls 95 percent of society's wealth; if particular people are advantaged or disadvantaged because of their birth or personal attributes rather than because of their accomplishments; if a third-time minor drug offender is sentenced to a long prison term or a confessed murderer is set free on a legal technicality; if civilian noncombatants are subjected to the violence and destruction of war? Because in every case these are matters of justice and injustice.

Trust: the bottom line

Together, truth and justice constitute the basis for trust. Therein lies their ultimate importance in distinguishing what is ethical from what is not. As Sissela Bok observed in her thoughtful and perceptive 1978 book *Lying:* "Trust is a social good to be protected just as much as the air we breathe or the water we drink. When it is damaged, the community as a whole suffers; and when it is destroyed, societies falter and collapse.... Trust and integrity are precious resources, easily squandered, hard to regain."

Trust is social glue. It is what unites rather than divides, what turns a gaggle of individuals into a community with a sense of oneness. If I am sure I can count on you to tell me the truth, to seek the truth where I am concerned, to treat me fairly, to care whether I get what I deserve and deserve what I get, then our relationship is more likely than not to be defined by trust. Where such trust exists—thinking, not blind, trust; lasting, not momentary, trust—the prevalence of ethical conflict and the burden of ethical choice are materially diminished. Restoring trust thus is the great task of ethics, and understanding ethics accordingly is the great task before humanity today.

The Six Pillars of Character

Michael Josephson

Editors' Note: Trustworthiness, respect, responsibility, fairness, caring, and citizenship have been identified by the Josephson Institute as "The Six Pillars of Character." These core values and principles, discussed by Michael Josephson here, can be used to improve the ethical quality of decision making.

Trustworthiness

Being trusted is a good thing: we're given greater leeway by those we deal with because they don't feel they need contracts to assure that we'll meet our obligations. They believe us and therefore they believe in us. That's satisfying. But there's a downside: we must constantly live up to the expectations of others and refrain from competitive, self-serving behaviors that tarnish if not destroy relationships, both professional and personal.

Another downside, of sorts: trustworthiness is the broadest and most complicated of the six core ethical values. It is concerned with all the qualities and behavior that make a person worthy of trust—qualities like integrity, honesty, reliability and loyalty.

Honesty

Obviously, honesty is one of the most fundamental of ethical values. We associate honesty with people of honor, and we admire and trust those who are honest. But honesty is a broader concept than many may realize.

Honesty in communications requires a good-faith intent to convey the truth as best we know it and to avoid communicating in a way likely to mislead or deceive. There are three dimensions:

- *Truthfulness* The obligation of truthfulness precludes intentional misrepresentation of fact (lying). Intent is the crucial distinction between truthfulness and truth itself. Being wrong is not the same thing as being a liar, although honest mistakes can still damage trust insofar as they may be evidence of sloppy judgment.

Reprinted from Michael Josephson's *Making Ethical Decisions* with permission of the Josephson Institute of Ethics. ©2002 www.charactercounts.org.

- *Sincerity/nondeception*   The obligation of sincerity precludes all acts, including half-truths, out-of-context statements, and even silence that are intended to create beliefs or leave impressions that are untrue or misleading.
- *Candor*   In relationships involving legitimate expectations of trust, honesty may also require candor, forthrightness and frankness, imposing the obligation to volunteer information that the other person needs to know.

Honesty in conduct prohibits stealing, cheating, fraud, subterfuge and other trickery. Cheating is a particularly foul form of dishonesty because one not only seeks to deceive but to take advantage of those who are not cheating. It's a twofer: a violation of trust and fairness.

All lies are dishonest, but not all lies are unethical. Huh? That's right, honesty is not an inviolate principle. Occasionally dishonesty is ethically justifiable, as when the police lie in undercover operations or when one lies to criminals or terrorists to save lives. But don't kid yourself: occasions for ethically sanctioned lying are rare and require serving a very high purpose indeed—not hitting a management-pleasing sales target or winning a game or avoiding a confrontation. We're talking about saving a life, that sort of thing.

Integrity

The word *integrity* comes from the word *integer*, meaning "one" or wholeness. This means there are no divisions in an ethical person's life, no difference *in the way* she makes decisions from situation to situation, no difference in the way she acts at work and at home, in public and alone. At one time or another, we all have allowed our behavior to depart from our conscience or to vary according to locale. Even so, almost all of us have lines we will not cross; our challenge is to draw the line around the Six Pillars.

Because she must know who she is and what she values, the person of integrity takes time for self-reflection so that the events, crises, and seeming necessities of the day do not determine the course of her moral life. She stays in control. She may be courteous, even charming, but she is never false. She never demeans [her]self with obsequious behavior toward those she thinks might do her some good. She is trusted because you know who she is: what you see is what you get.

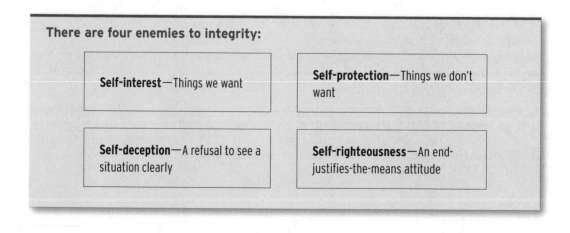

There are four enemies to integrity:

Self-interest—Things we want

Self-protection—Things we don't want

Self-deception—A refusal to see a situation clearly

Self-righteousness—An end-justifies-the-means attitude

Reliability (promise keeping)

When we make promises or other commitments which create a legitimate basis for another person to rely upon us to perform certain tasks, we undertake moral duties that go beyond legal obligations. The ethical dimension of promise keeping imposes the responsibility of making all reasonable efforts to fulfill our commitments. Because promise keeping is such an important aspect of trustworthiness, it is important to:

- *Avoid bad-faith excuses* Honorable people interpret their contracts and other commitments in a fair and reasonable manner and not in a way designed to rationalize noncompliance or create justifications for escaping commitments.

- *Avoid unwise commitments* Be cautious about making commitments that create ethical obligations. Before making a promise, consider carefully whether you are willing and likely to keep it. Think about unknown or future events that could make it difficult, undesirable or impossible. Sometimes, all we can do is promise to do our best.

- *Avoid unclear commitments* Since others will expect you to live up to what they think you have promised to do, be sure that when you make a promise, the other person understands what you are committing to do.

Loyalty

Loyalty is a special moral responsibility to promote and protect the interests of certain people, organizations or affiliations. This duty goes beyond the normal obligation we all share to care for others. Some relationships—husband-wife, employer-employee, citizen-country—create an expectation of allegiance, fidelity and devotion.

Limitations to loyalty Loyalty is a tricky thing. It is not uncommon for friends, employers, co-workers and others who have a claim on us to demand that their interests be ranked first, even above ethical considerations. Loyalty is a reciprocal concept, however, and no one has the right to ask another to sacrifice ethical principle in the name of a special relationship. Indeed, one forfeits a claim of loyalty when so high a price is put on continuance of the relationship.

Prioritizing loyalties Because so many individuals and groups make loyalty claims on us, it is often impossible to honor them all simultaneously. Consequently, we must rank our loyalty obligations in some rational fashion. In our personal lives, for example, most people expect us to place the highest degree of loyalty on our family relationships. It's perfectly reasonable, and ethical, to look out for the interests of our children, parents and spouses, even if we may have to subordinate our obligations to other children, neighbors, or co-workers in doing so.

Safeguarding confidential information The duty of loyalty requires us to keep secrets learned in confidence.

Avoiding conflicting interests Employees and public servants have an additional loyalty responsibility to make all professional decisions on their merits, unimpeded by conflicting personal interests. Their goal is to secure and maintain the trust of the public, to whom they owe their ultimate loyalty.

Respect

The way one shows respect varies, but its essence is the display of regard for the worth of people, including oneself. We have no ethical duty to hold all people in high esteem or admire them, but we are morally obligated to treat everyone with respect, regardless of who they are and what they have done—even if they don't *deserve* respect. The reason is not because these undeserving souls are human beings, but because we are. We have a responsibility to be the best we can be in all situations, even when dealing with the heinous.

Respect focuses on the moral obligation to honor the essential worth and dignity of the individual. Respect prohibits violence, humiliation, manipulation, and exploitation. It reflects notions such as civility, courtesy, dignity, autonomy, tolerance, and acceptance.

Civility, courtesy and decency   A respectful person is an attentive listener, although his patience with the boorish need not be endless (respect works both ways). Nevertheless, the respectful person treats others with consideration, conforming to accepted notions of taste and propriety, and doesn't resort to intimidation, coercion or violence except in extraordinary and limited situations to teach discipline, maintain order or achieve social justice. Punishment is used in moderation and only to advance important social goals and purposes.

Autonomy   An ethical person exercises personal, official, and managerial authority in a way that provides others with the information they need to make informed decisions about their own lives.

Tolerance   An ethical person accepts individual differences and beliefs without prejudice and judges others only on the content of their character.

Responsibility

Life is full of choices. Being responsible means being in charge of our choices and, thus, our lives. It means being accountable for what we do and who we are. It also means recognizing that what we do, and what we don't do, matters and we are morally on the hook for the consequences.

Responsibility makes demands on us. It imposes duties to do what we can, not because we are being paid or because we will suffer if we don't, but simply because it is our obligation to do so. The essence of responsibility is continuous awareness that our capacity to reason and our freedom to choose make us morally autonomous and, therefore, answerable for how we use our autonomy and whether we honor or degrade the ethical principles that give life meaning and purpose.

Beyond having the responsibility to be trustworthy, respectful, fair, and caring, ethical people show responsibility by being accountable, pursuing excellence, and exercising self-restraint. In other words, they demonstrate the *ability to respond* to expectations of performance.

Accountability   An accountable person is not a victim and doesn't shift blame or credit for the work of others. He considers the likely consequences of his behavior and associations. He recognizes the common complicity in the triumph of evil when nothing is done to stop it. He leads by example.

Pursuit of excellence   The pursuit of excellence has an ethical dimension when others rely upon our knowledge, ability or willingness to perform tasks safely and effectively.

- *Diligence*   It is hardly unethical to make mistakes or be less than "excellent" but there is a moral obligation to do one's best, to be diligent, reliable, careful, prepared, and informed.
- *Perseverance*   Responsible people finish what they start, overcoming rather than surrendering to obstacles and excuses.
- *Continuous improvement*   Responsible people are on the prowl for ways to do their work better.

Self-restraint   Responsible people exercise self-control, restraining passions and appetites (lust, hatred, gluttony, greed, fear, etc.) for the sake of reason, prudence and the duty to set a good example. They delay gratification if necessary and never feel it's necessary to "win at any cost." They realize they are as they choose to be, every day.

Fairness

Most would agree that fairness and justice involve issues of consistency, equality, impartiality, proportionality, openness, and due process. Most would agree that it is unfair to handle similar matters inconsistently. Most would agree that it is unfair to impose punishment that is disproportionate to the offense. Beyond that, there is little agreement. Fairness is another tricky concept, probably more subject to legitimate debate and interpretation than any other ethical value. Disagreeing parties tend to maintain that there is only one fair position (their own, naturally). But while some situations and decisions are clearly unfair, fairness usually refers to a *range* of morally justifiable outcomes rather than discovery of *the* fair answer.

Process   In settling disputes or dividing resources, how one proceeds to judgment is crucial, for someone is bound to be disappointed with the result. A fair person scrupulously employs open and impartial processes for gathering and evaluating information necessary to make decisions. Fair people do not wait for the truth to come to them; they seek out relevant information and conflicting perspectives before making important decisions.

Impartiality   Decisions should be made without favoritism or prejudice.

Equity   Fairness requires an individual, company, or society [to] correct mistakes, promptly and voluntarily. It is improper to take advantage of the weakness or ignorance of others.

Caring

Caring is the very heart of ethics. It is scarcely possible to be truly ethical and not be a caring person, genuinely concerned with the welfare of others. That is because ethics is ultimately about our responsibilities toward other people. If you existed alone in the universe, there would be no need for ethics, and your heart could be a cold, hard stone without consequence to anyone or anything.

It is easier to love "humanity" than it is to love people. People who consider themselves ethical and yet lack a caring attitude toward individuals tend to treat others as instruments of their will. They rarely feel an obligation to be honest, loyal, fair or respectful except insofar as it is prudent for them to do so, a disposition which itself hints at duplicity and a lack of integrity.

Implementation of ethical principles for public servants.

Ethical principles should be made a part of the work ethic of all government organizations. In order to maximize the incorporation of ethical principles into the day-to-day performance of public service, government organizations should take the following steps:

Exercise leadership

The members of any organization take their cues from the actions of those who hold top leadership positions in the organization. These leaders thus have a special responsibility within their organizations to:

- Advocate the core values and exemplify the guiding principles
- Evaluate their subordinates' performance in the light of these standards
- Seek others with strong ethical values to work in the organization.

Monitor and evaluate

In addition to assessing the ethical performance of individuals, there is also a need to monitor and evaluate the organization itself with respect to:

- How well the values and principles are understood and followed
- The extent to which they influence the organization's ethical climate.

Provide ongoing training

Ethics training should be broadened in focus beyond the current briefings on laws, regulations, and rules. Training sessions should include case studies utilizing the practical precepts. Continuous training is required to keep the core ethical values alive and relevant within a government agency.

Provide sources of advice

Employees with specific ethical dilemmas should have access to established sources of sensible, sympathetic, and reliable advice. These should be easy enough to use so that they can be employed for less than crucial, but still troubling, questions. The means of providing such guidance might include a hot line or off-the-record discussions with peers.

Assure compliance

The organization must be vigorous in insisting upon adherence to its declared ethical standards. It follows that unambiguous failures to observe them must be dealt with firmly.

Source: *Ethical Principles for Public Servants.* The Council for Excellence in Government, 1992. Reprinted with permission.

A person who really cares feels an emotional response to both the pain and pleasure of others. Oddly enough, though, it is not uncommon for people to be remarkably ungracious, intolerant, and unforgiving toward those they love—while at the same time showing a generous spirit toward strangers and business associates. Go figure.

Of course, sometimes we must hurt those we truly care for and some decisions, while quite ethical, do cause harm. But one should consciously cause no more harm than is reasonably necessary to perform one's duties.

The highest form of caring is the honest expression of benevolence. This is sometimes referred to as altruism, not to be confused with strategic charity. Gifts to charities to advance personal interests are a fraud. That is, they aren't gifts at all. They're investments, or tax write-offs.

Citizenship

The concept of citizenship includes civic virtues and duties that prescribe how we ought to behave as part of a community. The good citizen knows the laws and obeys them, yes, but that's not all. She volunteers and stays informed on the issues of the day, the better to execute her duties and privileges as a member of a self-governing democratic society. That is, she does more than her "fair" share to make society work, now and for future generations. And beyond respecting the law, reporting crimes, serving on juries, voting, and paying taxes, the good citizen protects the environment by conserving resources, recycling, using public transportation, and cleaning up litter. She never takes more than she gives.

When we say something is a civic duty, we imply that not doing that duty is unethical. Yet that can be a harsh and erroneous judgment. If one has a duty to be honest, caring, fair, respectful and responsible, then we mean it is ethically wrong to be the opposite of those things. But does that then mean that if one has a "civic duty" to stay informed that one is unethical if one is ignorant? Certainly we don't have to admire self-absorbed and lazy people who take their citizenship for granted. It is important, however, to make the distinction between what is ethically mandated and what is merely desirable and worthy of emulation. To a great extent, people have to live their own lives, in whatever degree of isolation they choose.

Moral Compassing

Stephen Covey

When managing in the wilderness of the changing times, a map is of limited worth. What's needed is a moral compass.

When I was in New York [once], I witnessed a mugging skillfully executed by a street gang. I'm sure that the members of this gang have their street maps, their common value—the highest value being "Don't fink or squeal on each other, be true and loyal to each other"—but this value, as it's interpreted and practiced by this gang, does not represent "true north," the magnetic principle of respect for people and property.

They lacked an internal moral compass. Principles are like a compass. A compass has a true north that is *objective and external*, that reflects natural laws or *principles*, as opposed to values that are subjective and internal. Because the compass represents the verities of life, we must develop our value system with deep respect for "true north" principles.

As Cecil B. DeMille said: "It is impossible for us to break the law. We can only break ourselves against the law."

Principles are proven, enduring guidelines for human conduct. Certain principles govern human effectiveness. The six major world religions all teach the same basic core beliefs—such principles as "You reap what you sow" and "Actions are more important than words." I find global consensus around what "true north" principles are. These are not difficult to detect. They are objective, basic, unarguable: "You can't have trust without being trustworthy" and "You can't talk yourself out of a problem you behave yourself into."

There is little disagreement in what the constitutional principles of a company should be when enough people get together. I find a universal belief in fairness, kindness, dignity, charity, integrity, honesty, quality, service, and patience.

Consider the absurdity of trying to live a life or run a business based on the opposites. I doubt that anyone would seriously consider unfairness, deceit, baseness, uselessness, mediocrity, or degradation as a solid foundation for lasting happiness and success.

People may argue about how these principles are to be defined, interpreted, and applied in real-life situations, but they generally agree about their intrinsic merit. They

From Stephen R. Covey, *Principle-Centered Leadership*. Copyright 1990 by Stephen R. Covey. Reprinted with permission from Franklin Covey Co.

may not live in total harmony with them, but they believe in them. And they want to be managed by them. They want to be evaluated by "laws" in the social and economic dimensions that are just as real, just as unchanging and unarguable, as laws such as gravity are in the physical dimension.

In any serious study of history—be it national or corporate—the reality and verity of such principles become obvious. These principles surface time and again, and the degree to which people in a society recognize and live in harmony with them moves them toward either survival and stability or disintegration and destruction.

In a talk show interview, I was once asked if Hitler was principle-centered. "No," I said, "but he was value-driven. One of his governing values was to unify Germany. But he violated compass principles and suffered the natural consequences. And the consequences were momentous—the dislocation of the entire world for years."

In dealing with self-evident, natural laws, we can choose either to manage in harmony with them or to challenge them by working some other way. Just as the laws are fixed, so too are the consequences.

In my seminars I ask audiences, "When you think of your personal values, how do you think?" Typically people focus on what they want. I then ask them, "When you think of principles, how do you think?" They are more oriented toward objective law, listening to conscience, tapping into verities.

Principles are not values. The German Nazis, like the street gang members, shared values, but these violated basic principles. Values are maps. Principles are territories. And the maps are not the territories; they are only subjective attempts to describe or represent the territory.

The more closely our maps are aligned with correct principles—with the realities of the territory, with things as they are—the more accurate and useful they will be. Correct maps will impact our effectiveness far more than our efforts to change attitudes and behaviors. However, when the territory is constantly changing, any map is soon obsolete.

A compass for the times

In today's world, what's needed is a compass. A compass consists of a magnetic needle swinging freely and pointing to magnetic north. It's also a mariner's instrument for directing or ascertaining the course of ships at sea, as well as an instrument for drawing circles and taking measurements. The word *compass* may also refer to the reach, extent, limit, or boundary of a space or time; a course, circuit, or range; an intent, purpose, or design; an understanding or comprehension. All of these connotations enrich the meaning of the metaphor.

Why is a compass better than a map in today's business world? I see several compelling reasons why the compass is so invaluable to corporate leaders:

- The compass orients people to the coordinates and indicates a course or direction even in forests, deserts, seas, and open, unsettled terrain.

- As the territory changes, the map becomes obsolete; in times of rapid change, a map may be dated and inaccurate by the time it's printed.

- Inaccurate maps are sources of great frustration for people who are trying to find their way or navigate territory.

Ethical principles and guiding questions.

Consequences	*What course of action will do the most good and the least harm?*
Utilitarian ethic	What course of action brings the greatest good for the greatest number of people?
Proportionality ethic	What are the good and bad results of this decision and do the good outweigh the bad?
Theory of justice	Does this action apply impartially to each employee and organizational unit?
Golden rule	If I were in the position of another person affected by my decision, would my actions be considered fair by that person?
Reversibility rule	Would I be willing to change places with the person affected by my contemplated action?
Protect health, safety, welfare	What course of action will best protect the health, safety and welfare of others?
Integrity	*What plan can I live with, which is consistent with the basic values and commitments in my organization?*
Virtuous character	Would this action be undertaken by someone of exemplary or virtuous character?
Disclosure rule	What course of action would I be comfortable with if it was examined by my friends, family and associates?
Professional ethic	Can my action be explained before a committee of peers?
Intuition ethic	Which course of action feels right to me?
Rights	*Which alternative best serves others' rights, including stakeholders' rights?*
Principle of equal freedom	Will my contemplated action restrict others from actions that they have a legitimate right to undertake?
Rights ethic	Will my action deprive any person affected by it of a right that must be respected?
Practicality	*Which course of action is feasible in the world as it is?*
Conventionalist ethic	What action will further my self-interest without violating the law?
Darwinian ethic	What course of action will enable me to succeed and survive in this organization?
Organizational vs. personal ethic	Is this action consistent with both organizational ethics and personal ethics and do organizational considerations override personal ones?
Organizational loyalty	What are the organizational goals and what can I do that is good for the organization?

Copyright Jonathan West.

- Many executives are pioneering, managing in uncharted waters or wilderness, and no existing map accurately describes the territory.

- To get anywhere very fast, we need refined processes and clear channels of production and distribution (freeways), and to find or create freeways in the wilderness, we need a compass.

- The map provides description, but the compass provides more vision and direction.

- An accurate map is a good management tool, but a compass is a leadership and an empowerment tool.

People who have been using maps for many years to find their way and maintain a sense of perspective and direction should realize that their maps may be useless in the current maze and wilderness of management. My recommendation is that you exchange your map for a compass and train yourself and your people how to navigate by a compass calibrated to a set of fixed, true north principles and natural laws.

Why? Because with an inaccurate map, you would be lost in a city. What if someone said "Work harder"? Now you're lost twice as fast. Now someone says "Think positively." Now you don't care about being lost. The problem has nothing to do with industry or with attitude. It has everything to do with an inaccurate map. Your paradigm or the level of your thinking represents your map of reality, your map of the territory.

The basic problem at the bottom of most ineffective cultures is the map in the head of the people who helped create that condition. It is an incomplete map, one based on quick-fix solutions and short-term thinking toward quarterly, bottom-line results, and it is based on a scarcity mentality.

The solution is to change from management by maps (values) to leadership by compass (natural principles). A political environment inevitably points to the style of top people—that's supposed to be true north. But the style is based upon volatile moods, arbitrary decisions, raw emotion, and ego trips. Sometimes true north is called an "information system" or a "reward system" and that governs behavior. What grows is what gets watered. Principle-centered leadership requires that people "work on farms" on the basis of natural, agricultural principles and that they build those principles into the center of their lives, their relationships, their agreements, their management processes, and their mission statements.

Strategic orientation

Map-versus-compass orientation is an important strategic issue, as reflected in this statement by Masaharu Matsushita, president of Japan's giant consumer electronics company: "We are going to win and the industrial West is going to lose because the reasons for your failure are within yourselves: for you, the essence of management is to get the ideas out of the heads of the bosses into the hands of labor."

The important thing here is the stated reason for our "failure." We are locked in to certain mind-sets or paradigms, locked in to management by maps, locked in to an old model of leadership where the experts at the top decide the objectives, methods, and means.

This old strategic planning model is obsolete. It's a road map. It calls for people at the top to exercise their experience, expertise, wisdom, and judgment and set ten-year strategic plans—only to find that the plans are worthless within eighteen months. In the new environment, with speed to market timetables of eighteen months instead of five years, plans become obsolete fast.

Peter Drucker has said: "Plans are worthless, but planning is invaluable." And if our planning is centered on an overall purpose or vision and on a commitment to a set of principles, then the people who are closest to the action in the wilderness can use that compass and their own expertise and judgment to make decisions and take actions. In effect, each person may have his or her own compass; each may be empowered to decide objectives and make plans that reflect the realities of the new market.

Principles are not practices. Practices are specific activities or actions that work in one circumstance but not necessarily in another. If you manage by practices and lead by policies, your people don't have to be the experts; they don't have to exercise judgment because all of the judgment and wisdom is provided them in the form of rules and regulations.

If you focus on principles, you empower everyone who understands those principles to act without constant monitoring, evaluating, correcting, or controlling. Principles have universal application. And when these are internalized into habits, they empower people to create a wide variety of practices to deal with different situations.

Leading by principles, as opposed to practices, requires a different kind of training, perhaps even more training, but the payoff is more expertise, creativity, and shared responsibility at all levels of the organization.

If you train people in the *practices* of customer service, you will get a degree of customer service, but the service will break down whenever customers present a special case or problem because in doing so they short-circuit standard operating procedure.

Before people will act consistently on the *principle* of customer service, they need to adopt a new mind-set. In most cases they need to be trained—using cases, role plays, simulations, and some on-the-job coaching—to be sure they understand the principle and how it is applied on the job.

With the compass, we can win

"A compass in every pocket" is better than "a chicken in every pot" or a car in every garage. With moral compassing we can win even against tough competition. My view is that the Japanese subordinate the individual to the group to the extent that they don't tap into the creative and resourceful capacities of people—one indication being that they have had only 4 Nobel Prize winners compared with 186 in the United States. The highest leadership principle is win-win interdependency, where you are both high on individual and high on team.

But once people start to realize that this "compass" is going to be the basis for evaluation, including leadership style of the people at the top, they tend to feel threatened.

The president of a major corporation once asked me to meet with him and his management team. He said that they were all too concerned with preserving their own management style. He said that the corporate mission statement had no impact on their style. These executives felt the mission was for the people "out there" who were subject to the law, but they were above the law.

The idea of moral compassing is unsettling to people who think they are above the law because the Constitution, based on principles, is the law: it governs everybody, including the president. It places responsibility on individuals to examine their lives and determine if they are willing to live by it. All are accountable to the laws and principles.

I'm familiar with several poignant examples of major U.S. corporations telling their consultants, "We can't continue to do market feasibility studies and strategic studies independent of our culture and people." These executives understand what Michael Porter has said: "A implementation with B strategy is better than A strategy with B implementation."

We must deal with people/culture issues to improve the implementation of strategy and to achieve corporate integrity. We must be willing to go through a constitutional convention, if not a revolutionary war, to get the issues out on the table, deal with them, and get deep involvement, resulting in wise decisions. That won't happen without some blood, sweat, and tears.

Ultimately the successful implementation of any strategy hinges on the integrity people have to the governing principles and on their ability to apply those principles in any situation, using their own moral compass.

The Ethical Professional
Cultivating scruples

James S. Bowman

> *In matters of style, swim with the current.*
> *In matters of principle, stand like a rock.*
> — *Thomas Jefferson*

Ever since George Washington required "fitness of character," service to country has been regarded as more than a matter of mere technical skill. Competence also included personal honor, a view shared by Theodore Roosevelt who believed that, "To educate a man in mind but not in morals is to create a menace to society." This component of the "professional edge"—excellence in ethical bearing as well as technical ability—has long been a hallmark of governance. The obligation and privilege to uphold this ethos remain in today's multisectored public service. When representing the state, governmental, non-profit, and business officials alike are stewards of the common good. The concern for ethics, then, is founded upon the capacity of government (and its agents) to exercise power, a function that is moral in nature insofar as policy decisions are the authoritative allocation of societal values.

Accordingly, public servants must not only do technical things right but also do ethically right things. Leaders without basic ethics skills are professionally illiterate. This is what makes the execrable corporate, not-for-profit, and governmental scandals of recent years so devastating—the worst form of incompetence does not involve not knowing how to do something, but rather not knowing why something is done. Many professionals in a variety of fields—management, law, securities, policy, accounting, banking—have demonstrated a lack of understanding of this fundamental precept. Muriel Siebert, the first woman appointed to the New York Stock Exchange, explains the episode:

From James S. Bowman, Jonathan P. West, Evan M. Berman, & Montgomery Van Wart, *The Professional Edge: Competencies in Public Service* (Armonk, NY: M. E. Sharpe, 2004), pp. 60-86. Copyright © 2004 by M. E. Sharpe, Inc. Reprinted with permission.

> I basically feel that Enron was a case of total moral bankruptcy. It was not just the company and its executives. It was not just the accountants. They had to get legal opinions from a law firm. They had to get the derivatives (i.e., a security or financial asset, such as an option or futures contract, whose value depends upon the performance of an underlying security) from banks and Wall Street firms. One group alone could not have done it. The money was vast, and the money was fast. (Holdstein 2002)

The centrality of ethics in management in all sectors of the economy is undeniable. It is not an imposition or constraint, but the foundation of everything a professional is or does.

Because controversy is inherent in decision making and there is "no one best way" to deal with ethical quandaries, professional practice requires that moral criteria be integrated into policymaking. What is needed is not only technical ability to analyze problems but also the capacity to grasp those problems in a manner consistent with professional rectitude. Yet professionals may be unprepared to deal with conflicts between ethical values (e.g., honesty, integrity, promise keeping) and nonethical values (wealth, comfort, success).

FBI agents not heeding terrorist warnings, firefighters setting fires, questionable Red Cross fundraising and blood safety practices, clergymen abusing children and their superiors covering up the problem, preemptive war making, Olympic judges rigging scores, stock analysts giving biased ratings, and corporate officers "restating" record numbers of audits all demonstrate that ethics is key to the identity and legitimacy of any organization. In the last case, for instance, "the core purpose of accounting is, after all, to verify authenticity, to certify to the public the integrity of the accounts of a business or public agency" (Frederickson 2002: 9). Instead these professionals, unlike hospital financial officer James Alderson, who uncovered the largest Medicare scandal in history, sacrificed the independence they claimed to possess. "Ethics," then, is not something mysterious and far removed from ordinary life; instead, it is about people making decisions every day. There is no doubt that everyone encounters ethical dilemmas; the only question is when and whether they are ready.

What is needed is a management approach to the subject that includes understanding why people behave the way they do. To assume anyone with good character can act honorably in professional situations is no more sensible than suggesting that someone can function as a physician without special training. While values are imprinted at an early age, the real question is how they are applied at the workplace. Professional socialization can equip leaders to anticipate problems, recognize when they occur, and provide frameworks for thinking about issues; it affects not only ethical awareness but also moral reasoning and behavior (Rest and Narvez 1994; Menzel 1997; Menzel with Carson 1997; Bruce 1996). Without this preparation, individuals may rely on technical proficiency (in fact, doing things right can become a dominant *moral* code), unexamined personal preferences, passive obedience to authority, and/or unquestioned organizational loyalty. Those serving the public may bring idealism and cynicism to their work. This chapter aims to reinforce the former and minimize the latter by briefly defining values and ethics, and then examining (1) professionals and moral development, (2) individual ethics, and (3) organizational integrity.

Values and ethics

The most important thing in life is to decide what is important. Values are what matter to someone; they describe who he or she is. They shape one's worldview and clarify the character of the individual and ultimately the community; shared values are a kind of "cement" that brings and holds people together. Conflicts are inevitable, even desirable; governance is about maintaining conditions in which civilization is possible. Indeed, the Greek root for ethics is *ethos*, which emphasizes the perfection of the individual and the community in which he or she is defined.

Ethics is the way values are practiced. As such, it is both a process of inquiry (deciding how to decide) and a code of conduct (a set of standards governing behavior). Ethics is a system of right and wrong and a means to live accordingly. It is a quest for, and understanding of, the good life. Grounded in values and predicated upon ethics, professional responsibility demands the discretion of practitioners. But upon what foundation are decisions made?

Professionals and moral development

The key theory of moral development was formulated by Lawrence Kohlberg (Table 1). This hierarchical, inclusive taxonomy posits that individuals develop moral maturity by moving gradually from stage to stage in each of three levels:

Table 1. Kohlberg's stages of moral development with behavioral orientation.

Level	Self-perception	Stage orientation	"Right" behavior	Reference frame
Preconventional	Outside group	1. Punishment and obedience	1. Avoid punishment; defer to power	1. Physical consequence of actions
		2. Instrumental— relativist	2. Satisfaction of needs	2. Human relations are like a marketplace
Conventional	Inside group	3. Good boy—nice girl	3. That which pleases/helps others	3. Majority or "natural" behavior
		4. Law and order	4. Duty, maintenance of social order	4. Authority and fixed rule of society
Postconventional	Above group	5. Social contract	5. In terms of individual rights, free agreement	5. Constitutional/ democratic agreement, social utility
		6. Universal- ethical	6. Choice of conscience, ethical principles	6. Universal imperatives, justice, human rights

Source: Adapted from L. Kohlberg, "From Is to Ought: How to Commit the Naturalistic Fallacy and Get Away with It in the Study of Moral Development," in *Cognitive Development and Epistemology*, ed. Theodore Mischel, pp. 164-65. Copyright © 1971, with permission from Elsevier.

- Preconventional level moral reasoning reflects punishment avoidance (Stage 1) or an instrumental orientation (Stage 2); the person is self-interested and either fears or uses others.

- Conventional level thinking regards right behavior as conformity to expectations of significant others (Stage 3) or allegiance to the broader social order (Stage 4); the person's point of reference is a group, either small and personal or large and political.

- Postconventional judgments are derived from the moral autonomy resulting from critically examined values in the social contract upon which the social order is constructed (Stage 5) or from adherence to transcendental ethical principles (Stage 6); the individual is an independent actor as moral precepts trump the social expectations found at level two and the self-interests in level one.

Growing from level one to level two is a common, though not inevitable, psychological development requiring little deliberation. Stages are not skipped, and evolution can stop at any point. Actual reasoning tends to reflect one dominant stage, although it may sometimes occur at one stage higher or lower. Kohlberg believed that most people are at the conventional level because the postconventional level requires an uncommon commitment and contemplation.

It is fitting, therefore, that professionals strive to make decisions at the highest level of moral development. They cannot form judgments solely from the self-interested level-one perspective. Level-two thinking also may be inadequate because some social roles are unjust (e.g., law enforcement officials in the Jim Crow U.S. South; physicians in Nazi Germany). Level-three reasoning, however, prevents abuse of professional skills for one's own advantage or for that of one's social group. The idea is not to deny self or collective interest, but to temper them in light of a higher claim of human dignity (Snell 1993). Professionalism, in short, requires dedication to technical and ethical excellence. It is unthinkable for the professional to do otherwise when grappling with important problems.

The professional and individual ethics

Approaches to ethics

The essential issue of ethics is, as Socrates said, "What ought one to do?" However, no unified theory, no one secular approach, resolves all moral dilemmas. In deciding what to do, it is likely that people have always considered potential outcomes of their decisions and/or relevant guidelines to tell them what is right. It follows that cognitive schools of thought generally contend that matters of right and wrong are a function of either:

(a) the expected results of an action (consequentialism or teleology) or

(b) the application of pertinent rules (duty ethics or deontology).

In consequentialism, the best decision results in "the greatest good for the greatest number"; what is right is that which creates the largest amount of human happiness. In duty ethics, however, certain actions are inherently right (truth telling) or wrong (inflicting harm), irrespective of supposed consequences; one must see one's obligation and do it. Actions are to conform to moral rules. In deciding what rule to apply, one asks, "Would I want everyone else to make the decision I did?" If the answer is "yes," then the choice is justified; if "no," it is not.

The claimed strength of these approaches to ethics is that they are superior to an intuitive understanding of right or wrong—to say nothing of sheer expediency. In weighing expected results, the decision maker acts as an engineer calculating the costs and benefits of an action; in choosing among rules, she plays the role of a judge. Yet these theories have undue confidence in the power of reason: predicting consequences in human affairs is hazardous and choosing among conflicting duties is daunting. Moreover, both can be seen as rationalistic efforts that ignore the person making the decision. Ethics involves more than following general norms such as consequences or duty (Bowman 2003). Since antiquity, people have also relied upon their personal characters when confronted with dilemmas.

In this theory, known as virtue ethics, the primary faculty is moral intuition, not intellect. Reason may be essential in decision making, but the source of morality is human sentiment. Ethical questions are not simply technical ones to be resolved by projecting assumed results or established rules to a situation. Virtue ethics, instead, is a way of life, not merely a method of analysis. It is about right character more than right procedure. Indeed, reason easily leads into error insofar as many do not have the capacity or training for discursive reasoning (consider the convincing—and opposing—jury closings on *The Practice* or *Law and Order* television courtroom dramas).

This school of thought, accordingly, is a more personal, subjective approach to morality than cognitive ethics. Answers to questions of "What to do" have little to do with results and rules, and everything to do with what kind of person one is. An individual must *be* before he can *do*. Personal character is forged through experience by developing praiseworthy habits. The role of theory is not to get the professional out of a jam, but to help build one's fiber. Excellence in character ensures that the professional has "the right stuff" to do the right thing at the right time.

Yet no general theory of human virtue exists; virtues seem to vary from time to time and place to place as some virtues may not apply to all (e.g., men vs. women, young vs. old). Further, the virtue school lacks a theory of action. Virtues may generate instructions for action (the virtue of justice, for instance, provides the motivation to act justly), but what does a just person do in a given dilemma? The theory, finally, lacks integrity; one may be good but not know how to do good. Worse, confusing the two can easily lead to self-righteousness; if one believes he is good, then it is not hard to think that what he does is good.

The ethics triangle

If philosophers cannot agree on competing models (results-and-rules cognitive approaches and virtue ethics), then why should public servants? The reason is that they must be able to defend their judgments: professionals, by definition, are obligated to develop virtues, respect rules, and consider results. A decision-making tool, the "ethics triangle" (Svara 1997), recognizes the complementarity and interdependence of the imperatives in these three schools of thought. It emphasizes that cognition without virtue is as insufficient as virtue without cognition (Figure 1).

Each point of the triangle provides a distinct filter to clarify and reframe different aspects of a situation. Operating inside the triangle helps prevent the shortcomings of each approach as its angles inform and limit one another. Consider these examples:

- exaggerating advantages of a proposal to secure support
- insisting on one's own way at the risk of unit cohesiveness
- cutting corners in established processes
- showing disloyalty when times are tough
- concealing errors
- engaging in favoritism
- failing to report violations of agency policy
- denying responsibility for a mistake.

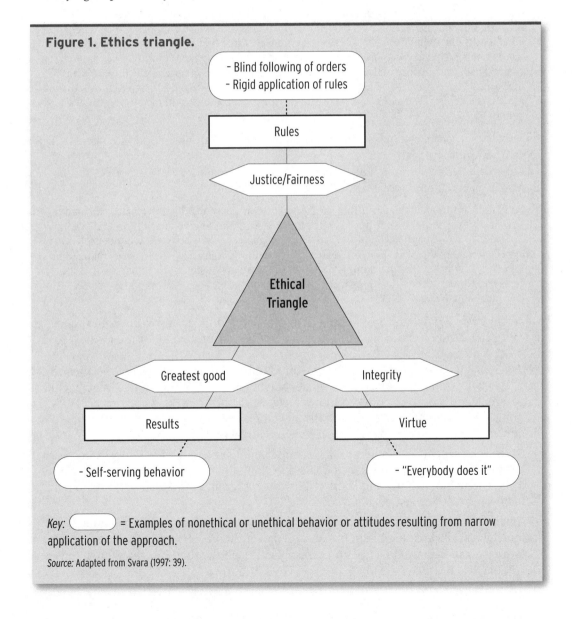

Figure 1. Ethics triangle.

Key: ⬭ = Examples of nonethical or unethical behavior or attitudes resulting from narrow application of the approach.

Source: Adapted from Svara (1997: 39).

Considering the results point of the triangle, "the greatest good for the greatest number" is achieved by refusing to engage in these actions because of the negative consequences from their exposure. Using a rules-based interpretation, the duty to avoid such behavior is clear. Under virtue ethics, finally, excellence in individual and community character is nourished by doing the right thing in each case.

Here is an actual case that occurred during the buildup for the 2003 attack on Iraq:

> A few months before I retired from the military, part of my responsibility was to submit monthly Unit Readiness Reports (URRs) to higher headquarters. Unit commanders are responsible to ensure that their units are combat ready 24/7. They must maintain 80 percent or greater readiness every month; how they get there is entirely their responsibility. I discovered that every month the number of soldiers trained and passing physicals was increased. When the URR numbers are less than 80 percent, commanders and staff would paper drill ("pencil whip") selective training events that never took place. I mentioned to the commander that the numbers were incorrect; his guidance was "we'll make it up next month." The unit had recently had a mandatory military ethics class instructed by the commander himself. When the reports were submitted to higher headquarters with the commander's signature and one of the staff members, I refused to sign them (anonymous personal communication, February 1, 2003).

Like the hypothetical examples earlier, the ethics triangle can be helpful in analyzing how to deal with this situation.

More complex issues—such as the genuine ethical dilemma below—produce more interesting, sometimes conflicting, findings.

> Bob has heard from his manager that their organization's staff will be downsizing; it could be as little as 5 percent or as much as 30 percent. However, the supervisor told Bob that "we're all under strict orders to keep it quiet" so that the agency's best employees will not seek other jobs. Ron, one of the finest professionals in Bob's unit, upon hearing downsizing rumors, told Bob that he was sure that he could get another job at a new business if a reduction in force occurred. However, their openings will close soon. Ron asked Bob, "Will there be layoffs?" (Bowman and Williams 1997: 522)

Generally speaking, when considering the results point of the triangle, the critical question is, "Which decision has the most utility in serving the greatest good for the greatest number?" In contemplating duty-based ethics from the rules part of the triangle, the key question is "What decision best carries the weight of universality?" (i.e., "What if everyone did that?"). Finally, from the virtue ethics angle, one might ask, " Who am I?" "What would a person of integrity do?" or "How can I best achieve excellence in this circumstance?" Although the synthesis developed from triangulation analysis does not tell one what to do or how to do it, it offers guidance about how to handle the situation:

- Because all schools of thought in the triangle imply that confidential information is to be respected, an honest answer to Ron's question might be, "I don't know what the level of reduction will be, but some reduction will occur. Ron, I want to keep you and help you, but you must decide what to do."

- Given that duty and virtue ethics emphasize truth-telling, the fair treatment of individuals suggests that the information Bob has should not be withheld, especially for organizational convenience and expediency; it follows that Bob should tell Ron what he has heard.

- Because credible arguments hold for the above options, the deliberations stimulated by the triangle could elicit moral imagination, which seeks a solution that both respects privileged organizational information and honors individuals. That is, promoting an ethical department through open communication could assist Bob in dealing with his manager (a discussion limited to rumors is insufficient) while demonstrating personal integrity (to tell Ron, but not the entire staff, is improper). Accordingly, Bob could tell Ron that he himself has heard rumors, too, and that he will seek clarification from his superiors—the only ones that can provide such information.

This analysis, then, is useful in teasing out the underlying logic by which actions are justified.

Of course, none of these strategies will satisfy everyone, but that is hardly the point; the triangle cannot produce a final, perfect decision for all seasons. Instead the decision-making process highlights a key function of ethical management: generating alternative viewpoints, systemically evaluating them, and crafting a considered judgment. The result is not a muddled compromise but a conscious attempt to reconcile conflicting values. This is difficult to do, and that is why these decisions are not easily made. This eclectic technique for adjudicating matters of right and wrong is very demanding. Yet in light of the shortcomings of each point of the triangle, there is little alternative; such an ethic is necessary given the complexity of the human condition. When choices are guided by benevolence, creativity, and an ethic of compromise and social integration—a moral tenet of democracy—there is at least the satisfaction that the problem has been fully examined and that the result can be rationally defended.

The goal is to strive for balance; governance is not geometry, but the art of the possible. It is an imperfect world where no one gets all he or she wants. In ethics, as in the rest of life, there are no magic answers. Differences between theories, nonetheless, should not lead to despair or the conclusion that one is as good as another. Better to have an imprecise answer to the right question than a precise answer to the wrong question.

Indeed, a narrow, overreaching application of a single approach at the extremes of the triangle (Figure 1) at the expense of the others holds considerable dangers: expediency (consequentialism), rigid rule application (duty ethics), and self-justification (virtue ethics). Attempts at rationalizing the eight dubious behaviors listed at the start of the subsection illustrate these risks. Instead the task is to consider the issues from each viewpoint and make an informed judgment. Professionals can do no less. Ethical quandaries are maddeningly intractable—and hauntingly unavoidable. Still, if they cannot be conclusively resolved, then that only demonstrates how fundamental they are; the fact that decisions are hard does not stop them from being made.

The ethics triangle, then, like a good map, offers choices, not formulas. Just as a map outlines a journey, the triangle provides help in making the inevitable compromises. As Aristotle admonished, do not expect more precision from the subject matter than it can allow. Professional ethics is more like an art than a science; instead of expecting definitive technical solutions, an aesthetic perspective appreciates that conflict is essential and productive. "Great art is beautiful precisely because of tension, not in spite of it" (Anon. 2002). Like the artist, the professional creatively combines differing influences. The need for judgment is not eliminated, but rather the triangle enables the skilled management of ethical ambiguity and independent thinking.

Organizational ethics

Individual-centered ethics is necessary, but not sufficient, for understanding the full scope of professional ethics. Because employees are susceptible to workplace influences, organizations are also important (recall the Greek emphasis on the citizen and community). People may make judgments based on personal standards, but institutions define and control the situations in which decisions are made. That is, organizations are major agencies of social control; ethical behavior is not only a psychological phenomenon but also a sociological one. As Myles's Law of Bureaucracy dictates ("Where you stand depends upon where you sit"), what employees ought to do is affected by their organizational roles.

Some resist acknowledging institutional factors for fear of diluting personal moral responsibility, but this concern is based on a false dichotomy. Recognizing the role of organization does not exculpate wrongdoers; it simply recognizes that "no man is an island," and that both the individual and the collectivity of which he is a part share important obligations. In order for either one to exercise responsibility in an informed manner, their interdependence must be seen and acted upon.

Kohlberg's six stages of individual moral development, in fact, can also be applied to organizations. Stage-1 institutions focus on survival as their moral beacon; any strategy will be employed to ensure it. Those in Stage 2 define success by manipulating others; victory justifies the tactics used. Stage-3 companies, nonprofits, and public agencies conform to the practices of peer institutions; prevailing industry customs dictate what is right and wrong. Stage-4 organizations take direction from legitimate authority to determine standards; their moral compass is based on society's legal structure. Units representing the next stage rely on tolerance, open discussion, and participatory management in uphold-

---

Exhibit 1. Comparing organizational strategies.

Low road

Ethos: Conformity with external standards

Objective: Prevent criminal conduct

Leadership: Lawyer-driven

Methods: Training, limited discretion, controls, penalties

Assumption: People driven by material self-interest

High road

Ethos: Self-governance according to chosen standards

Objective: Enable responsible conduct

Leadership: Management-driven

Methods: Education, leadership, accountability

Assumption: People guided by humanistic ideals

Source: Adapted from Paine (1994: 113).

ing—or changing—the social contract under which they operate; standards are derived through critical analysis and consensus. Finally, Stage-6 businesses, not-for-profits, and governmental departments profess ideals such as justice and individual rights; balanced judgment among competing interests, based on universal principles, determines right behavior. When laws violate these principles, principles ultimately prevail.

For purposes of analysis, these stages can be condensed into two organizational approaches (see Exhibit 1). The personal, negative, punitive, "low road" compliance strategy derives from Kohlberg's lower stages. This policy is clearly important, for without it a comprehensive ethics program may lack credibility. Yet it concentrates on individuals, defines ethics as staying out of trouble, emphasizes "symptom-solving," and often uses ethics to control behavior instead of to encourage improvement. If this approach represents the lowest common denominator, then the "high road" strategy symbolizes the highest common denominator. A structural, affirmative, commitment system based on the more mature stages of Kohlberg's framework is aimed at deterring rather than merely detecting problems by promoting right behavior. Instead of stressing blame and punishment, the approach focuses on reform and development. A robust ethics strategy, described below, will likely include elements of both plans, although not necessarily in equal proportion.

Creating an ethical institutional culture is no more easily achieved than resolving individual moral conundrums (White and Lam 2000; Trevino et al. 1999; Gilman 1999). In an organizational age, instruments of leadership are often corporate in nature. Indeed, the cornerstone of a comprehensive ethics program is a code of ethics. While their value is

---

Exhibit 2. Debating codes of ethics and conduct.

Standard affirmative arguments contend that codes:

- acknowledge the moral character of democracy
- honor transcendental ideals of self-government
- provide a symbolic basis for public expectations
- inspire moral behavior in public service
- offer a "shield" of protection for employees
- furnish a frame of reference to legitimize the discussion of workplace ethics.

Standard negative arguments maintain that codes:

- lack utility because they are either too vague (aspirational codes of ethics) or too precise (legal codes of conduct)
- contain contradictory provisions and/or have no priorities among them
- foster the official hypocrisy and public cynicism that they are designed to prevent, if not enforced
- focus on employee obligations to the employer to the exclusion of organizational responsibilities to foster ethics
- emphasize proscribed, at the expense of prescribed, behavior.

certainly arguable (see Exhibit 2), codes can play significant aspirational and operational roles when seen as a means to a larger end. The real issue is how these documents are developed and what goes with them in order to make them meaningful in daily management. Like any organizational initiative, the impetus to create (or reinvigorate) an agency code must have authentic leadership support. The actual strategy, produced and implemented by a representative employee taskforce, begins with a self-generated needs assessment to gather information, encourage participation, conduct workshops, and create a shared vocabulary. Depending on the results, the initiative could include:

- advice mechanisms and reporting channels (e.g., establishing an independent advisory ethics board available to all, grievance procedures, toll-free whistleblower numbers [see, e.g., www.hotlines. com], support structures to ensure due process, an ombudsman)
- decision-making tools (e.g., rotating appointments of an "angel's" advocate tasked to raise ethical issues in staff meetings, or formulating "ethical impact statements" prior to major decisions)
- promotion activities (posting of the code in the department, as well as reprinting it in agency newsletters and reports; recognizing exemplary cases in an awards program)
- personnel system changes (revising recruitment, training, and performance evaluation processes, including identification of ethical dimensions of jobs in position descriptions and whistle-blower protections against retaliation)
- periodic ethics audits (conducting document reviews, vulnerability assessments, employee interviews and surveys, evaluations of existing systems) to provide an ongoing appraisal of program effectiveness.

The objective is to make the code a living document by offering opportunities to participate in its development and evolution, infusing its values into the routines of the organization, providing procedures for its interpretation, and ensuring its enforcement.

While it may be true that little of importance occurs without individuals, little is lasting without institutions. Thus a good place to start is to:

- change the chief executive officer's title to the chief ethics officer,
- hook up an ethics hotline in her office,
- increase executive exposure to criminal and civil liability,
- include outside directors on nonprofit and business boards,
- create "open book" management systems,
- rotate auditors on a periodic basis,
- strengthen conflict-of-interest rules,
- adopt a "three strikes and you're out" corporate death penalty (revocation of corporate charter with the third criminal conviction), and
- support calls for a national commission on white-collar crime.

What is needed, in short, is an actual commitment to an ethical infrastructure rather than just an announcement about an actual commitment. Indeed, one Defense Supply Center employee believes, "Each organization is different and has diverse motivations. We should ask ourselves if ethics initiatives are more for public relations than for establishing an ethical organization. For those of us who have been around for a while, and watched programs *du jour* come and go, one develops a healthy skepticism about the intentions of organizations" (anonymous personal communication, January 26, 2003).

While no strategy will be without criticism, if all proposals are rejected until perfection is guaranteed, then improvement is unlikely. Public and private organizations should plant and cultivate standards by which a professional can measure his or her behavior, encourage correction of deficiencies, and minimize institutional conditions that lead to unethical behavior. The issue is not whether norms of conduct will develop in an organization, but rather what they are, how they are communicated, and whether all are fully conscious of the ethical dimensions of work. The idea is to nourish a transparent institutional culture by offering incentives for ethical behavior, reducing opportunities for corruption, and increasing the risk of untoward conduct.

Like the top of a jigsaw puzzle box, such an initiative can provide a point of departure and serve as an enabling device to strive for professional ideals. It must have the leadership's dedication, be "home grown" by employees themselves, and include a clear policy statement, explanatory guidelines, due process procedures, and employee training, as well as sanctions and rewards. That is, there must be top-down commitment to, and bottom-up participation in, processes designed for continuous improvement. Such a program makes common rationalizations of questionable behavior (e.g., "What I want to do is not 'really' unethical" or "Because the idea will help the organization, I will support it") much more difficult (Gellerman 1986). Organizations, paradoxically, are at their most dangerous when they are successful because people become arrogant and that prevents learning. In the absence of an ethics initiative, business-as-usual expediency and an "anything goes" mentality is likely to dominate, condoning untoward behavior, reinforcing amorality, and discouraging ethical action.

Conclusion

This article, after defining values and ethics, discussed moral development theory and the strengths and weakness of three major approaches to ethics—results, rules, and virtue—as part of the mosaic of understanding moral philosophy. Because individual professionals must justify their decisions, the ethics triangle, which emphasizes the interdependence of these approaches, was presented and used in case studies. As Stephen K. Bailey (1965) believed, the dilemma—and glory—of public service is to be consistent enough to deserve respect from others (and oneself) and pliable enough to accomplish ethical objectives.

Ultimately, the challenge of every public servant is to resolve to act solely in the public interest and to shun the many opportunities that threaten this resolve. The quest to improve social circumstances, to fulfill human potential, is to lead the good life. The state of mind required to achieve this is eloquently described by Max Weber:

> [I]t is immensely moving when a mature person...is aware of a responsibility for the consequences of his conduct and really feels such responsibility with heart and soul. He then acts by following an ethic of responsibility and somewhere he reaches the point where he says: "Here I stand; I can do no other." That is something genuinely human and moving....In so far as this is true, an ethic of ultimate ends and an ethic of responsibility are not absolute contrasts but rather supplements, which only in unison constitute a genuine person—a person who can have the "calling" for politics. (Carney 1998)

Insofar as the whole point of leading organizations is to recognize the vitality inherent in conflict and to harmonize pressures in praiseworthy ways, attention then shifted to organizational ethics. Moral development theory was applied and condensed to delineate components of an ethical infrastructure. Such programs can reinforce an exemplary organizational climate, but they cannot create it—that remains the function of leadership.

References

Anon. 2002. "An Aesthetic Theory of Conflict in Administrative Ethics." Unpublished manuscript.

Bailey, S. 1965. "Relationship Between Ethics and Public Service." In *Public Administration and Democracy: Essays in Honor of Paul Appleby*, ed. R. Martin, 282-98. Syracuse, NY: Syracuse University Press.

Bowman, J. 2003. "Virtue Ethics." *Encyclopedia of Public Administration and Public Policy*, ed. J. Rabin, 1259-63. New York: Dekker.

Bowman, J., and R. Williams. 1997. "Ethics in Government: From a Winter of Despair to a Spring of Hope." *Public Administration Review* 57: 517-26.

Bruce, W. 1996. "Codes of Ethics and Codes of Conduct: Perceived Contribution to the Practice of Ethics in Local Government." *Public Integrity Annual*: 23-30.

Carney, G. 1998. "Working Paper: Conflict of Interest: Legislators, Ministers and Public Officials." Available at: www.transparency.org/working_papers/carney/4-conclusions.html (accessed June 4, 2003).

Frederickson, H. G. 2002. "Arthur Anderson, Where Art Thou?" *Public Administration Times* (October): 9.

Gellerman, S. 1986. "Why 'Good' Managers Make Bad Ethical Choices." *Harvard Business Review* 64 (July-August): 85-90.

Gilman, S. 1999. "Effective Management of Ethical Systems: Some New Frontiers." In *Fighting Corruption*, ed. V. Mavaso and D. Balia, 95-114. Pretoria: University of South Africa Press.

Holdstein, W. 2002. "An Insider's Advice on Corporate Ethics." *New York Times*, November 24, BU: 5.

Kohlberg, L. 1971. "From Is to Ought: How to Commit the Naturalistic Fallacy and Get Away With It in the Study of Moral Development." In *Cognitive Development and Epistemology*, ed. Theodore Mischel, 164-65. New York: Elsevier.

Menzel, D. 1997. "Teaching Ethics and Values in Public Administration: Are We Making a Difference?" *Public Administration Review* 57: 224-30.

Menzel, D., with C. Carson. 1997. "Empirical Research on Public Administration Ethics: A Review and Assessment." *Public Integrity* 1, no. 3: 239-64.

Rest, J., and D. Narvez. 1994. *Moral Development in the Professions*. Hillsdale, NJ: Erlbaum.

Snell, R. 1993. *Developing Skills for Ethical Management*. London: Chapman and Hill.

Svara, J. 1997. "The Ethical Triangle." *Public Integrity Annual* 2: 33-41.

Trevino, L., G. Weaver, D. Gibson, and B. Toffler. 1999. "Managing Ethical and Legal Compliance: What Works and What Hurts." *California Management Review* 40 (2): 131-51.

White, L., and L. Lam. 2000. "A Proposed Infrastructural Model of the Establishment of Organizational Ethics Systems." *Journal of Business Ethics* 28: 35-42.

Part 2

Implementation:
Ethical Leadership

An Ethics–Based Approach to Leadership

Montgomery Van Wart

The ethics-based approach offers a stark contrast to the power-based approach to leadership studies. The power-based approach assumes that the primary source of wisdom is the leader or that knowledge is for the leader's benefit, that the leader is the critical decision maker and implicitly the most important, and that the leader's success is the principal consideration (Exhibit 1). In contrast, an ethics-based approach assumes that the leader is not likely to have all wisdom and that followers either have important contributions to make or may even have all the facts and knowledge necessary to the leader's decisions. Second, the approach assumes that followers have approximately the same importance as leaders themselves, and sometimes followers have even greater importance than leaders. Followers accomplish the work and they are the responsibility of the leader. Rather than increasing personal influence, leaders are involved in empowerment. Finally, this approach stresses that leaders must deemphasize their personal interests to be effective. While the power-based approach does not endorse use of power for personal ends, it tends to neglect that aspect in its study of influence.

Leadership styles are based on the level of social consciousness, self-discipline, and courage of the leader. The most common symptom of leaders with *unethical styles* is that they use their positions for their personal benefit or for a special group at the expense of others. Also, unethical leaders may use their positions and power to promote the interests of friends at the expense of more qualified people or to seek retribution against those who cross them. Less egregious but still unethical are those leaders who simply use their positions as platforms for ego-boosting rather than accomplishing good; such leaders tend to hoard all the credit for accomplishments. Moreover, it is generally considered unethical when leaders ignore major responsibilities or decisions that they think may reflect poorly on themselves or because they are simply lazy or sloppy.

From Montgomery Van Wart, *Dynamics of Leadership in Public Service: Theory and Practice* (Armonk, NY: M. E. Sharpe, 2005), pp. 377-384. Copyright © 2005 by M. E. Sharpe, Inc. Reprinted with permission.

Many leaders are *ethically neutral* in their style. They may be unaware of subtle ethical issues, or if they are aware, fail to take the time to reflect on them. A senior manager may not know, because he is not receptive to receiving information about his supervisors, that one of them frequently uses a demeaning style with employees. Or the senior manager may know about the problem but ignore it. Sometimes managers in the private and public

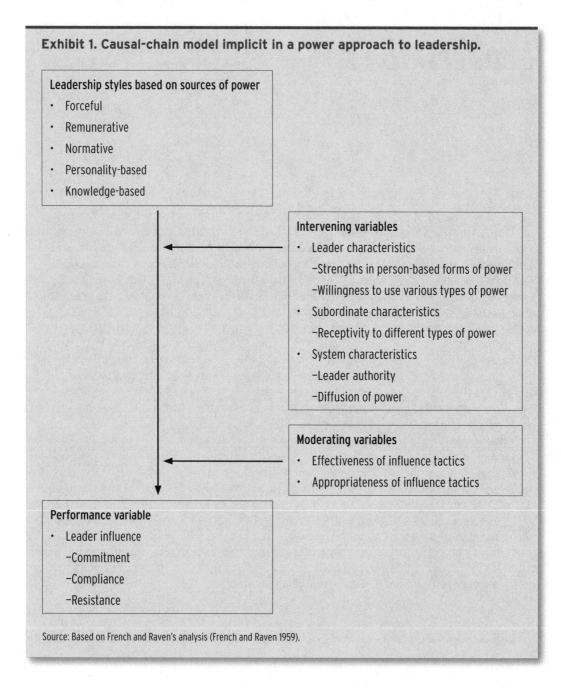

Exhibit 1. Causal-chain model implicit in a power approach to leadership.

Leadership styles based on sources of power

- Forceful
- Remunerative
- Normative
- Personality-based
- Knowledge-based

Intervening variables

- Leader characteristics
  - Strengths in person-based forms of power
  - Willingness to use various types of power
- Subordinate characteristics
  - Receptivity to different types of power
- System characteristics
  - Leader authority
  - Diffusion of power

Moderating variables

- Effectiveness of influence tactics
- Appropriateness of influence tactics

Performance variable

- Leader influence
  - Commitment
  - Compliance
  - Resistance

Source: Based on French and Raven's analysis (French and Raven 1959).

sectors pride themselves on the technical and "neutral" execution of their duties. What are the authoritative guidelines and bureaucratically assigned duties? Managers operating in this mode generally try to emphasize the procedural nature of work, the rules, and technical fairness. Ethics, apart from rule breaking, is not a part of their job. Thus, ethically neutral leaders can range from those who are unresponsive or unaware of moderate ethical issues to those who attempt to structure and conceive of their work as procedural and essentially value free. Ethically neutral leaders are themselves free of improper behavior, but they do not actively encourage an ethical climate.

The analysis of ethical leadership is nearly as old as philosophy itself. Most of Aristotle's work on ethics is set in a leadership context (Aristotle 1953). His virtue-based perspective of ethics emphasizes the rational process that leaders exercise. People of good character—*ethical leaders*—engage in three primary practices. First, people of good character recognize ethical issues. They understand that many values invariably compete in social settings, and that leaders are often the arbiters of who gets what in terms of allocating of values. For example, a seemingly simple decision about extending hours has many ramifications. What will be the effect on the employees, the clients, the quality of work, the manager's own ability to coordinate the hours and get people to staff less desirable times, the cost of operations, and so forth? Second, ethical leaders take the time to reflect on issues that often pit one important value against another. Consider the leader evaluating a problem supervisor: A demeaning supervisor is also extremely hard working, organized, and informed. He is himself the best worker and he leads the most productive unit. Nonetheless, the ethical conundrum is that leaders should not put down or degrade their subordinates and clutch all power to themselves in the name of the organization. Third, ethical leaders find ways to integrate the collective good into appropriate decisions. Using the previous example, changing the supervisor's style, without diminishing productivity or the supervisor's substantial contributions, is not an easy task. Integrating appropriate but differing sets of values may mean hard work for the ethical leader. It may also mean finding workable compromises that optimize several of important values.

A number of theorists have been interested in identifying not only ethical leaders but also highly ethical, or *exemplary,* leaders (Cooper and Wright 1992; Hart 1992). What characterizes the person of high character? This is an especially important question for public sector leadership because stewardship of the public good is inherently a social process and often very challenging to enact. Two additional elements are generally articulated: contribution and courage.

Making a substantial contribution to a group, organization, community, or system takes sustained hard work, perseverance, and involvement of many people, which in turn requires trust, empathy, and nurturance. One type of substantial contribution might be the accomplishment of a specific project or good work of some magnitude. A city library director might seek authorization for and implement expanded auxiliary services such as after-school programs in a disadvantaged area, despite its lack of popularity with a policy board dominated by wealthier neighborhoods. A second type of substantial contribution involves raising the moral consciousness of followers or the community. Burns (1978) asserted that it was the responsibility of political leaders to actively guide the transformation of society by stressing justice, liberty, and equality. Leaders them-selves should be transformed by the process so that their morality also ascends to a higher, more socialized level. In a similar vein, Heifetz (1994) proposes a facilitative role for leaders in the process of moral consciousness raising. He believes that such leaders articulate the value conflicts of workers, organizations, and communities in rapidly changing environments. Exemplary leaders enable groups to sustain dialogues until coherent decisions can be reached that benefit all in win-win solutions. Leaders do not select the answers or make decisions occur; leaders allow answers and decisions to emerge by mobilizing people to tackle the tough issues. This means that they must bring attention to the critical issues, foster honest and candid discussion, manage competing perspectives, and facilitate the decision-making process in a timely way.

The final or highest level of exemplary leadership is often perceived as the willingness to make sacrifices for the common good and/or to show uncommon courage. David K. Hart (1992) discusses such leaders as they confront moral episodes. Sacrifice is denying oneself commodities that are generally valued in order to enhance the welfare of others or the common good. Leaders who sacrifice may give extraordinary time, do without financial emoluments, pass up career advancement, or forsake prestige as a part of their passion to serve others. The best leaders may be those who are able to make sacrifices but nonetheless feel joy at the opportunity to help (Block 1993; DePree 1989). Greenleaf (1977) calls these servant leaders. Servant leaders are highly concerned about empathy, development of others, healing, openness, equality, listening, and unconditional acceptance of others. When they act, they do so with quiet persuasion that places a high threshold on inclusion. They avoid the unequal power paradigm typical in hierarchical organizations and instead use the *primus inter pares* (first among equals) paradigm (Greenleaf 1977, 61-62). Indeed, they assert that the hierarchical model of leadership is often damaging to leaders. Some of the challenges "strong" leaders often face are:

- "To be a lone chief atop a pyramid is abnormal and corrupting."

- "A self-protective image of omniscience often evolves from... warped and filtered communication."

- "Those persons who are atop the pyramids often suffer from a very real loneliness."

- "...in too many cases the demands of the office destroy these [leaders'] creativity long before they leave office."

- "Being in the top position prevents leadership by persuasion because the single chief holds too much power."

- "In the end the chief becomes a performer, not a natural person, and essential creative powers diminish."

- "[A single chief] nourishes the notion among able people that one must be boss to be effective. And it sanctions, in a conspicuous way, a pernicious and petty status-striving that corrupts everyone." (Greenleaf 1977, 63-64)

However, some leaders are willing to make exceptional and painful sacrifices or decisions that require great courage. Making a tough decision may lead to social stigmatization. Revealing unpleasant truths about powerful people, interests, or groups may result in loss of job or even the ruin of a career.... While most leaders do not experience many of these moments, when they do, opportunities for greatness or conspicuous mediocrity and/or failure emerge. Yet, sometimes a decision is not so much dangerous to one's career as it is so enormous and controversial that it would be far less trouble simply to ignore it. The courage of such decisions can result in ethical greatness if the leader's ethical integrity is mature. For example, Thomas Jefferson despised executive privilege but nonetheless doubled the size of the country with a unilateral executive order when he made the Louisiana Purchase in 1803, an act nearly as defining as the American Revolution itself. For a general model of ethical leadership that differentiates good and exemplary characteristics, see Exhibit 2.

Models of ethical leadership are generally proposed as universal theories. The one exception may be the highest level of exemplary leadership, which requires acts of extraordinary courage or sacrifice. Such challenges/opportunities are relatively rare.

The quality of ethical leadership is moderated by three factors. First, how conscious are leaders of ethical issues and how active are such leaders in reflecting on them? This cognitive element must be joined with a caring ethic that motivates leaders to integrate competing communal values in wholesome ways. Second, ethical leaders are not occasionally ethical; they are constant in practicing ethical reflection. This self-discipline is even more important for persons aspiring to be of high character. Great self-discipline is normally required to accomplish important moral projects or increase the moral awareness of the community. Third, the degree of courage that a leader has will affect his/her ability and courage to make substantial personal sacrifices and potential administrative martyrdom.

The performance variables for ethical leadership are dissimilar to other approaches that generally emphasize efficiency of production or follower satisfaction. Various theorists in

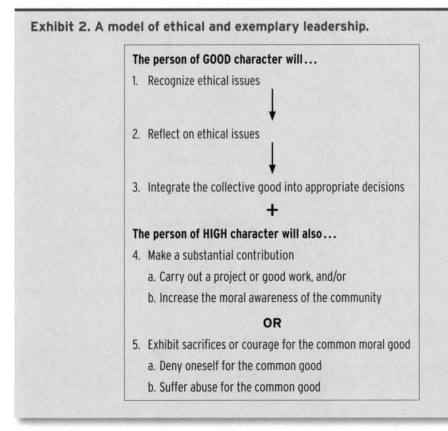

Exhibit 2. A model of ethical and exemplary leadership.

The person of GOOD character will...

1. Recognize ethical issues

2. Reflect on ethical issues

3. Integrate the collective good into appropriate decisions

+

The person of HIGH character will also...

4. Make a substantial contribution

   a. Carry out a project or good work, and/or

   b. Increase the moral awareness of the community

OR

5. Exhibit sacrifices or courage for the common moral good

   a. Deny oneself for the common good

   b. Suffer abuse for the common good

this general approach propose different goals, but increasing the common good and the empowerment of followers are the most frequent. These goals contrast especially with the power-based approach to leadership. Furthermore, ethics-based approaches implicitly emphasize the quality of decision making as demonstrated by the more thoughtful, comprehensive methods they recommend (Cooper 1990). See Exhibit 3 for the implicit causal chain for ethics-based approaches.

Because it takes such a different path than most other approaches, ethics-based leadership has a number of strengths. For example, it prominently raises the question: For whom is leadership exercised? *In this approach, the context of leadership as a social phenomenon to enhance the common good must be the first consideration.* Other approaches with their more instrumental perspective may emphasize productivity, success, or influence, but this can allow some leaders to exercise excessive narcissism in the name of efficiency or control. Indeed, in many business contexts leaders are taught that social responsibilities are constraints to be avoided or ignored (Henry 2003, 54). Often, other approaches add an ethical component, but it generally seems to be a codicil to the

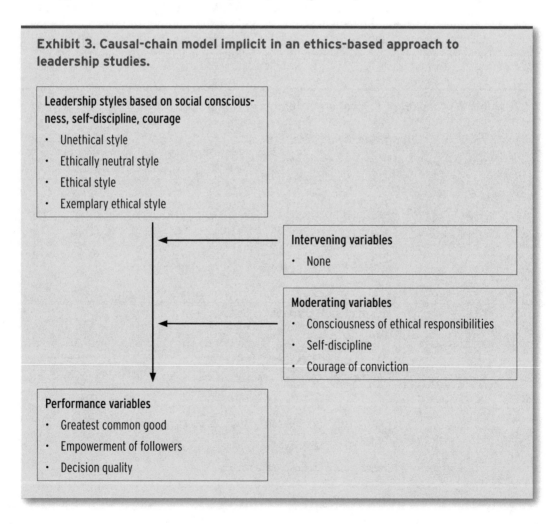

Exhibit 3. Causal-chain model implicit in an ethics-based approach to leadership studies.

Leadership styles based on social consciousness, self-discipline, courage
- Unethical style
- Ethically neutral style
- Ethical style
- Exemplary ethical style

Intervening variables
- None

Moderating variables
- Consciousness of ethical responsibilities
- Self-discipline
- Courage of conviction

Performance variables
- Greatest common good
- Empowerment of followers
- Decision quality

theory. Ethics-based leadership is also inspiring because of the examples it cites and the challenges it lays out. Theoretically, ethics-based leadership provides valuable insights and recommendations with respect to the courage needed and the nature of leader character. One major weakness is that it offers little insight into the more pragmatic aspects of leadership. Ethical conundrums are, hopefully, relatively rare in a manager's routine. Moreover, ethics-based leadership frequently has an abstract, philosophical quality. This is partly a result of its intellectual heritage and partly due to the highly generalized normative base that it advocates.

References

Aristotle. 1953. *The Ethics of Aristotle.* Trans. J.A.K. Thompson. New York: Viking Penguin.

Block, P. 1993. *Stewardship: Choosing Service Over Self Interest.* San Francisco: Berrett-Koehler.

Burns, J. 1978. *Leadership.* New York: Harper and Row.

Cooper, T. 1990. *The Responsible Administrator.* San Francisco: Jossey-Bass.

Cooper, T., and Wright, D., eds. 1992. *Exemplary Public Administrators: Character and Leadership in Government.* San Francisco: Jossey-Bass.

DePree, M. 1989. *Leadership Is an Art.* New York: Doubleday.

French, J. and Raven, B. 1959. "The Bases of Social Power." In *Studies in Social Power,* ed. D. Cartwright. Ann Arbor: University of Michigan.

Greenleaf, R. 1977. *Servant Leadership: A Journey into the Nature of Legitimate Power and Greatness.* New York: Paulist Press.

Hart, D. 1992. "The Moral Exemplar in an Organizational Society." In *Exemplary Public Administrators: Character and Leadership in Government,* ed. T. Cooper and D. Wright, ch. 12. San Francisco: Jossey-Bass.

Heifetz, R. 1994. *Leadership Without Easy Answers.* Cambridge, MA: Belknap Press.

Henry, N. 2003. *Public Administration and Public Affairs.* 9th ed. Upper Saddle River, NJ: Prentice Hall.

Leadership Ethics

Peter G. Northouse

Leadership is a process whereby the leader influences others to reach a common goal. The *influence* dimension of leadership requires the leader to have an impact on the lives of those being led. To make a change in other people carries with it an enormous ethical burden and responsibility. Because leaders usually have more power and control than followers, they also have more responsibility to be sensitive to how their leadership affects followers' lives.

Whether in group work, organizational pursuits, or community projects, leaders engage subordinates and use them in their efforts to reach common goals. In all of these situations, leaders have the ethical responsibility to treat followers with dignity and respect—as human beings with unique identities. This "respect for persons" demands that leaders be sensitive to followers' own interests, needs, and conscientious concerns (Beauchamp & Bowie, 1988). While all of us have an ethical responsibility to treat other people as unique human beings, leaders have a special responsibility because the nature of their leadership puts them in a special position, where they have a greater opportunity to influence others in significant ways.

Ethics is central to leadership, and leaders help to establish and reinforce organizational values. Every leader has a distinct philosophy and point of view. All leaders "have an agenda, a series of beliefs, proposals, values, ideas, and issues that they wish to 'put on the table'" (Gini, 1998). The values promoted by the leader have a significant impact on the values exhibited by the organization (cf. Carlson & Perrewe, 1995; Schminke, Ambrose, & Noel, 1997; Trevino, 1986). Again, because of their influence, leaders play a major role in establishing the ethical climate of their organizations.

In short, ethics is central to leadership because of the nature of the process of influence, the need to engage followers to accomplish mutual goals, and the impact leaders have on establishing the organization's values.

The following section provides a discussion of some of the work of several prominent leadership scholars who have addressed issues related to ethics and leadership. Although many additional viewpoints exist, those presented are representative of what is currently the predominant thinking in the area of ethics and leadership.

Abridged from Peter G. Northouse, "Leadership Ethics," in *Leadership: Theory and Practice*, 3d ed., pp. 306-316, copyright 2004 by Sage Publications, Inc. Reprinted by permission of Sage Publications, Inc.

Heifetz's perspective on ethical leadership

Based on his work as a psychiatrist and his observations and analysis of many world leaders (e.g., President Lyndon Johnson, Mohandas Gandhi, and Margaret Sanger), Ronald Heifetz (1994) has formulated a unique approach to ethical leadership; it emphasizes how leaders help followers to confront conflict and to effect changes from conflict. Heifetz's perspective is related to ethical leadership because it deals with values—values of workers, and the values of the organizations and communities in which they work. According to Heifetz, leadership involves the use of authority to help followers deal with the conflicting values that emerge in rapidly changing work environments and social cultures. It is an ethical perspective because it speaks directly to the values of workers.

For Heifetz (1994), leaders must use authority to mobilize people to face tough issues. The leader provides a "holding environment" in which there is trust, nurturance, and empathy. Within a supportive context, followers can feel safe to confront and deal with hard problems. Specifically, leaders use authority to get people to pay attention to the issues, to act as a reality test regarding information, to manage and frame issues, to orchestrate conflicting perspectives, and to facilitate the decision-making process (Heifetz, 1994, p. 113). The leader's duties are to assist the follower in struggling with change and personal growth.

Burns's perspective on ethical leadership

Burns's theory of transformational leadership places a strong emphasis on followers' needs, values, and morals. Transformational leadership involves attempts by leaders to move followers to higher standards of moral responsibility. This emphasis sets transformational leadership apart from most other approaches to leadership because it clearly states that leadership has a moral dimension (cf. Bass & Steidlmeier, 1999).

Similar to that of Heifetz, Burns's (1978) perspective argues that it is important for leaders to engage themselves with followers and help them in their personal struggles regarding conflicting values. In the process, the connection between the leader and the follower raises the level of morality in both the leader and the follower.

The origins of Burns's position on leadership ethics are rooted in the works of such writers as Abraham Maslow, Milton Rokeach, and Lawrence Kohlberg (Ciulla, 1998). The influence of these writers can be seen in how Burns emphasizes the leader's role to attend to the personal motivations and moral development of the follower. For Burns, it is the responsibility of the leader to help followers assess their own values and needs in order to raise them to a higher level of functioning, to a level that will stress values such as liberty, justice, and equality (Ciulla, 1998).

Burns's position on leadership as a morally uplifting process has not been without its critics. It has raised many questions. How do you choose what is a better set of moral values? Who is to say that some decisions represent higher moral ground than others? If leadership, by definition, requires raising individual moral functioning, does this mean that the leadership of a leader such as Adolf Hitler is not actually leadership? Notwithstanding these very legitimate questions, Burns's perspective on leadership is unique in how it makes ethics the central characteristic of the process. His writing has placed ethics at the forefront of scholarly discussions of what leadership means and how leadership should be carried out.

Greenleaf's perspective on ethical leadership

In the early 1970s, Robert Greenleaf developed a somewhat paradoxical approach to leadership called *servant leadership.* It is an approach that has gained increased popularity in recent years (cf. Block, 1993; De Pree, 1989, 1992). With its strong altruistic ethical overtones, servant leadership emphasizes that leaders should be attentive to the concerns of their followers and empathize with them; they should take care of them and nurture them.

Greenleaf (1970, 1977) argued that leadership was bestowed on a person who was by nature a servant. In fact, the way an individual emerges as a leader is by first becoming a servant. A servant leader focuses on the needs of followers and helps them to become more knowledgeable, more free, more autonomous, and more like servants themselves. They enrich others by their presence.

In addition to serving, the servant leader has a social responsibility to be concerned with the "have-nots" and to recognize them as equal stakeholders in the life of the organization. Where inequalities and social injustices exist, a servant leader tries to remove them (Graham, 1991). In becoming a servant leader, a leader uses less institutional power and less control, while shifting authority to those who are being led. Servant leadership values everyone's involvement in community life because it is within a community that one fully experiences respect, trust, and individual strength. Greenleaf places a great deal of emphasis on listening, empathy, and unconditional acceptance of others.

In the novel *The Journey to the East,* by Herman Hesse (1956), there is an example of leadership that was the inspiration behind Greenleaf's formulation of servant leadership. The story is about a group of travelers on a mythical journey who are accompanied by a servant who does menial chores for the travelers but also sustains them with his spirits and song. The servant's presence has an extraordinary impact on the group, but when the servant becomes lost and disappears, the group of travelers falls into disarray and abandons their journey. Without the servant, they are unable to carry on. It was the servant who was leading the group. He emerged as a leader by caring for the travelers.

A common theme running through all three of the perspectives (i.e., Heifetz, Burns, and Greenleaf) is that the leader-follower relationship is central to ethical leadership. In addition, they all emphasize that it is critically important for leaders to pay close attention to the unique needs of their followers.

In many ways, the ideas presented by these leadership scholars are parallel to and consonant with the *ethic of caring* set forth by Gilligan (1982), who contended that personal relationships should be the beginning point of ethics. In the past 20 years, the "caring principle" has become recognized by scholars as one of the predominant moral principles. From a caring perspective, a leader's actions are morally correct if they express care in protecting the people with whom the leader has special relationships (Schumann, 2001). An ethic of caring is extremely important in organizations because it is the main ingredient in building trust and cooperative relationships (Brady, 1999).

Principles of ethical leadership

In this section, we turn to a discussion of five principles of ethical leadership, the origins of which can be traced back to Aristotle. The importance of these principles has been discussed in a variety of disciplines including biomedical ethics (Beauchamp & Childress,

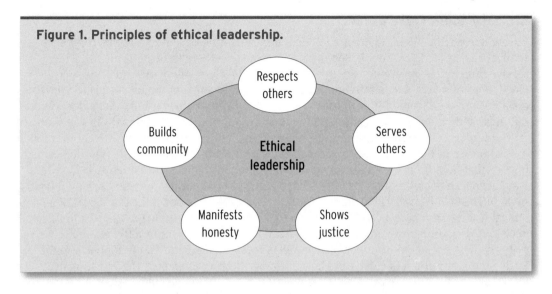

Figure 1. Principles of ethical leadership.

1994), business ethics (Beauchamp & Bowie, 1988), counseling psychology (Kitchener, 1984), and leadership education (Komives, Lucas, & McMahon, 1998), to name a few. Although not inclusive, these principles provide a foundation for the development of sound ethical leadership: *respect, service, justice, honesty,* and *community* (see Figure 1).

Ethical leaders respect others

Philosopher Immanuel Kant (1724-1804) argued that it is our duty to treat others with respect. To do so means always to treat others as ends in themselves and never as means to ends. As Beauchamp and Bowie (1988) pointed out, "Persons must be treated as having their own autonomously established goals and must never be treated purely as the means to another's personal goals" (p. 37). They go on to suggest that treating others as ends rather than as means requires that we treat other people's decisions and values with respect because failing to do so would signify that we were treating them as a means to our own ends.

Leaders who respect others also allow them to be themselves, with creative wants and desires. They approach other persons with a sense of unconditional worth and valuable individual differences (Kitchener, 1984). Respect includes giving credence to others' ideas and confirming them as human beings. At times, it may require that leaders have to defer to others. As Burns (1978) suggested, leaders should nurture followers in becoming aware of their own needs, values, and purposes and assist them in integrating these with the leader's.

Respect for others is a complex ethic that is similar to but goes deeper than the kind of respect that parents teach children when they are little. Respect means that a leader listens closely to his or her subordinates, is empathic, and is tolerant of opposing points of view. It means treating subordinates in ways that confirm their beliefs, attitudes, and values. When a leader exhibits respect to subordinates, subordinates can feel competent about their work. In short, leaders who show respect in fact treat others as worthy human beings.

Ethical leaders serve others

[Elsewhere we have] contrasted two ethical theories—one based on a concern for self (ethical egoism) and another based on the interests of others (ethical altruism). The service principle is clearly an example of altruism. Leaders who serve are altruistic; they place their followers' welfare foremost in their plans. In the workplace, altruistic service behavior can be observed in activities such as mentoring, empowerment behaviors, team building, and citizenship behaviors, to name a few (Kanungo & Mendonca, 1996).

The leader's ethical responsibility to serve others is very similar to the ethical principle in health care of beneficence. Beneficence is derived from the Hippocratic tradition, which implies that health professionals ought to make choices that benefit patients. In a general way, beneficence asserts that providers have a duty to help others pursue their own legitimate interests and goals (Beauchamp & Childress, 1994). Similar to health professionals, ethical leaders have a responsibility to attend to others, be of service to them, and make decisions pertaining to them that are beneficial and not harmful to their welfare.

In the past decade, the service principle has received a great deal of emphasis in the leadership literature. It is clearly evident in the writings of Greenleaf (1977), Gilligan (1982), Block (1993), Covey (1990), De Pree (1989), and Kouzes and Posner (1995), all of whom maintained that attending to others is the primary building block of moral leadership. Further emphasis on service can be observed in the work of Senge (1990) in his well-recognized writing on learning organizations. Senge contended that one of the important tasks of leaders in learning organizations is to be the steward (servant) of the vision within the organization. Being a steward means clarifying and nurturing a vision that is greater than one's self. This means not being self-centered but integrating one's self or vision with others in the organization. Effective leaders see their own personal vision as an important part of something larger than themselves—a part of the organization and the community at large.

In short, whether it be Greenleaf's notion of waiting on the have-nots or Senge's notion of giving oneself to a larger purpose, the idea behind service is contributing to the greater good of others. In practicing the principle of service, ethical leaders must be willing to be follower centered, must place others' interests foremost in their work, and must act in ways that will benefit others.

Ethical leaders are just

Ethical leaders are concerned about issues of fairness and justice. They make it a top priority to treat all of their subordinates in an equal manner. Justice demands that leaders place issues of fairness at the center of their decision making. As a rule, no one should receive special treatment or special consideration except when their particular situation demands it. In instances where individuals are treated differently, the grounds for differential treatment need to be clear, reasonable, and based on sound moral values.

For example, many of us can remember being involved with some type of athletic team while we were growing up. The coaches we liked were the ones we thought were fair with us. No matter what, we did not want the coach to treat anyone differently than the rest. In situations where someone came late to practice with a poor excuse, we wanted that person disciplined just as we would have been disciplined. If a player had a personal problem and needed a break, we wanted the coach to give it. Without question, the good coaches

---

Figure 2. Principles of distributive justice.

These principles are applied in different situations

To each person

- an equal share
- according to individual need
- according to that person's rights
- according to individual effort
- according to societal contribution
- according to merit

---

were those who never had favorites and those who made a point of playing everyone on the team. In essence, what we wanted was that our coach be fair and just.

When resources and rewards or punishments are distributed to employees, the leader plays a major role. The rules that are used and how they are applied say a great deal about whether the leader is concerned about justice and how he or she approaches issues of fairness.

Rawls (1971) stated that a concern with issues of fairness is a requirement for all people who are cooperating together to promote their common interests. It is similar to the Golden Rule: Do unto others as you would have them do unto you. If we expect fairness from others in how they treat us, then we should treat others fairly in our dealings with them. Issues of fairness become problematic because there is always a limit on goods and resources, and there is often competition for those limited things available. Because of the real or perceived scarcity of resources, conflicts often occur between individuals about fair methods of distribution. It is important for leaders to clearly establish the rules for distributing rewards. The nature of these rules says a lot about the ethical underpinnings of the leader and the organization.

Beauchamp and Bowie (1988) have outlined several of the common principles that serve as guides for leaders in how to distribute the benefits and burdens fairly in an organization (see Figure 2). Although not inclusive, these principles point to the reasoning behind why leaders choose to distribute things the way they do in organizations. In a given situation, a leader may use a single principle or a combination of several principles in treating subordinates.

To illustrate the principles described in Figure 2, consider the following hypothetical example. Imagine you are the owner of a small trucking company, which employs 50 drivers. You have just opened a new route, and it promises to be one that pays well and has an ideal schedule. Only one driver can be assigned to the route, but seven drivers have applied for it. Each feels he or she should have an *equal opportunity* to get the route. One of the drivers recently lost his wife to breast cancer and is struggling to care for three young children *(individual need)*. Two of the drivers are minorities and one of them feels strongly that he has a *right* to the job. One of the drivers has logged more driving hours for 3 consecutive years and she feels her *effort* makes her the logical candidate for the new route. One of the drivers serves on the National Safety Board and has a 20-year accident-free driving record (*societal contribution*). Two drivers have been with the company since its inception and their *performance* has been meritorious year after year.

As the owner of the company, your challenge is to assign the new route in a fair way. Although many other factors could influence your decision (e.g., seniority, wage rate, or employee health), the principles described in the figure provide a set of guides for deciding who is to get the new route.

Ethical leaders are honest

When we were children, a phrase we frequently heard from grownups was "never tell a lie." To be good meant we must tell the truth. For leaders the lesson is the same. To be a good leader, leaders need to be honest.

The importance of being honest can be understood more clearly when we consider the opposite of honesty: dishonesty (cf. Jaksa & Pritchard, 1988). Dishonesty is a form of lying, a way of misrepresenting reality. Dishonesty may bring with it many objectionable outcomes, and foremost is the distrust it creates. When leaders are not honest, others come to see them as undependable and unreliable. People lose faith in what leaders say and stand for; their respect for leaders is diminished. As a result, the leader's impact is compromised because others no longer trust and believe in the leader.

When we relate to others, dishonesty also has a negative impact. It puts a strain on how people are connected to each other. When we lie to others, we are in essence saying that we are willing to manipulate the relationship on our own terms. We are saying that we do not trust the other person in the relationship to be able to deal with information we have. In reality, we are putting ourselves ahead of the relationship by saying that we know what is best for the relationship. The long-term effect of this type of behavior is that it weakens relationships. Dishonesty, even when used with good intentions, contributes to the breakdown of relationships.

But being honest is not just about telling the truth. It has to do with being open with others and representing reality as fully and completely as possible. However, this is not an easy task because there are times when telling the complete truth can be destructive or counterproductive. The challenge for leaders is to strike a balance between being open and candid while at the same time monitoring what is appropriate to disclose in a particular situation. It is important for leaders to be authentic but at the same time it is essential that they be sensitive to the attitudes and feelings of others. Honest leadership involves a wide set of behaviors.

Dalla Costa (1998) made the point clearly in his book *The Ethical Imperative* that being honest means more than "not deceiving." For leaders within organizations, being honest means "do not promise what you can't deliver, do not misrepresent, do not hide behind spin-doctored evasions, do not suppress obligations, do not evade accountability, do not accept that the 'survival of the fittest' pressures of business release any of us from the responsibility to respect another's dignity and humanity" (p. 164). In addition, Dalla Costa suggested that it is imperative that organizations recognize and acknowledge the necessity of honesty and reward honest behavior within the organization.

Ethical leaders build community

[We have] defined leadership as the process of influencing others to reach a common or communal goal. This definition has a clear ethical dimension because it refers to a *common* goal. A common goal requires that the leader and followers agree on the direction to be taken by the group. Leaders need to take into account their own and followers' purposes, while working toward goals that are suitable for both of them. This factor, concern for others, is the distinctive feature that delineates *authentic* transformational leaders from *pseudo*-transformational leaders (Bass & Steidlmeier, 1999). Concern for the common good means that leaders cannot impose their will on others. They need to search for goals that are compatible with everyone.

Burns (1978) placed this idea at the center of his theory on transformational leadership. A transformational leader tries to move the group toward a common good that is beneficial for both the leaders and the followers. In moving toward mutual goals, both the leader and follower are changed. It is this feature that makes Burns's theory unique. For Burns, leadership has to be grounded in the leader-follower relationship. It cannot be controlled by the leader, such as Hitler's influence in Germany when Hitler coerced people to meet his own agenda—and followed goals that did not advance the goodness of humankind.

An ethical leader takes into account the purposes of everyone involved in the group and is attentive to the interests of the community and the culture. Such a leader demonstrates an ethic of caring toward others (Gilligan, 1982) and does not force others or ignore the intentions of others (Bass & Steidlmeier, 1999).

Rost (1991) went a step further and suggested that ethical leadership demands attention to a civic virtue. By this he means that leaders and followers need to attend to more than their own mutually determined goals. They need to attend to the *community's* goals and purpose. As Burns (1978, p. 429) wrote, transformational leaders and followers begin to reach out to wider social collectivities and seek to establish higher and broader moral purposes. All of our individual and group goals are bound up in the common good and public interest. We need to pay attention to how the changes proposed by a leader and followers will affect the larger organization, the community, and society. An ethical leader is concerned with the common good—in the broadest sense.

References

Bass, B. M., & Steidlmeier, P. (1999). Ethics, character, and authentic transformational leadership behavior. *Leadership Quarterly, 10*(2), 181-217.

Beauchamp, T. L., & Bowie, N. E. (1988). *Ethical theory and business* (3rd ed.). Englewood Cliffs, NJ: Prentice Hall.

Beauchamp, T. L., & Childress, J. F. (1994). *Principles of biomedical ethics* (4th ed.). New York: Oxford University Press.

Block, P. (1993). *Stewardship: Choosing service over self-interest.* San Francisco: Berrett-Koehler.

Brady, F. N. (1999). A systematic approach to teaching ethics in business. *Journal of Business Ethics, 19*(3), 309-319.

Burns, J. M. (1978). *Leadership.* New York: Harper & Row.

Carison, D. S., & Perrewe, P. L. (1995). Institutionalization of organizational ethics through transformational leadership. *Journal of Business Ethics, 14*(10), 829-838.

Ciulla, J. B. (1998). *Ethics, the heart of leadership.* Westport, CT: Greenwood.

Covey, S. R. (1990). *Principle-centered leadership.* New York: Fireside.

Dalla Costa, J. (1998). *The ethical imperative: Why moral leadership is good business.* Reading, MA: Addison-Wesley.

De Pree, M. (1989). *Leadership is an art.* New York: Doubleday.

De Pree, M. (1992). *Leadership jazz.* New York: Dell.

Gilligan, C. (1982). *In a different voice: psychological theory and women's development.* Cambridge MA: Harvard University Press.

Gini A. (1998) Moral leadership and business ethics. In J. B. Ciulla (Ed.), *Ethics, the heart of leadership* (pp. 27-46). Westport, CT: Greenwood.

Graham, J. W. (1991). Servant-leadership in organizations: Inspirational and moral. *Leadership Quarterly, 2*(2), 105-119.

Greenleaf, R. K. (1970). *The servant as leader.* Newton Centre, MA: Robert K. Greenleaf Center.

Greenleaf, R. K. (1977). *Servant leadership: A journey into the nature of legitimate power and greatness.* New York: Paulist.

Heifetz, R. A. (1994). *Leadership without easy answers.* Cambridge, MA: Harvard University Press.

Hesse, H. (1956). *The journey to the East.* London: P. Owen.

Jaksa, J. A., & Pritchard, M. S. (1988). *Communication ethics: Methods of analysis.* Belmont, CA: Wadsworth.

Kanungo, R. N., & Mendonca, M. (1996). *Ethical dimensions of leadership.* Thousand Oaks, CA: Sage.

Kitchener, K. S. (1984). Intuition, critical evaluation and ethical principles: The foundation for ethical decisions in counseling psychology. *The Counseling Psychologist, 12*(3), 43-55.

Komives, S. R., Lucas, N., & McMahon, T. R. (1998). *Exploring leadership: For college students who want to make a difference.* San Francisco: Jossey-Bass.

Kouzes, J. J, & Posner, B. Z. (1995). *The leadership challenge: How to keep getting extraordinary things done in organizations* (2nd ed.). San Francisco: Jossey-Bass.

Rawls, J. (1971). *A theory of justice.* Boston: Harvard University Press.

Rost, J. C. (1991). *Leadership for the twenty-first century.* New York: Praeger.

Schminke, M., Ambrose, M. L., & Noel, T. W. (1997). The effect of ethical frameworks on perceptions of organizational justice. *Academy of Management Journal, 40*(5), 1190-1207.

Schumann, P. L. (2001). A moral principles framework for human resource management ethics. *Human Resource Management Review, 11,* 93-111.

Senge, P. M. (1990). *The fifth discipline: The art and practice of the learning organization.* New York: Doubleday.

Trevino, L. K. (1986). Ethical decision making in organizations: A person-situation interactionist model. *Academy of Management Review, 11*(3), 601-617.

Political Prudence and the Ethics of Leadership

J. Patrick Dobel

A vital policy initiative fails due to skilled opposition. A fine program disintegrates under pressure of an unanticipated backlash. A powerful and strong institution collapses when its long-time leader departs. A new leader full of good intentions soon flees office overcome by frustration and ineffectiveness. These all-too-familiar examples highlight the haunting reality that good intentions, moral conviction, and even technical competence do not guarantee success in political and administrative life. This disjunction of ethics and achievement has inspired many to despair of the relationship between ethics and leadership, best summed up by Niccoló Machiavelli, "the man who wants to act virtuously in every way necessarily comes to grief among so many who are not virtuous. Therefore if a prince wants to maintain his rule he must learn how not to be virtuous" (Machiavelli, 1973, 15). This realist view argues that leaders cannot afford ethics in a world of serious responsibilities, powerful institutions, and committed adversaries (Morgenthau, 1959; Walz, 1957; Cohen, 1987). The realist view competes with an alternative moral conception of leadership in the natural law and the Kantian traditions, which argues that leaders should follow the requirements of ethics (Gierke, 1934; Kant, 1957).

The leadership literature reflects this split between realpolitik and moralism. Classic studies focus upon the tactical and personality dimensions of successful leadership (Neustadt, 1976; Tucker, 1995). A number of writers, however, call for an explicit recognition of the moral nature of leadership (Burns, 1978; Gardner, 1990; Terry, 1995). These studies succeed in identifying the moral nature of leadership but seldom provide consistent guidelines about where leadership ethics should focus. Recent theorists have argued that a virtue-based ethics focuses upon the moral quality of the person and can inform an ethics of leadership (Galston, 1991; Norton, 1991; Cooper, 1987; Cooper and Wright, 1992). From the time of Aristotle, theorists have argued that of all the virtues, prudence represents the linchpin of political judgment and that any theory of leadership needs to develop an account of prudence (Coll, 1991; Dunn, 1985; 1990, esp. 199-215; Dobel, 1990).

Reprinted with permission from *Public Administration Review* 58, no. 1(1998):74-81.

Building on this tradition, I will argue that political prudence is a central moral resource for political leaders. This article presents an account of political prudence focusing upon its operational requirements. These requirements provide a moral framework to guide and evaluate actions. This article will discuss the relationship between virtue and leadership, prudence as a virtue derived from the requirements of political achievement, and the normative responsibilities and obligations that flow from political prudence.

Virtue and leadership

Leadership entails ethics because leaders have responsibilities. Persons in positions of leadership make a difference; they can bring about changes in behavior that would not occur without their presence and actions. Leading is not always linked to official authority; in fact, leadership opportunities exist throughout political and organizational life. Individuals or institutions rely on leaders to accomplish tasks. Fellow citizens, colleagues, and subordinates depend on the leader and are vulnerable to the consequences of his or her actions. They rely on the leader's competence and promises. Citizens depend on official leaders to protect their security, welfare, and basic interests. Colleagues and other officials depend on leaders to enable them to perform their work. Leaders who hold office are responsible for respecting that reliance, vulnerability, and dependence.

The ethics of responsibility requires leaders to attend to the consequences of their actions (Weber, 1969).[1] Their first responsibility, however, resides in what Adam Smith called self-mastery. All virtues and the personal capacity to live up to promises, obey the law, and follow directives depend upon this primary moral capacity (Smith, 1976, III, 6, 3).

People in positions of responsibility have an obligation to control their passions and overcome temptations. Without this basic self-discipline they could abuse their power for their own purposes. Thoughtless, rash, or impulsive actions could harm or exploit those who depend on the leader or cause the leader to fail in performing vital responsibilities. When internal or external stimuli affect leaders, they should have the self-control not to react instantly. Their actions should be based on reflection, not driven by reactive emotions. Without self-command, moral life remains impossible (Smith, 1976, VI, 3, 1-19). Self-mastery, however, only lays the groundwork for ethical leadership.

Virtue ethics extends self-mastery to the way people should develop their character and patterns of reaction and engagement with life. It attempts to identify the characteristics required by a person who has responsibilities (Cooper, 1987). A virtue embodies a pattern of habitual perception and behavior. The patterns and habits arise from how a person is raised, but also from his or her training and self-development. To possess a virtue such as prudence means that a person's emotions and perceptions are trained and aligned with moral purposes so that they support rather than subvert responsible judgment. Personal actions play out over time as choices that react back and form habits. The choices build a pattern of judgments that habitually identify and internalize the morally important aspects of a situation (Sherman, 1989). Personal virtues are not immutable. People can train themselves over time to approach problems in different manners, to judge according to different standards, and to choose different ways (Budziszewski, 1988).

A virtue-based ethics reinforces leadership ethics because it focuses on the responsibility of the person. Without this focus, the exercise of power reduces to what Vaclav Havel called the "innocent power" of the individual actor who becomes an "innocent tool of an 'innocent' anonymous power, legitimized by science, cybernetics, ideology, law, abstraction and objectivity—that is, by everything except personal responsibility to human beings as persons and neighbors" (Havel, 1986, 136-158).

Responsible political leaders should exercise judgment that unites moral and practical concerns in a world of conflict (Anderson, 1977; Beiner, 1983; Steinberger, 1993, chs. 1, 2, 5). A leader's virtues define the stable cognitive and emotional responses to that world which guide, inform, and sustain judgment and action. This involves not just trained emotions but also a trained perception where an individual identifies the morally salient aspects of a situation and frames a judgment around these aspects (Sherman, 1989). Virtues do not replace laws, norms, or duties in political life, but they give life to these moral imperatives. When situations grow complicated or no self-evident moral answers emerge, virtues provide the stability of judgment and endurance to pursue moral commitment across time and obstacles.

Virtues alone cannot sustain a full political ethics. Many virtues such as courage, temperance, justice, generosity, and mercy cluster around political action. But virtues understood as simple dispositions without judgment can be blind and fall prey to Aristotle's reminder that any aspect of life carried to an extreme can become a vice (Aristotle, 1969, II). They require judgment in their exercise. If a person wishes to be generous, she or he still needs to decide when to be generous, to whom, and how much. Similarly, multiple virtues, like principles, might confront other virtues and it will often be unclear what concrete action is required of a moral commitment or virtue.[2] Finally, virtues can be subsumed by other less desirable ends. For example, a soldier may behave with courage but serve an evil cause; evil dictators can act with mercy; greedy individuals can show generosity to friends. Virtues alone cannot provide the moral foundations of all action (Smith, 1976, VI, iii, 12). They co-exist in dialogue with norms, principles, and conceptions of the good society that bound them and give them a direction. Consequently, classical discourse about political judgment cites prudence as the central virtue because it gives concrete "shape" to the moral aspirations, responsibilities, and obligations of a person (Aquinas, 1967, qu. 47, art. 2, 5, 7; Pieper, 1966).

Unfortunately, modern accounts of political prudence have done little to bolster prudence's traditional role. Building on Hobbes, the modern accounts generally postulate prudence as a form of extended rational self-interest (Hobbes, 1967, chs. 22-25; Grundstein, 1986; Smith, 1976, VI 3). Prudence reduces to algorithmic accounts of how to maximize goals within constraints and over time or becomes the engine for garnering consent among self-interested agents. It suffers from a very high level of abstraction and offers little help in the formation of the goals themselves (Parfit, 1986; Bricker, 1986). Adam Smith referred to such prudence as important but limited, a virtue commended with "cold esteem," but incapable of sustaining a full moral life (Smith, 1976, VI, i, 14).

This article builds on an older account of political prudence, which Alberto Coll (1991) identifies as "normative prudence." Normative prudence focuses upon the obligation of the leader to achieve moral self-mastery, attend to the context of the situation, and through deliberation and careful judgment seek the ends of political excellence.

Political prudence

Most virtues can best be understood as the normative practices entailed in seeking excellence in a domain of human conduct. The standards of excellence derive from the ends of the activity within the domain of conduct (MacIntyre, 1984; Cooper, 1987). This article argues that political prudence encompasses the logic of excellence in political achievement and extends the range of moral concerns and justifications. Excellent political achievements consist of outcomes that: (1) gain legitimacy, (2) endure over time, (3) strengthen the political community, (4) unleash minimum unforeseen consequences, (5) require reasonable use of power resources, and (6) endure without great violence and coercion to enforce the outcome (Dobel, 1988, 29-44).

Political prudence consists of a family of justifications derived from excellent achievement in the domain of politics. Prudent judgment identifies salient moral aspects of a political situation which a leader has a moral obligation to attend to in making a decision. This approach moves the understanding of prudence beyond recitation of examples and extracts reference points that give an intellectual content to virtue's demands.

Political prudence encompasses seven overlapping dimensions of political achievement clustered into three related areas. The first area clusters around the capacities a leader should cultivate to act with prudence: (1) disciplined reason and openness to experience, and (2) foresight and attention to the long term. The second area clusters around the modalities statecraft leaders should master: (3) deploying power; (4) timing and momentum, and (5) the proper relation of means and ends. The third area clusters around the attributes of political outcomes to which prudent statecraft should attend: (6) the durability and legitimacy of outcomes, and (7) the consequences for community. To be politically prudent, a leader should attend to each of the seven dimensions. Failure to account for them means a leader is guilty of negligence.[3]

Disciplined reason and openness

The Latin derivation of prudence means to view or see and reinforces the emphasis upon self-mastery. Prudence requires disciplined reason—the ability to see and think clearly and not be overcome by passions or egocentricity. Talleyrand suggested that good leaders should bear little malice and hold few grudges in politics (Cooper, 1932, 43, and passim). Emotion-driven decisions undisciplined by reflection can lead to irresponsible judgments, failure, or great loss for little gains. Everyone who depends upon a leader relies upon the leader to remain clear-eyed and think through actions.

Prudent reason builds upon openness and attention to the complexity of reality. Good judgment requires good information and a willingness to learn. Prudent leaders strive to see the world clearly and seek out knowledge of the physical, social, and economic world around them. Additionally, reason and openness lead to deliberation and learning. Cardinal Richelieu, like Machiavelli, urged public officials not to listen to flatterers and friends in making official judgments. A clear sign of prudence is the willingness of a person to seek the advice and help of skilled experts in making policy. Richelieu emphasized the need to build a capacity for honest and expert advice into institutions and encourage individuals to speak the truth, not hide it (Richelieu, 1961; Machiavelli, 1973, XVII, XVIII). This approach requires self-knowledge so leaders can hire to complement their knowledge and strengths. This capacity to learn from and utilize others more capable than oneself highlights the centrality of reason, deliberation, and openness to prudent judgment. It also guards against the self-deception to which many leaders fall prey (Goldhamer, 1978; Janis, 1982).

Attention to openness also means that a prudent leader does not close off options needlessly or prematurely, or overcommit to one solution. Any action might generate unanticipated consequences and harms. Prudence requires that leaders be willing to rethink actions and confront the problems as well as the good of their actions. A consistent enemy of prudent judgment is ideological rigidity, which interprets all information within one frame of reference and drives to one outcome regardless of costs. To be driven by emotion, vengeance, anger, ambition, or pride violates the responsibilities of leadership and the requirements of prudence.

Much prudent knowledge focuses upon historical knowledge. Such knowledge involves discovering as much as possible about the history of institutions, allies, and adversaries. A leader should try to learn their practices and understandings, to be able to work with them and avoid being manipulated or making ignorant mistakes. Leaders have special obligations to understand the level of trustworthiness as well as the intentions and capacities of people, especially adversaries. This obliges leaders to develop a capacity to project themselves into the minds of others and know their cultural and historical background (Neustadt and May, 1986). Not exploring and understanding the historical aspects of a case violates political prudence.

Foresight and the long term

The Latin derivation of the term prudence also suggests that prudent leaders exercise foresight. They try to anticipate future issues and scan the power and interests of the actors in their political world. For Machiavelli, the hallmark of a good leader was the capacity to foresee and address political problems early (Machiavelli, 1973, III). Foresight also requires that leaders try to think through the consequences of action and avoid actions where probable negative consequences will overwhelm the good sought. In a similar way, this foresight and attending to reality causes leaders to give special consideration to preparation for reasonable contingencies and to dealing with the power and hostility of others. Successful foresight also enables leaders to act when opportunity arises.

Foresight drives a leader to a long-term view. Thinking of the long term disciplines reason to think more clearly and be less overwhelmed by the passions of the moment or the clamor of groups demanding immediate solutions. Although everyone is dead in the long run, this discipline of reflection focuses upon issues of durability and legitimacy and drives prudence beyond the narrow self-interest of a particular person. For instance, the moment of victory truly tests prudent statecraft. When Napoleon defeated Austria at Ulm, Talleyrand could not convince him to treat Austria well. Napoleon's short-term ambition sowed the seeds of the long-term alliances against him. After the German victory at Sadowa, on the other hand, Bismarck persuaded the Kaiser to treat Austria leniently and sowed the seeds of a future alliance (Cooper, 1932, 149). The long-run perspective will compete with and conflict with the short-term requirements of power and maintaining a coalition to attain a goal. At the Versailles conference the British prime minister, Lloyd George, usually allied with President Woodrow Wilson, constantly fought to ameliorate the worst impositions upon Germany. At several points, however, he acceded to issues like war reparations and the war-guilt clause either to hold France in the coalition or satisfy his parliamentary supporters (Lentin, 1993).

Viewing from the long term enables a leader to link achievements to the discovery and unfolding of what one's moral commitments require in a constrained situation. When Dag Hammarskjold became secretary general of the United Nations, he worked with great care to build the office of the secretary general into a significant actor in the international arena. The institution had no real resources and little stature. With a constant attention to "the long run," he created an important role by building on the rhetorical and legal possibilities of the United Nations Charter, incessantly practicing self-disciplined civility, and creating a crucial role as an intermediary who enabled leaders to escape from the rhetoric and confrontation in which they were enmeshed as in the Lebanon crisis of 1958. Every action he took was predicated on the notion that "only partial results can be expected in each generation" and humans and institutions must "grow" into solutions to problems (Jones, 1993). Prudent leaders understand that preparation for windows of opportunity, building coalitions, and building acceptance of policies all depend on sustained efforts that often play out as momentum and direction of movement rather than as a static and determinable outcome.

Deploying power

In political life power determines the range of possibilities for achievement. Too often people in positions of authority disdain the exercise of power as contaminating them or the office. They believe their technical competence or authority should ensure their position. No one with responsibilities, however, can stand above the play of power. All official life is rife with politics, and official or unofficial leadership requires skillful mastery of the art of acquiring and deploying power. Political achievement depends upon attention to one's own power as well as the ability to perform the hard work of marshaling power and resources to the achievement of goals.

A leader should also understand and appreciate the power of adversaries and allies. When Konrad Adenauer became president of a war-devastated Germany after World War II, he presided over a desperately weakened country with little effective power. Yet he developed his own power base by gaining the trust and respect of his allies as well as playing on their own fears to gain their aid in Germany's redevelopment and to gain support for Germany's rearmament and reintegration into the Western European community (Hodge, 1993). Good leaders understand power in all its manifestations and know how to create it even when none exists. Power must also endure for achievements to endure, and the deployment of power should look toward durability as well as initial success. When Nancy Hanks took over the fledgling National Endowment for the Arts in the late 1960s, the agency struggled with little support and much skepticism. Hanks built allies within the executive office, Congress, and the arts community and worked to build a rhetorical mission that connected arts funding with the aspirations of democratic life. Her nonpartisan institution building enabled the endowment to flourish through numerous changes of administration and controversy (Wyszomirski, 1987).

Titian's painting *An Allegory of Prudence* embodies the Renaissance understanding of the prudent leader that highlights these concerns. A man's head has three facets, youth, maturity, age. Each aspect of the man looks in a different direction surrounded by an animal avatar. A dog looks to the rear, a lion looks across the plane to the viewer, and a boar looks forward. The dog respects history and what came before; the lion looks to the present with strength and fortitude; the boar seeks to divine the future and anticipate the consequences of action. In more colloquial terms, prudent leaders cover their rear, their flanks, and their front.

Timing and momentum

Given the importance of circumstances and power to achievement, the ability to time one's actions to accord with the greatest strength of a position and the weakest position of an opponent is crucial. Sometimes this takes years of patient preparation working to attain a particular alignment of power and produce the cultural and political conditions for acceptance. It may mean working patiently for a shift in the terms of debate or an incident that galvanizes support around an issue, as President Lyndon Johnson did when he used John Kennedy's assassination to make the civil rights bill a testimony to a martyred leader. Similarly, President Harry Truman and Secretary of State George Marshall used the communist threat in Eastern Europe as the opportunity to overcome domestic opposition and isolationism and push the Marshall Plan to reconstruct Europe after World War II (Pogue, 1987, chs. 12-15). Political leadership involves the ability to act with care and wait with patience, then move with quickness and surety when the opportunity arises. As Machiavelli suggests, the lion and the fox should dwell in the same person or leadership cadre (Machiavelli, 1973, XVIII).

Prudent leadership does not mean cautious or cramped leadership. Although it is profoundly important to avoid harm and loss, Saint Thomas Aquinas argued that prudence actively seeks to accomplish good (Aquinas, 1967, 47). A prudent leader's intelligence looks for opportunities that permit action to be taken consonant with goals and power. Principles, laws, and norms seldom dictate one clear action in concrete situations. As long as one does not expect a utopian fulfillment of all goals, then every action and attainment will only approximate moral aspirations. Achievements often consist of a direction and unfolding of goals, of initiating and sustaining momentum towards greater achievement later. For ten years Congress could not revise the Clean Air Act because of the complex politics involved. Senator George Mitchell, Democratic majority and minority leader during this period, was committed to a revision that did not destroy the law's intent. He spent much of that decade laying down the foundations of a compromise one step at a time by authorizing reports or keeping various issues alive in subcommittees. When President Bush signaled his willingness to work for a bill and break a decade of gridlock, Mitchell pulled together the various strands which he had woven together over the years to make a compromise possible (Cohen, 1992). Patience and timing do not reduce to opportunism or quiescence but represent a dialogue between possibilities and ideals.

Statecraft never achieves final or perfect solutions. Given the constraints of politics and the power of others, most outcomes comport only partially with one's moral aspirations. They will be imperfect. In such a world, leaders need to think in terms such as movement, direction, and momentum as they adapt and learn from the possibilities and from experience (Behn, 1991). An achievement may not be perfect, but when thinking of the long term, of the need to build the foundations of legitimacy and durability, a leader may often settle for movement along a road. Timing also involves the capacity to remember, as Titian hints, that the past, the future, and the present must always be seen as a continuum. Actions should account for the past, attend to the present with its constraints and opportunities, and aim with care and humility to future consequences. Any leader who does not account for all these dimensions of time risks moral negligence.

Means and ends

The tradition of normative prudence emphasizes the importance of aligning the means and the ends. In the press of daily politics, pressures to reach an end often override qualms about the means. Linking the two is crucial to prudent leadership. This has three dimensions. The first dimension is finding the right means to attain an end. The means of influence are many and varied, and the right combination of deliberation, persuasion, incentives, coercion, and authority is crucial. Misfits between means and ends will result in failure. Just as important the means used affect the quality of relations in an organization or politics at the end.

Second, the means used, the resources expended, and the opportunities forgone should be proportionate to the end sought. Additionally, the means must substantially contribute to the end and not be gratuitous, wasteful, or inefficient. While the use of coercion is most often cited as the test case for the requirements of proportionality and contribution, these standards apply to all dimensions of political action. In 1986, the Reagan administration sought to deter leaks and spying by pushing a program to require lie detector tests of all government officials with access to classified material. Secretary of State George Shultz fought the program to the point of threatening resignation. He believed the proposed solution would undercut his entire leadership style of building trust on trust. It would sabotage the culture of the State Department and put innocent people at risk while not deterring trained spies. In all these terms the lie detector test failed the proportionality test (Shultz, 1993, 712, 800-804).

Third, prudent leaders recognize that means profoundly affect the end. Ends achieved with morally problematic means can be undermined by the illegitimacy, resentment, and anger that are the moral residuals of excessive and immoral methods to attain goals. The means used can also rebound and affect the quality of humanity of the people pursuing the policy. The United States learned during the Vietnam War that the means used can undermine the legitimacy of the leaders and institutions pursuing the policy. Additionally the means used, as in forming a coalition, rebound forward upon the outcome of the goals. Mitchell's final bill on clean air was shaped by the needs to keep the coalition together, ranging from tax breaks for ethanol to subsidies to end acid rain (Cohen, 1992).

Coercion looms as the most dangerous means and poses special concerns. Politics often appear to take on a Mephistophelian character because it seems to reduce to issues of coercion and violence. But all prudent political achievement should breed accomplishments that endure and gain legitimacy with an economical use of coercion. The more sustained coercion is required to enforce an achievement, the less likely it is that the achievement has earned legitimacy or will endure over time.

Coercion, however, is often necessary to define the boundaries of acceptable behavior. The threat of coercion is often crucial to give others the incentive to comply with an outcome. At other times, government coercion can deter, defend, and set boundaries on regime behavior and protect individuals from exploitation. Prudent leaders, however, recognize coercion and violence as dangerous means that can entangle and poison the ends sought. They should be used with economy and care (Wolin, 1960). Gains wrought by coercion have their own dynamic and exact a never-ending cost from a society in terms of resources spent, investment deferred, and social strictures imposed.[4] Over time, coercion can silence and induce grudging acceptance, but it also elicits violent counteractions. Forced compliance strategies can create a world of illusory agreement and brittle acceptance, but unending application of coercion generates moral problems and is inconsistent with the core of prudence.

Durability and legitimacy

Excellent political achievement endures. Fleeting success or actions that arouse backlashes to what a leader sought to achieve should not qualify as acts of excellent political achievement. A prudent leader will work to ensure that achievements will endure and gain legitimacy in the eyes of the individuals who must live with them. Political achievement earns its legitimacy with people by the provision of benefits, respect for the people's interests and commitments, and links to their cultural terms of right. David Lilienthal served as a founding commissioner of the Tennessee Valley Authority (TVA). The public corporation was approved after a ten-year congressional battle and faced great opposition and skepticism. Lilienthal, much like Nancy Hanks at the National Endowment for the Arts, worked with other members of the TVA Board to develop a legitimizing rhetoric of grass roots democracy coupled with strong consultation to anchor the TVA. The TVA focused its mission on the provision of basic needs that benefited the local constituencies and wedded them to it. The rhetoric blunted the conservative opposition to public provision of such services while the benefits cemented local and regional support. This combination stabilized the mission and support of the TVA for its first several decades (Hargrove, 1987). Prudent leaders should always attend to their government's legitimacy and credibility. These are essential social and political resources for the society, and leaders are responsible not to squander but to protect, restore, and augment them.

When Konrad Adenauer worked to establish democratic practices in Germany after World War II, he realized that provision of economic welfare and prosperity would earn the government trust and legitimacy in a way nothing else could. Adenauer, allied with his brilliant finance minister, Ludwig Erhard, devoted time and energy to forge a viable and vibrant economy even as he used fear of the communists to unite his state and garner American support and aid for his fledgling state (Hodge, 1993; Ellwood, 1992). Together they helped create a strong viable democracy and the greatest European political success of the postwar era.

The means used also affect the quality and durability of the outcome. When George Washington led the fight for independence in the United States, he instructed his soldiers not to steal or forcibly take supplies but wherever possible to buy them and respect the property rights of the landowners. At the same time, he treated the loyalists with leniency to prevent long-term alienation from the new state. He believed that only such treatment could build loyalty and legitimacy for the beleaguered American government (Flexner, 1974). In perhaps his greatest act of prudence, he retired from the presidency after two terms. This set an indelible precedent, ensured a peaceful transition of power for a revolutionary regime, and ended all aspirations for a monarchical government (Wills, 1984).

In all these cases, durability depends upon connecting the achievement to the perceived interests of the parties and citizens involved and realizing the intimate connection of ends to means. Accomplishments or policies, however well-intentioned or morally defensible, will not endure if they do not ground themselves in the interests of those affected. Without this focus, many solutions will erode, dissipate, or require greater and greater amounts of coercion to maintain.

Building community

Prudent leaders hold special responsibilities to maintain and strengthen community foundations. Excellent political achievements do not stand in isolation but sustain the legitimacy of institutions and build community. Vaclav Havel has argued that "those who find themselves in politics therefore bear a heightened responsibility for the moral state of society, and it is their responsibility to seek out the best in that society, and to develop and strengthen it." Havel discusses the special obligation of leaders to sustain an inclusive society where diverse groups and interests can engage in political and civil conflict and cooperation. The conditions of social integration, the capacity of members and groups within a society to interact peacefully, and to act with a modicum of civility and respect towards each other, cannot be controlled by leaders, but they can be influenced by example and policy (Havel, 1992, 4-6). President Nelson Mandela of South Africa responded to just these concerns about long-term community when, after years of imprisonment and with terrorism and tensions rising, he became the first black leader of his country. He initiated a careful campaign of national reconciliation designed simultaneously to reassure the once dominant white minority and provide hope and rewards for the newly enfranchised black majority. The policies attempted the very difficult feat of creating a political community where civil war once raged, and establishing trust where little existed (Mandela, 1994).

This obligation to strengthen the communal affiliations and bonds among members of the society should inform and constrain judgments as a substantive demand of political prudence. The possibility of political community depends upon trust. Trust for each other and trust in institutions are the social resources and capital that leaders and major institutions should work to create and sustain. Without trust among citizens, institutions, and leaders, the capacity of the society to act for common purposes declines. The cost of common endeavors increases as does the interaction costs of all social relations. Like all social capital, trust is created by interactions over time and is solidified by the meaningful creations of social welfare from the pattern of interactions and communal affiliations. Prudent leadership entails special responsibilities to maintain this dimension of community and its common possibilities (Dunn, 1990).

Prudent leadership

Prudence does not encompass all public ethics. It does, however, expand the range of moral resources available to leaders and avoids the overdrawn distinctions between politics and morality. The morality of statecraft is neither demonic nor romantic, but built upon the foundations and circumstances of human ethics. To the extent that all moral action is underdetermined and takes place in a world of limited resources and constraints set by circumstances, all morality is imperfect. All relational morality strives for the best outcome "all things considered" or "given the circumstances." Politics does not differ fundamentally from the morality by which most people live everyday. Political leadership may be shaped by the responsibility to others and by the lack of mutuality or problems posed by hostility and threats, but it differs from everyday morality in degree, not in kind.

Understanding prudence as a shaping and active virtue connected to foresight and dynamic judgment means that prudence does not reduce to caution or conservatism. The British historian G. M. Trevelyan described Lord Grey's actions in the Reform Act of 1832, which abolished the rotten boroughs in Britain and extended the suffrage, as "one of the most prudent acts of daring in history." Trevelyan added that a "a more perfect bill (judged by 20th century standards) would have failed to pass in 1832, and its rejection would sooner or later have been followed by a civil war" (Trevelyan, 1920, 268, 372). As many prudent leaders do, Lord Grey saw the need to act boldly to avoid severe problems, and then he carefully set out to gain the greatest good permitted by the circumstances of the time as well as building a coalition and solution that would endure and earn its own legitimacy despite its imperfections. In a similar vein, when Secretary of State George Shultz recognized the fundamental shift that had occurred in the Soviet Union with the advent of Mikhail Gorbachev, he began the arduous task of changing President Ronald Reagan's ideological hostility toward the Soviet Union. Shultz worked to persuade a recalcitrant administration to change 40 years of unremitting enmity towards the Soviet Union to one of cautious support of reform (Shultz, 1993). Political prudence possesses extraordinary versatility, and it has been a modern mistake to narrow its application to self-interest or a cautious and tepid disposition.

Prudence understood as shaping solutions within constraints also questions the importance of "circumstances" or "necessity" as the overpowering moral force they often appear to be in justifications. What often distinguishes a great from a good leader is his or her capacity to understand that circumstances themselves can be subject to prudent action and change. The argument so often offered as a justification or really an "excuse" for action by "necessity" assumes: (1) that the public purposes remain immutable; (2) that the action required is the only way to achieve the fixed purpose; (3) that the circumstances and time constraints require one to do only *this* action at *this* time to achieve those goals.

According to the insights of political prudence, individuals choose that goal from among many. Individuals choose to accept one particular shape as the content of that goal. Individuals choose to accept the circumstances as determinative and do not choose to try and change them or the rules of the game. Statecraft, however, demonstrates that enemies can become friends with effort, imagination, and self-interest; coalitions can be restructured, and resources can be rearranged and redirected to meet goals. Richard Nixon's opening to China demonstrated his grasp that the rules of the Cold War were limitations on action, not laws of history. Through careful preparation, he waited for the right opportunity and transformed the relations of the United States to the dominant partners of the communist world. In forging the Marshall Plan, President Truman and Secretary of State George Marshall helped change the political landscape and co-opt the opposition by connecting European exports to the midwestern farmers. This gained conservative support, just as the later creation of a food stamp program for the poor transformed political constraints by using vouchers, solidifying the support of conservative midwestern farm states for the program. Political prudence understood in this way narrows tremendously the argument from necessity and rejects an unimaginative acceptance of "circumstances" or "conditions" as permanent necessities.

Political prudence deeply informs ethical leadership. Starting with the obligation for self-mastery, it generates a checklist of concerns that responsible leaders have a moral obligation to account for in their judgments. Political prudence is not simply a disposition of character to act, or a narrative of exemplars. It is a virtue linked to the moral responsibilities of political leadership to discern the prudential aspects of a situation. Political prudence's intellectual content arises from the full dimensions of excellence in political achievement. The nature of political achievement generates a family of justifications for action which carry moral weight and to which leaders have an obligation to attend. They should structure perception and reflection in a situation. These justifications provide guidance for the leader, but they also provide standards of judgment for others to assist or criticize actions of leaders. They are: (1) disciplined reason and openness to experience and knowledge; (2) foresight and attention to the long term; (3) deployment of power and resources; (4) timing, momentum, and direction; (5) the proper alignment of means and ends; (6) the durability and legitimacy of outcomes; and (7) building and sustaining community.

If leaders account for each aspect, they have lived up to part of their ethical responsibilities as leaders; if they fail, they are guilty of moral negligence and irresponsibility. Political prudence does not cover all morality, neither does it guarantee success. Negligent leaders can succeed by accident, by luck, or by the incompetence of others. Paradoxically, even prudent leaders can fail. Political prudence flows from the responsibilities of leadership and power and provides a necessary but not sufficient ground for ethical leadership.

Notes

1. John Dunn (1990, 193-216) has correctly discussed the need to "democratize prudence" and its obligations beyond those who have assumed responsibility in various positions.

2. The traditional understanding of normative prudence sees it as contributing to the correct choice of moral action on two levels. First, it helps humans sort out and balance decisions when multiple normative imperatives conflict. Second, it comprehends efforts to give reality to moral commitments and responsibilities. Although these two levels are conceptually distinct, they may interact. For instance, if several principles or goods conflict, a leader may choose to act on the one that he or she believes is most feasible, or will endure the longest, or involves the least amount of violence. The dimensions of prudence then legitimately affect that realm of judgment. This article focuses on the second level of judgment and explores the dimensions involved in political achievement.

3. Both Aquinas and Aristotle develop more elaborate lists of characteristics necessary to judge with prudence (Coll, 1991, 36-44). Their characteristics deeply inform the approach I have developed, which attempts to provide more operational terms for them.

4. Paul Kennedy (1987) provides an insightful account of the cost of the projection of power and coercion for dominant powers

References

Anderson, Charles W. (1977). *Statecraft: An Introduction to Political Choice and Judgment.* New York: Wiley.

Aquinas, Thomas (1967). *Prudence.* Vol. 36, Part 2 of the Second Part (2a 2ae) of *Suma Theologica.* Thomas Gilby, O. P., ed. and trans., London: Blackfriers.

Aristotle (1969). *The Nicomachean Ethics.* Sir David Ross, trans. Oxford: Oxford University Press.

Behn, Robert D. (1991). *Leadership Counts: Lessons for Public Managers from the Massachusetts Welfare, Training, and Employment Program.* Cambridge, MA: Harvard University Press.

Beiner, Ronald (1983). *Political Judgment.* Chicago: University of Chicago Press.

Bricker, Phillip (1986). "Prudence." *Journal of Philosophy* 77: 381-401.

Budziszewski, J. (1988). *The Nearest Coast of Darkness: A Vindication of the Politics of Virtues.* Ithaca, NY: Cornell University Press.

Burns, James MacGregor (1978). *Leadership.* New York: Harper and Row.

Cohen, Marshall (1987). "Moral Skepticism and International Relations." In Kenneth Kipnis and Diane T. Meyers, eds., *Political Realism and International Morality: Ethics in the Nuclear Age.* Boulder, CO: Westview Press.

Cohen, Richard E. (1992). *Washington at Work: Back Rooms and Clean Air.* New York: MacMillan.

Coll, Alberto R. (1991). "Normative Prudence as a Tradition of Statecraft." *Ethics and International Affairs* 5: 33-51

Cooper, Duff (1932). *Tallyrand.* New York: Harper.

Cooper, Terry (1987). "Hierarchy, Virtues, and the Practice of Public Administration." *Public Administration Review* 47(4): 320-328.

Cooper, Terry L., and Dale N. Wright, eds. (1992). *Exemplary Public Administrators: Character and Leadership in Government.* San Francisco, CA: Jossey-Bass.

Dobel, J. Patrick (1988). "Reflection and Good Reasons in Policy Analysis." In Edward Bryan Portis and Michael B. Levy, eds., *The Handbook of Political Theory and Policy Science.* New York: Greenwood Press, 29-44.

Dobel, J. Patrick (1990). "Integrity in Public Service." *Public Administration Review* 50(3): 354-366.

Doig, Jameson W., and Erwin C. Hargrove, eds. (1987). *Leadership and Innovation: A Biographical Perspective on Entrepreneurs in Government.* Baltimore, MD: The Johns Hopkins University Press.

Dunn, John (1985). *Rethinking Modern Political Theory.* Cambridge: Cambridge University Press.

Dunn, John (1990). *Interpreting Political Responsibility.* Cambridge: Cambridge University Press.

Ellwood, David W. (1992). *Rebuilding Europe: Western Europe, America and Postwar Reconstruction.* London: Longmans.

Flexner, James Thomas (1974). *Washington: The Indispensable Man.* Boston, MA: Little Brown.

Galston, William (1991). *Liberal Purposes: Goods, Virtues, and Diversity in the Liberal State.* Cambridge: Cambridge University Press.

Gardner, John W. (1990). *On Leadership.* New York: Free Press.

Gierke, Otto (1934). *Natural Law and the Theory of Society: 1500-1800.* Ernest Barker, trans., Cambridge: Cambridge University Press.

Goldhamer, Herbert (1978). *The Advisors.* New York: Elsevier.

Grundstein, Nathan (1986). *The Futures of Prudence: Pure Strategy and Aristotelian and Hobbesian Strategists* Hudson, OH: Enterprise Achievement Associates.

Hargrove, Erwin (1987). "David Lilienthal and the Tennessee Valley Authority." In Jameson W. Doig and Erwin C. Hargrove, eds., *Leadership and Innovation: A Bibliographical Perspective on Entrepreneurs in Government.* Baltimore, MD: The Johns Hopkins University Press, 2-62.

Havel, Vaclav (1986). *Living in Truth.* Jan Valdislav, trans., London: Faber and Faber.

Havel, Vaclav (1992). *Summer Meditations.* New York: Vintage Books.

Hobbes, Thomas (1967). *The Leviathan.* Oxford: Oxford at the Clarendon Press.

Hodge, Carl Cavanagh (1993). "Konrad Adenauer and the Diplomacy of German Rearmament." Paper presented at the International Conference on Ethics and Statecraft, University of British Columbia, October 6-10.

Janis, Irving L. (1982). *Groupthink.* Boston, MA: Houghton Mifflin Company.

Jones, Dorothy V. (1993). "Dag Hammarskjold and the Ethics of the Long Term." Paper presented at the International Conference on Ethics and Statecraft, University of British Columbia, October 6-10.

Kant, Immanuel (1957). *Perpetual Peace.* L. W. Beck, trans., New York: Bobbs Merrill.

Kennedy, Paul (1987). *The Rise and Fall of Great Powers: Economic Change and Military Conflict from 1500 to 2000.* New York: Vintage.

Kipnis, Kenneth, and Diane T. Meyers, eds. (1987). *Political Realism and International Morality: Ethics in the Nuclear Age.* Boulder, CO: Westview Press.

Lentin, Antony (1993). "Several Types of Ambiguity: Lloyd George at the Paris Peace Conference." Paper presented at the International Conference on Ethics and Statecraft, University of British Columbia, October 6-10.

Machiavelli, Niccolo (1973). *The Prince.* George Bull, trans., New York: Penguin Books.

MacIntyre, Alasdair C. (1984). *After Virtue: A Study in Moral Theory.* 2nd ed. South Bend, IN: Notre Dame University Press.

Mandela, Nelson (1994). *Long Road to Freedom: The Autobiography of Nelson Mandela.* Boston, MA: Little, Brown, and Company.

Morganthau, Hans (1959). *Politics Among Nations*, 2nd ed. New York: Alfred A. Knopf.

Neustadt, Richard E. (1976). *Presidential Power: The Politics of Leadership with Refections on Johnson and Nixon.* New York: Wiley.

Neustadt, Richard E., and Ernest R. May (1986). *Thinking in Time: The Uses of History by Decision Makers.* New York: Free Press.

Norton, David (1991). *Democracy and Moral Development: A Politics of Virtue.* Berkeley: University of California Press.

Parfit, Derek (1986). "Prudence, Morality and the Prisoner's Dilemma." In Jon Elster, ed., *Rational Choice.* New York: New York University Press, 34-59.

Pieper, Josef (1966). *The Four Cardinal Virtues.* South Bend, IN: Notre Dame University Press.

Pogue, Forrest C. (1987). *George C. Marshall: Statesman 1945-59.* New York: Viking.

Richelieu, Armand Jean du Plessis (1961). *The Political Testament of Cardinal Richelieu.* Henry Bertram Hill, trans. Madison: University of Wisconsin Press.

Sherman, Nancy (1989). *The Fabric of Character: Aristotle's Theory of Virtue.* Oxford: The Clarendon Press.

Shultz, George P. (1993). *Turmoil and Triumph: My Years as Secretary of State.* New York: Scribner.

Smith, Adam (1976). *The Theory of the Moral Sentiments.* Indianapolis, IN: Liberty Press.

Steinberger, Peter J. (1993). *The Concept of Political Judgment.* Chicago: University of Chicago Press.

Terry, Larry D. (1995). *Leadership of Public Bureaucracies: The Administrator as Conservator.* Thousand Oaks, CA: Sage Publications.

Toulmin, Stephen, and Albert Jones (1988). *The Abuse of Casuistry.* Berkeley: University of California Press.

Trevelyan, G. M. (1920). *Lord Gray of the Reform Bill.* London: Longmans.

Tucker, Robert C. (1995). *Politics as Leadership.* Rev. ed. Columbia: University of Missouri Press.

Walz, Kenneth (1957). *Man, State, and War.* New York: Columbia University Press.

Weber, Max (1969). "Politics as a Vocation." In H. H. Gerth and C. Wright Mills, eds., *From Max Weber: Essays in Sociology.* Oxford: Oxford University Press.

Wills, Garry (1984). *Cincinnatus: George Washington and the Enlightenment.* New York: Doubleday.

Wolin, Sheldon (1960). "Machiavelli: Politics and Economy of Violence." In *Politics and Vision: Continuity and Innovation in Western Political Thought.* Boston, MA: Little, Brown and Company, 195-238.

Wyszomirski, Margaret Jane (1987). "The Politics of Art: Nancy Hanks and the National Endowment for the Arts." In Jameson W. Doig and Erwin C. Hargrove, eds., *Leadership and Innovation: A Biographical Perspective on Entrepreneurs in Government.* Baltimore, MD: The Johns Hopkins University Press, 207-245.

Demonstrating Ethical Leadership by Measuring Ethics

A survey of U.S. public servants

Muel Kaptein, Leo Huberts, Scott Avelino, and Karin Lasthuizen

"The most frustrating thing about the recent scandals is that I was not aware of what was going on. I thought we were in control. In reality, the organization was decaying at its core, and many of my managers and employees knew this. But no one told me." These are the words of the director of a large Dutch public organization in the wake of a much-publicized debacle that shocked Dutch society.[1] This manager is no exception. Managers are often in the dark about the scale of unethical conduct in their organizations until it is too late (Punch 1996). In many cases, however, there are signs of unethical conduct and employees who try to draw management's attention to the issue (Perry 1993), but management either does not pay attention or does not recognize the warning signs for what they are. Or, perhaps more troubling, sometimes employees express concern about a certain matter but one or more managers look the other way, sweep it under the rug, or shoot the messenger (Bird 1996).

It is risky to subscribe to the view that "no news is good news" (Cohan 2002). From a moral and legal point of view, managers are increasingly held responsible not only for what they know, but also for what they could and should have known (Kaptein and Wempe 2002). As one manager of a Dutch government department remarked: "It's not what I know that scares me—it's what I don't know."

Without an understanding of the ethical quality of the organization, management cannot determine whether it is in control or at risk, and whether current oversight activities are effective or other measures are needed. It is therefore of great importance for the management of an organization to be aware of the organization's ethical quality, and

From *Public Integrity*, vol. 7, no. 4 (Fall 2005): 299-311. Copyright © 2005 by American Society for Public Administration (ASPA). Reprinted with permission of M. E. Sharpe, Inc. The views and opinions expressed by the first and third authors are their own and do not necessarily represent the views of KPMG International or its member firms.

this raises the question of how management can measure organizational ethics. To date, there has been little research on this subject (e.g., Kaptein 1998; Petrick and Quinn 1997; Rosthorn 2000; Treviño and Weaver 2003). The present article distinguishes and discusses a number of aspects relevant to obtaining an overview of the ethical quality of an organization. The focus is on the survey technique as instrument for measuring ethics because of its potential to generate valuable information. Involving employees in the measurement of organizational ethics also demonstrates ethical leadership.

Methodology

There have been many empirical studies on unethical conduct within organizations. Most of these focus on only one form of unethical conduct. For instance, Cherrington and Cherrington (1985) examined theft in the workplace, and Chappell and Di Martino (2000) investigated violent behavior at work. Other studies consider several different forms of unethical conduct but include only one or a few organizations in their sample. Weaver, Treviño, and Cochran (1999), for instance, investigated the ethical quality of six organizations, and Vardi and Weitz (2004) investigated misconduct in a few Israeli organizations. To date, there has been almost no empirical research on the ethical quality of a cross-section of U.S. public organizations. One exception is the recent study by Feldheim and Wang (2004), who conducted a national survey of ethical behavior of civil servants in early 2000. They mailed a survey to the chief administrative officer in every U.S. city with a population larger than 50,000.

The Feldheim and Wang study made the central assumption that the person who completed the survey would have insight into the kind of unethical conduct that took place in the organization. However, perceptions of the ethics of an organization may differ from one level to the next, and thus the perceptions of top management may not be representative of the organization as a whole. It therefore seemed desirable to complement the findings of Feldheim and Wang with a survey of U.S. public servants that would present a picture of organizational ethics as perceived from the bottom up. The following research methodology was employed to gather this information.

In 2000, KPMG commissioned one of the largest database firms in the world, National Family Opinion, to create a representative database on U.S. employee perceptions and behavior with respect to integrity in the workplace. A questionnaire with 133 data-collection points was sent to a representative sample of the working population consisting of 3,075 adults. This sample was obtained from a panel of the U.S. population, consulted frequently by the National Family Opinion for all types of surveys and carefully composed to be representative of the workforce. With a return of 2,390 completed questionnaires, a response rate of 78 percent was achieved. Almost 15 percent of the respondents ($n = 344$) worked in the public sector. Of the respondents, 57 percent were male and 43 percent were female. Thirty percent performed a supervisory function.

Figure 1 depicts the structure of the questionnaire. First, different types of unethical conduct were listed and the respondents indicated their frequency. Second, the respondents were asked to identify the potential consequences of each type of misconduct for the organization, its employees, and its external stakeholders. In order to manage ethics effectively, it is crucial to know the extent to which the organization encourages ethical conduct. For this reason, the questionnaire included items pertaining to three organiza-

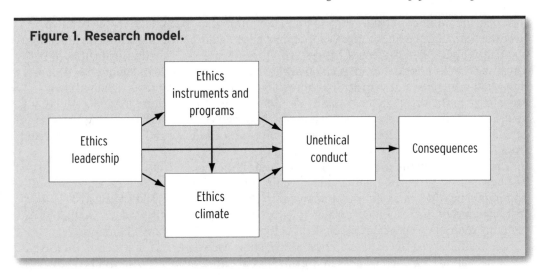

Figure 1. Research model.

tional factors: the existence and content of ethics programs, the ethical climate of the organization, and the ethics of management. The results are presented below, starting with the design and implementation of pertinent programs.

Design and implementation of ethics programs

For many organizations, the first step in managing ethics is to establish a code of conduct, or a document of some kind that articulates the organizational values, principles, and standards. In the Netherlands, for example, almost all national government departments and 47 percent of the 100 largest local governments have codes of conduct (Ethicon 2004). Of the U.S. local governments surveyed by Feldheim and Wang (2004), 68.5 percent said they had a code of ethics.

To implement a code of conduct, ethics and compliance programs can be rolled out consisting, for example, of employee training, communication programs, security measures, hotlines, disciplinary and enforcement mechanisms, and response protocols (Kaptein 1998, 2002; Lawton 1998; Paine 1994; Preston and Sampford 1998; Weaver et al. 1999). The study by Feldheim and Wang (2004) shows that 28.2 percent of the local governments said that ethics training was required for all their managers, and 31.9 percent said that they regularly conducted workshops in which ethics was discussed.

As for determining the effectiveness of these efforts, the answer remains elusive for some organizations, and others prefer not to know the answer at all. Only 33.1 percent of the respondents in the Feldheim and Wang study (2004) said that the ethics of the organization and its employees was reviewed on a regular basis. The approaches to measurement vary from superficial checkboxes to meaningful organizational analysis. To begin with, organizations could look at design indicators, such as whether each department or unit has a code of conduct, an ethics hotline, or provides ethics training. Although monitoring design indicators is worthwhile, it says little about the extent to which these measures are actually "alive." Therefore, organizations should also consider the implementation of these instruments, such as the percentage of employees who have received the code, the number of calls to the hotline, the number of disciplinary cases handled over the year, and the opportunities for employees to gain knowledge of the organization's standards. Eighty-five percent of the respondents indicated that their organization provided them with information that clarified the organization's code of conduct as well as its overall principles and values. Sixty-three percent of the respondents acquired their knowledge of the organization's standards from policy and procedure manuals, 49 percent from internal memos (including e-mail), 34 percent from internal training sessions provided by the organization, 25 percent from posters and bulletin boards, and 18 percent from remarks and speeches by senior managers.

The results show that most organizations inform their employees about their ethical responsibilities. However, training and coaching are also important in creating awareness and improving the moral skills of employees to deal with ethical issues (Paine 2003). If just one-third of the respondents receives ethics training or attends workshops, there is certainly room for improving the implementation of ethical programs. Monitoring participation in ethics programs and employee satisfaction with them is a first step to increase awareness about the effectiveness of organizational efforts. However, as will be shown in the following sections, more information needs to be obtained to truly understand institutional ethics.

Frequency of unethical conduct

Next to design and implementation indicators, organizations could also proactively monitor actual compliance levels—for instance, by investigating whether there is evidence of corruption or misuse of confidential information. In the survey, respondents were asked to indicate on a five-point scale, from "never" to "always," how often in the last twelve months they had observed ethical infringements in their work environment. Table 1 shows the percentage of respondents in the public sector that observed at least one infringement. The results for business organizations (n = 1,529) are also included for the sake of comparison.

The questionnaire included eighteen types of ethical infringements. It was found that the frequency at which these different types of violations occur differed widely among public organizations. The implications, from a probability standpoint, can be unsettling. In a public sector organization with 1,000 employees, it is likely that in the past year some 340 employees have observed instances of sexual harassment or conduct creating a hostile work environment, 260 employees have witnessed false or misleading information being given to the public or media, and 110 employees have witnessed an offer of improper gifts, favors, or entertainment to influence others.

While there are some differences, the frequencies of the selected types of behavior are comparable in public and private organizations. The types of unethical conduct found in public sector organizations are apparently not sector-specific. This is evidenced by a 40 percent observance rate of employment discrimination in the public sector compared to 36 percent in the private sector, and a 38 percent and 36 percent observance rate of violation of employee rights to privacy in the public and private sector respectively. These similarities suggest that public and private organizations might benefit from sharing information on these violations and strategies to curb them.

A number of differences are also worth noting. Public sector organizations are characterized by a greater number of "activities posing a conflict of interest," instances of

Table 1. Rate of observed misconduct in one year (*n* = 344).

	Public sector		Private sector
Employment discrimination	40%	(11%)	36%
Violation of workplace health and safety rules	39%	(6%)	37%
Violation of employee rights to privacy	38%	(10%)	36%
False/misleading promises to customers/clients	36%	(7%)	39%
Carelessness with confidential/proprietary information	35%	(8%)	31%
Sexual harassment or hostile work environment	34%	(6%)	34%
Activities posing a conflict of interest	27%	(5%)	21%
False/misleading information to public or media	26%	(7%)	18%
Environmental breaches	18%	(4%)	17%
Alcohol and drugs abuse in and around the workplace	16%	(4%)	19%
Falsification/improper manipulation of financial data	15%	(4%)	11%
Making false/misleading statements to government regulators	15%	(4%)	9%
Unfair competition/antitrust	11%	(3%)	19%
Offering improper gifts, favors, or entertainment to influence others	11%	(3%)	14%
Dishonesty/unfair treatment of suppliers	10%	(2%)	13%
Embezzling funds or stealing from the organization	9%	(1%)	10%
Improper political contribution to domestic officials	4%	(<1%)	4%
Trading company shares based on insider information	2%	(<1%)	5%

Notes: The items are measured on a five-point scale of 1 (never), 2 (rarely), 3 (sometimes), 4 (often), and 5 (always). The cumulative percentages of 2, 3, 4, and 5 are listed in the table, with the cumulative percentages of 4 and 5 in parentheses

"giving false/misleading information to the public or media," and "making false/misleading statements to government regulators." The frequency with which these three types of behavior occur in the public and private sectors differs by more than 5 percent.

In the absence of research on unethical behavior, managers may be less likely to be aware of ethical violations within their organizations. In view of the prevalence of misconduct, management should be suspicious if no incidents are reported in their organization. A police organization, for example, was confounded by the fact that relatively many incidents occurred in some regional departments and none in other departments (Kaptein and Van Reenen 2001). An in-depth analysis revealed an inverse relationship between the number of incidents reported to the board and the number of incidents employees had knowledge of in their departments. The departments that had not reported any incidents had the most observed instances of unethical conduct. It turned out that the number of incidents reported, rather than being a reflection of the actual number of incidents, indicated the willingness of management to deal with ethical issues openly and transparently.

In view of the results, which show a high prevalence of different types of misconduct, managers should bear in mind that such violations may also be occurring in their organization. They will therefore periodically examine the level of ethical misconduct in their organization in order to establish whether it is acceptable. In assessing the seriousness of the different types of ethical infringements, it is advisable to reflect on their potential consequences. This is discussed below.

Consequences of unethical conduct

To avoid paying a disproportionate amount of attention to relatively immaterial ethical issues and neglecting the serious ones, organizations should balance their efforts on some sort of risk assessment, such as the likelihood and consequences of each type of violation (Davies 2000; Lasthuizen, Huberts, and Kaptein 2002). A single case of large-scale fraud, for instance, can have a much greater impact than a hundred cases of petty inventory theft. Moreover, ten incidents of sexual harassment can be more damaging than a hundred illegitimate expense claims. The more serious the consequences, the more stringent the prevention measures required. Sixty percent of the respondents from the public sector said that their organization would lose significant public trust if the infraction they had observed were to find its way into the media. This holds true for all organizations (49%) but even more so for public organizations (60%).

Just as unethical conduct has negative effects for an organization (Cooper 2001; Fijnaut and Huberts 2002), ethical conduct has positive consequences (Feldheim and Wang 2004; Kaptein 2005). The results of the survey show, for example, that a reputation for sound ethical practice enhances the ability of organizations to attract and retain good employees. On average, 79 percent of the public sector employees surveyed would recommend their organization to prospective employees. Among those who believe that ethical misconduct is widespread, only 19 percent would recommend their organization.

Causes, climate, and leadership

Organizations should not only obtain insight into the scope of unethical conduct and its potential consequences, they should also examine its causes. The occurrence of unethical conduct cannot be explained merely in terms of the deviance of a few ill-inclined individuals, sometimes referred to as the proverbial rotten apples. The barrel itself, the organizational context, can also be the source of unethical conduct (Bowman 1990; della Porta and Vannucci 1999; Hoffman and Moore 1990; Klockars, Ivkovic, and Haberfeld 2004; Treviño and Youngblood 1990). Being attuned to the organizational context allows management to detect whether and where the organization is at risk. Knowing and understanding the organizational context is an important point of departure in improving the ethical conduct of management and employees (Kaptein and Wempe 2002; Paine 2003; Treviño and Nelson 1995).

Ethical transgressions in organizations are attributable to a diverse range of factors that includes unclear standards, pressure to perform, and intolerance of criticism (Huberts 1998; Jackall 1988; Punch 1996). In an ethics survey of the federal government in the Netherlands, Kaptein (1998) found that leakage of confidential information to the media

Table 2. Perceived ethical leadership in public organizations (*n* = 344).

	Rate of observance
Employees feel comfortable reporting an observed violation to their supervisor	77%
Management is fully committed to upholding the organizational standards of conduct	73%
Management would respond appropriately if they become aware of improper conduct	60%
Employees will bring observed violations to the attention of their supervisor	58%
Management sets reasonable performance goals	59%
Managers are positive role models	56%
Employees believe that management is approachable if they have questions or need to deliver bad news	48%
Management know what type of behavior goes on in the organization	46%
Employees who report a violation to management will not experience retaliation	43%
Employees feel comfortable seeking advice from senior management if they have a question/concern about standards	43%
Offenders will be disciplined consistently and fairly by management	36%

Note: The items are measured on a five-point scale of 1 (strongly disagree), 2 (disagree), 3 (unsure/no opinion), 4 (agree), and 5 (strongly agree). The cumulative percentages of 4 and 5 are listed.

was strongly related to inadequate opportunities for civil servants to discuss conflicting views on solving socio-political problems. In order to get political support for their views, they passed on confidential information to journalists and political representatives. Instead of making more rules and imposing heavier sanctions, the department decided to give civil servants more opportunities to discuss their views with their supervisors and the board.

The presence or absence of strong leadership and role models also has an impact on the organizational climate and the way employees behave (Treviño and Weaver 2003). In addition to measuring the ethical climate of the organization, it is particularly important for management to focus on employee perceptions of the ethical quality of leadership. Table 2 depicts a number of leadership qualities identified by respondents in public organizations.

Seventy-seven percent said they felt comfortable reporting a violation to their supervisor, but the results were less reassuring for other aspects of the ethical leadership climate. Management was a positive role model for 56 percent of the respondents, while 48 percent reported that management is approachable if they had questions or needed to deliver bad news. In addition, 43 percent reported that they felt comfortable seeking advice from senior management if they had a question or concern about ethical values and principles.

Only 36 percent of the respondents held the opinion that management would discipline offenders fairly and consistently.

Based on these results, one may conclude that a large number of U.S. public organizations do not always send the right messages on ethical conduct to their employees. In light of this, management would be well advised to regularly ask itself whether it is clearly explaining the meaning of responsible conduct to employees, giving them sufficient support to act responsibly, and encouraging open discussion of ethical dilemmas. It must also consider whether it is able to detect and address unethical conduct, and how it deals with reports of alleged misconduct. Information of this kind can be obtained by means of a questionnaire. An overview of the advantages and risks of employing an ethics survey is provided below.

Ethics review

The results of the survey of U.S. public servants clearly show that public organizations face the risk of unethical behavior undermining their performance, credibility, and legitimacy. Managers can only manage organizational ethics if they have a clear idea of the effectiveness of current efforts (e.g., codes of conduct and compliance programs) aimed at preventing unethical behavior and stimulating ethical behavior. Because management is not omniscient and organizational hierarchies may prevent employees from freely communicating violations, it is advisable to conduct ethics audits to determine whether management's view of the organization is a true reflection of the state of affairs.

In order to implement an effective ethics or compliance program and take adequate measures to prevent unethical conduct, it is important that managers have insight into the nature, scope, and seriousness of existing problems. Examining the causes of and interdependencies between different forms of ethical misconduct enables management to put measures in place to prevent similar behavior in the future. Ethical risks differ from organization to organization because their organizational activities, cultures, and environments are not the same. In consequence, each organization needs to review its ethics in view of its particular situation.

An ethics review can also be used to assess the effectiveness of implemented policies and to benchmark them. Schiphol Airport in the Netherlands, for example, conducted a survey of its ethical climate before and after developing a code of conduct. Based on these surveys, the organization concluded, eighteen months later, that the extent to which ethical dilemmas were discussable had improved by 21 percent, clarity of standards had increased by 19 percent, and the number of employees who believed that management set a good example had increased by 17 percent (Kaptein and Wempe 1998). An integrity review, in itself, is an instrument that promotes effectiveness. If managers know that the ethics of their department will be evaluated periodically, they have even more reason to work on ethical issues (Blanchard and Peale 1988).

There are several reasons for conducting an ethics review among employees. First, by involving employees, the organization shows not only that ethics receives managerial attention, but also that employee opinions count. Second, consulting employees stimulates their awareness of ethical issues in their own functions. Third, conducting an ethics review fosters support among employees for tackling ethical issues. Furthermore, employees may be aware of types of unethical conduct that their managers know nothing about.

A final important argument for consulting employees is that the ethics of an organization is strongly influenced by how employees experience the organizational context. As noted above, this perception is their reality and affects their behavior.

Survey

Several methods are available for assessing the ethics of organizations (Kaptein and Wempe 2002). Together with more objective data (e.g., cases of theft, number of complaints, incidence of bribery), an opinion survey can generate information to determine the ethical quality of the organization. The main advantages are efficiency, confidentiality, comparability, and the opportunity to use advanced statistical methods to analyze the results. Employing a questionnaire to measure the perceptions of managers and employees can be helpful in predicting and explaining misconduct as well as estimating the risks and impacts of different types of misconduct. The information becomes more valuable if used to track an organization's progress over time and draw comparisons with similar organizations. Comparing differences and similarities in the patterns and causes of unethical conduct in similar organizations often generates interesting questions and also may yield useful answers. These answers might be found in the empirical data on the organizational climate and the perception of ethical leadership in this field.

Of course, measuring ethics by means of a survey has some pitfalls. If respondents fear that their anonymity might be compromised, they will give socially desirable answers or even refrain from filling out the questionnaire (Randall and Fernandes 1991). The same holds true for situations where management commitment is inadequate and respondents doubt that reviews will be followed up. Another risk arises if the results indicate that management's ethics is one of the main problems and management refuses to take the results seriously, ignores them, or even trashes the report. Table 3 summarizes the major advantages and risks of an ethics survey. To minimize these risks, an ethics survey can be presented and employed as a tool for moving forward instead of looking backward—that is, as a tool for taking pro-active and preventative measures instead of merely identifying offenders and taking reactive or repressive measures. Respondents should perceive the survey as non-threatening—a common responsibility to enhance the integrity of the organization, and not a means to tattle on colleagues or management.

Conclusions and implications

This article has presented a number of reasons for paying attention to ethics management in public organizations and has illustrated the usefulness of questionnaires in measuring the ethics of an organization with reference to the outcome of a survey of public servants. The results show that they face different types of unethical conduct with different frequencies. The infringements that occur most frequently include employment discrimination, violation of workplace health and safety rules, violation of privacy, false and misleading promises to clients and citizens, and carelessness with confidential information. These problems could have disastrous consequences. Sixty percent of the respondents indicated that their organization would lose a significant amount of public trust if the infraction they had knowledge of was published. The results also show that although most organizations provide their employees with information that clarifies the code of conduct and the overall principles and values, the organizational climate is not always conducive to ethical

Table 3. Advantages and risks of an ethics survey.

Advantages	Risks
• Management communicates the importance of ethics	• Respondents may have no trust in management commitment to develop its own ethics and the ethics of the organization
• Management communicates that employee opinions are important	• Survey seen as an intrusion on the trust of management in employees, of employees in management, or between employees
• Survey creates awareness among respondents about the ethics of their work environment	• Respondents fear anonymity will be compromised
• Survey creates support among respondents to develop the ethics of the organization	
• Employees and management may have different opinions and perceptions about organizational ethics	
• Confidentiality	
• Efficiency	
• Comparability and benchmarking	
• Use of advanced statistical methods to analyze data	

conduct. The most noticeable organizational weaknesses are (1) managers do not discipline offenders fairly and consistently, (2) employees feel uncomfortable seeking advice from senior management, and (3) employees feel they will be retaliated against if they report an offense.

Two of the major challenges to the ethics of public agencies are (1) heightening management's awareness of irregularities within the organization, and (2) enhancing management's appreciation of the impact of the organizational climate on ethical conduct. In order to assess ethical risks, management must develop skills and methods for identifying unethical conduct proactively, obtain insight into possible causes, and establish whether incidents are the result of an unlucky coincidence or reflect a more systematic organizational failure. These challenges point to the importance of having a system in place that monitors the ethics of the organization on a regular basis. In this respect, employing a questionnaire to measure the opinions of managers and employees can be helpful in predicting and explaining misconduct as well as estimating the risks and impacts of different types of problems. The information generated can be used to track organizational progress over time and to compare the agency's performance with similar organizations.

Although relevant research is progressing, there is as yet very little scientific knowledge about the structural and cultural causes of ethics violations (Treviño and Weaver 2003). This is also true for the relationship between dimensions of leadership, on the one hand, and unethical behavior, on the other (Van Wart 2003). Therefore, more work needs to be done on the relationship between leadership, the ethics climate, and unethical behavior. Empirical data, such as the data gathered through surveys, can be used to test this relationship using correlation and regression procedures. They can also be employed to help identify the leadership characteristics that encourage or prevent different types of offenses. Another important question asks which mix and type of leadership, climate, and ethics program leads to the lowest rate of ethical violations and the least damaging consequences. Still another type of question concerns the reliability of ethics surveys. Our survey found a great number of violations in the work environment of the respondents. But to what extent do employee perceptions correspond with the actual number of violations, what factors distort their perceptions, and to what extent does a questionnaire in itself influence perceptions and survey outcomes? The topic of ethical leadership and the use of questionnaires to measure ethics should both be given a more prominent place in the fields of organizational ethics, integrity, and leadership.

Note

1. This interview took place on 14 October 2003 during an ethics and integrity workshop at a large Dutch public organization in the province of South Holland. The confidentiality of the interview prohibits us from naming the person or organization represented.

References

Bird, Frederick B. 1996. *The Muted Conscience: Moral Silence and the Practice of Ethics in Business.* Westport, Conn.: Quorum Books.

Blanchard, Kenneth, and Norman Vincent Peale. 1988. *The Power of Ethical Management: Why the Ethical Way Is the Profitable Way in Your Life and in Your Business.* New York: Morrow.

Bowman, James S. 1990. "Ethics in Government: A National Survey of Public Administration." *Public Administration Review* 50:345-353.

Chappell, Duncan, and Vittorio Di Martino. 2000. *Violence at Work.* Geneva: International Labor Organization.

Cherrington, David J., and J. Owen Cherrington. 1985. "The Climate of Honesty in Retail Stores." In *Employee Theft: Research, Theory, and Applications,* edited by W. Terres, pp. 27-39. Rosemont: London House.

Cohan, J. A. 2002. "'I Didn't Know' and 'I Was Only Doing My Job': Has Corporate Governance Careened out of Control? A Case Study of Enron's Information Myopia." *Journal of Business Ethics* 40, no 3:275-299.

Cooper, Terry L., ed. 2001. *Handbook of Administrative Ethics.* 2nd ed. New York: Marcel Dekker.

Davies, David. 2000. *Fraud Watch.* Bottom-Line Business Guides. London: ABG Professional Information.

della Porta, Donatella, and Alberto Vanucci. 1999. *Corrupt Exchanges: Actors, Resources, and Mechanisms of Political Corruption.* New York: Aldine de Gruyter.

Ethicon. 2004. *Codes of Conduct within Governmental Organizations.* Available at www.b-sm.org.

Feldheim, MaryAnn, and Xiaohu Wang. 2004. "Ethics and Public Trust: Results from a National Survey." *Public Integrity* 6, no. 1:63-75.

Fijnaut, Cyrille, and Leo Huberts, ed. 2002. *Corruption, Integrity and Law Enforcement.* Dordrecht: Kluwer Law International.

Hoffman, W. Michael, and Jennifer Mills Moore. 1990. *Business Ethics: Readings and Cases in Corporate Morality.* New York: McGraw-Hill.

Huberts, Leo 1998. "What Can Be Done Against Public Corruption and Fraud? Expert Views on Strategies to Protect Public Integrity." *Crime, Law and Social Change* 29, nos. 2-3:209-224.

Jackall, Robert. 1988. *Moral Mazes: The World of Corporate Managers.* New York: Oxford University Press.

Kaptein, Muel. 1998. *Ethics Management: Auditing and Developing the Ethical Content of Organizations.* Dordrecht: Kluwer Academic.

———. 2002. "Guidelines for the Development of an Ethics Safety Net." *Journal of Business Ethics* 41, no. 3:217-234.

———. 2005. *The Six Principles of Managing with Integrity: A Practical Guide for Leaders.* New York: Spiro Press.

Kaptein, Muel, and Piet Van Reenen. 2001. "Integrity Management of Police Organizations." *Policing: An International Journal of Police Strategies & Management* 24, no. 3:281-300.

Kaptein, Muel, and Johann Wempe. 1998. "Twelve Gordian Knots When Developing an Organizational Code of Ethics." *Journal of Business Ethics* 17:853-869.

———. 2002. *The Balanced Company: A Theory of Corporate Integrity.* Oxford: Oxford University Press.

Klockars, Carl B., S. Kutnjak Ivkovic, and M. R. Haberfeld. 2004. *The Contours of Police Integrity.* Thousand Oaks, Calif.: Sage.

Lawton, A. 1998. *Ethical Management for the Public Services.* Buckingham, Pa., and Philadelphia: Open University Press.

Lasthuizen, Karin, Leo Huberts, and Muel Kaptein. 2002. "Integrity Problems in the Police Organization: Police Officers' Perceptions Reviewed." In *Policing in Central and Eastern Europe: Deviance, Violence, and Victimization,* edited by M. Pagon, pp. 25-37. Ljubljana: College of Police and Security Studies.

Paine, Linda S. 1994. "Managing for Organizational Integrity." *Harvard Business Review* 72:107-117.

———. 2003. *Values Shift.* New York: Prentice-Hall.

Petrick, Joseph A., and John F. Quinn. 1997. *Management Ethics: Integrity at Work.* Thousands Oaks, Calif.: Sage.

Perry, James L. 1993. "Whistleblowing, Organizational Performance, and Organizational Control." In *Ethics and Public Administration,* edited by H. George Frederickson, pp. 79-99. Armonk, N.Y.: M. E. Sharpe.

Preston, Noel, and Charles Sampford (with C.-A. Bois). 1998. *Ethics and Political Practice: Perspectives on Legislative Ethics.* London: Routledge.

Punch, Maurice. 1996. *Dirty Business: Exploring Corporate Misconduct.* London: Sage.

Randall, Donna M., and Maria F. Fernandes. 1991. "The Social Desirability Response Bias in Ethics Research." *Journal of Business Ethics* 10:805-817.

Rosthorn, John 2000. "Business Ethics Auditing: More Than a Stakeholder's Toy." *Journal of Business Ethics* 27:9-19.

Treviño, Linda Klebe, and Katherine A. Nelson. 1995. *Managing Business Ethics: Straight Talk about How to Do It Right.* New York: John Wiley.

Treviño, Linda Klebe, and Gary R. Weaver. 2003. *Managing Ethics in Business Organizations: Social Scientific Perspectives.* Stanford: Stanford University Press.

Treviño, Linda Klebe, and Stuart A. Youngblood. 1990. "Bad Apples in Bad Barrels: A Causal Analysis of Ethical Decision-Making Behavior." *Journal of Applied Psychology* 75:378-385.

Van Wart, Montgomery 2003. "Public-Sector Leadership Theory: An Assessment." *Public Administration Review* 63, no. 2:214-228.

Vardi, Yoav, and Ely Weitz. 2004. *Misbehavior in Organizations: Theory, Research and Management.* Mahwah, N.J.: Lawrence Erlbaum.

Weaver, Gary R., Linda Klebe Treviño, and P. L. Cochran. 1999. "Integrated and Decoupled Corporate Social Performance: Manager Commitments, External Pressures, and Corporate Ethics Practices. *Academy of Management Journal* 42, no. 5:539-552.

Part 3

Implementation:
Ethics Management

The Corruption Continuum

How law enforcement organizations become corrupt

Neal Trautman

Scandals can be prevented. They result from an evolution of predictable and preventable circumstances. Virtually every significant case of employee misconduct has involved warning signs that leaders either ignored or failed to recognize as important.

Leaders themselves are at the core of both the causes of and the solutions to corruption. Past research has repeatedly confirmed that most scandals start with relatively small unethical acts and grow to whatever level the leadership allows.

It now is understood that administrators play a much more direct and powerful role in the prevention or promotion of misconduct than previously thought. The "rotten apple" theory that some administrators have proposed as the cause of their demise has usually been nothing more than a self-serving facade, intended to draw attention away from their own failures.

Few events are more devastating to an organization than a scandal, and understanding how they begin and evolve is necessary to prevent them. Yet, a much more important requirement for stopping corruption is that administrators have the courage to acknowledge that they have integrity needs.

The continuum

Phase 1. Administrative indifference toward integrity

Many administrators are instantly resentful and defensive at the inference that they are or have ever been indifferent to ethics and integrity. But actions speak louder than words. The reality is that most workplaces are filled with employees who never have had ethics training, and the vast majority of workers in America feel far more stress from rampant backstabbing, internal politics, hidden agendas, and blatant unfairness than they do from simply doing their jobs.

Reprinted with permission of the author from *Public Management* magazine, June 2000, published by the International City/County Management Association, 777 North Capitol Street, N.E., Washington, DC 20002. The author retains copyright to this article.

At first glance, it seems illogical that the upper administration of an organization would not be deeply committed to maintaining a high level of organizational integrity. After all, employee misconduct leads to civil suits, negative publicity, ineffectiveness, and devastated morale. Chief administrators who have found themselves terminated will confirm that these and similar circumstances were used to justify their terminations.

It is widespread indifference that serves as the breeding ground for future misconduct. Pitfalls in the daily operations of a law enforcement agency that are the most revealing of integrity-related indifference include these indicators:

- A low quality of recruitment and hiring.
- The perception that discipline or promotion is unfair.
- Disgruntlement among field training officers.
- Supervisors who treat people with a lack of respect.

Phase 2. Negligence of obvious ethical problems

Because it is clearly in the best interests of an administrator to prevent misconduct, why aren't leaders more dedicated to stopping unethical behavior? In this phase of the continuum, leaders who are not committed to integrity can be categorized into three distinct levels according to their behaviors:

- At the least harmful level are administrators who don't devote resources to enhancing or maintaining ethical standards but are not negative role models themselves.
- At the second level of severity are leaders who intentionally look the other way and ignore acts of indiscretion by workers, even though these acts continue to grow in seriousness and frequency.
- Finally, the most despicable leaders are those who cover up misconduct rather than admit the truth and attempt to rectify a situation.

The failure of leadership to address internal integrity needs is more than just indifference at this phase because the needs are more recognizable and serious. Intentionally ignoring obvious ethical problems primarily arises out of one of two problems: a lack of knowledge or a certain self-centeredness. Although these leadership failures usually lead to devastating consequences, they can be prevented and corrected.

Lack of knowledge In this instance, misconduct occurs because administrators don't know what they can do to prevent or stop it. This is a circumstance in which leaders have the courage and desire to enhance integrity yet lack the knowledge, skill, or ability to carry out their good intentions. Their lack of training doesn't excuse them from being responsible, but it is the primary reason that misconduct has been able to flourish. They must still hold themselves accountable for ensuring that they learn how to implement and maintain the state of the art in misconduct prevention.

Self-centeredness The second reason why some leaders don't do more about clear ethical problems is that they believe that bringing attention to their integrity needs could hurt them personally. Encouraged by the hope that they will escape scrutiny and criticism if no one brings attention to the situation, they make their self-centeredness more important than maintaining integrity. Examples include doing nothing even though they know that:

- Discrimination or harassment is occurring.
- Sex among employees who are married to other people or with a supervisor exists.
- There is a general lack of accountability: some officers may have a number of citizen complaints or use-of-force incidents, for example.
- Some supervisors are degrading and intimidating employees.
- New officers are allowed to complete the field training officers' (FTO) program even though feedback from field training officers warrants termination. This, the single most demoralizing event that can occur within an FTO program, takes place because administrators don't want the city or county officials to feel that their hiring process was ineffective.

Administrators must always rise above the belief that they may look like hypocrites if they mandate ethics training. The reality is that if the organization has evolved to this phase in the continuum, they *will* look hypocritical. Here lies yet another example of why courage is the greatest quality of leadership. There can be no place for leaders who are afraid to improve integrity because an improvement may bring harsh criticism for past misconduct they have condoned by ignoring it.

Phase 3. Hypocrisy and fear dominant in the culture

This phase of the continuum is only possible after an administration has orchestrated several years of indifference and deliberately ignored the ethical needs of its organization. This phase is characterized by several clear symptoms that must be resolved, or the likelihood of significant corruption will be imminent.

Fear   By this stage of the evolution, fear has manifested itself in several forms. The most harmful consequence of fear occurs when an administration's role-modeling of ignoring integrity problems prompts the majority of supervisors to ignore them, too.

Although this idea is never found in a policy manual, every manager or supervisor knows at this point in the continuum that politics and hidden agendas decide which leaders will continue to be promoted and which will be ostracized or pushed aside. Thus, if you want to prosper or even merely survive as a leader, you are forced to abide by the unwritten rules of internal politics. The frustration of being treated with such disrespect and hypocrisy causes supervisors to discredit administrators in front of employees. What began as indifference has now grown into to a cancer, destroying morale, productivity, and dedication.

Extreme bitterness   Because all employees want to be treated with dignity and respect, an indication that serious misconduct has begun within a workplace is that employees have become deeply resentful over the way they are treated. Overt warning signs of this degree of resentfulness are:

- Constant, harsh criticism from large groups of people.
- Open defiance of administrators.
- Workers who rationalize doing unethical things during conversations with each other.

Hopelessness When workers no longer believe there is any hope for improvement or relief from their unbearable working conditions, they can justify carrying out unethical acts that would have been unthinkable to them in the past. If people are robbed of their dignity by insecure supervisors and find themselves surrounded by the "Everyone else is doing it" mentality, misconduct is guaranteed.

Confirmation of this fact can be found in the most extensive research ever conducted on serious law enforcement misconduct. The circumstances surrounding the decertifications of 2,296 local and state officers in the United States between 1990 and 1995 were analyzed by the National Institute of Ethics. Among the realities was this profile: 91 percent of all decertified officers had not been promoted, had been employed an average of 7.2 years, and were resentful.

Phase 4. Survival of the fittest

This ultimate level of the continuum of corruption is dominated by the pervasive intention of most employees to do whatever it takes just to survive. While the particular circumstances dictate the specific forms of misconduct, several common denominators exist among organizations that have reached this phase:

- The administrator's lack of knowledge on how to prevent unethical acts, combined with his or her refusal to address such prevention, blocks any attempt to enhance integrity.
- Good, honest employees fear the corrupt, dishonest ones.
- A long tradition of ignoring misconduct has convinced employees that leaders want misconduct covered up, rather than exposed or corrected.
- The code of silence is both condoned and privately encouraged.
- FTOs are resentful and bitter.
- There is a predominant, unwritten priority to "keep corruption out of the newspapers" at all costs.
- Officers that should be fired, arrested, and decertified are allowed to resign quietly.
- Chief administrators believe they would be fired if the truth about corruption were known, so they hide misconduct rather than try to resolve it.
- No one thinks the situation will get any better.

The best solutions to corruption

Truly great leaders do much more than merely supervise or administer. They are remembered for their courage to stand steadfast, doing what is right and just. They are individuals who always have remained uncompromised in their integrity.

The most effective solutions to corruption must be instilled with straight forwardness and honesty. Before implementing the following recommendations, however, a leader should be certain to determine whether any existing integrity needs are pervasive enough that instituting the improvements could make the administration look hypocritical. The most common example of this mistake is conducting ethics training before leaders have even begun to address the fact that some employees are being treated with a blatant lack of respect and dignity.

Solution 1. Ensure high-quality background investigations

The most important element of any organization's hiring process is the background check. The best predictor of future behavior has been and will always be past performance. Consequently, the most crucial requirement for superior background investigations is a sincere commitment from the upper administration to do what it takes to guarantee them.

Solution 2. Ensure a high-quality FTO program

It is a disheartening fact that the national standard of field training programs has remained stagnant for several decades. Most programs struggle with a variety of serious problems, like low levels of communication, standards, FTO selection procedures, compensation, and support from administrators. Unfortunately, the state of the art for field training is a much more efficient model than is the actual national standard. Implementing the cutting edge of field training helps to ensure that FTOs are not angry and frustrated. As a result, a positive organizational culture within the patrol division will be much more likely.

Solution 3. Fight political interference

Political favoritism and interference have always been detriments to law enforcement. Although these problems generally aren't as extreme today as they were in the 1800s, they still can be severe obstacles to professionalism. Today's interference typically attacks two aspects of a government, by lowering hiring standards and interfering with promotions. The best solution is usually to educate local officials about the consequences of allowing these two things to happen.

Solution 4. Ensure consistent, fair accountability

A continued lack of accountability is destructive to the culture of an organization. Ethical accountability will be one of the most-used means of preventing unethical acts in the next decade. Acknowledging that there is little or inconsistent accountability in an organization is particularly painful for many administrators, as these leaders are probably the ones who are to blame.

The upper administration is the only correct place to start when a person truly wants to improve accountability because these administrators are usually offenders themselves. They must set an example by holding themselves accountable for starting to resolve integrity needs.

Solution 5. Conduct effective ethics training

Even though this is law enforcement's greatest training need, most agencies have never conducted internal ethics training. The specific topics that will be best for most agencies are the major causes of misconduct; the Continuum of Compromise® (Gilmartin and Harris); ethical-dilemma simulation training, which anchors a decision-making process into an attendee's long-term memory; study of the researched facts about bad cops; intervention to save fellow officers; the need for ethical courage; and the Corruption Continuum®. Every effort should be made to teach these topics through interactive, hands-on video case studies.

Solution 6. Accept nothing less than positive leadership role models

Supervisors act as trainers, counselors, and mentors for all employees. As a result of their constant contact and formal power, they become major role models. The importance of this relationship is vital in developing such traits as sincerity, loyalty, honesty, respect, and dedication. Role modeling is a leader's greatest single source of power.

Actions do speak louder than words. It is impossible for any company, association, or agency to be filled with integrity if line supervisors are unethical, for role modeling also can be used to instill corrupt behavior.

Solution 7. Prevent officers from feeling victimized

The Continuum of Compromise®, as developed by Kevin Gilmartin and Jack Harris, shows that officers perceiving a sense of victimization can commit progressively worsening unethical acts. Their perception of being victims makes it easier for them to rationalize their misconduct.

Solution 8. Implement an effective employee intervention process

Employee intervention now can be implemented through two distinct tools: computer software and internal training. Software will permit the tracking of performance, so there can be intervention for those whose performance has been outstanding, as well as for those who could benefit from assistance in correcting performance deficiencies.

The other contemporary form of intervention is training. When an officer begins to exhibit misconduct, other officers are usually the only ones who can intervene to prevent them from destroying their own careers.

Fatal Choices

The routinization of deceit, incompetence, and corruption

David W. Haines

The following case material is drawn from some fifteen years of experience in federal and state agencies. The work ranged from policy and research analysis, to management consulting, to senior management. A few general comments are needed about the case material. First, the topics are deceit, incompetence, and corruption. These strong labels would not be used by most of the people in the organizations from which the material comes—in itself an important part of the dynamic that will be discussed. Second, the purpose of the discussion that follows is not to evaluate the specific personal actions described but to understand the organizational reactions to them. It is the organizational reactions that are the fatal choices. Most of the individual actions in the cases that follow are in themselves rather minor. It is the organizational choices about them that transform these failings—or inadvertent lapses—into serious organizational weaknesses. Third, the material is sensitive. Therefore, much of the context has been removed from the examples to protect the identity of the people involved. As a result, much of the organizational ambience is lost. One benefit, however, is a focus not on local explanations for the examples but on the emergence of problems of this kind in almost every organization. In removing and modifying identifiers, after all, it has been necessary to make sure that each of these events could have taken place in multiple organizations.

Finally, while the introductory discussion stressed rationality in government, the term has a more specific meaning in the case material: availability and accuracy of information. This narrow definition is helpful in providing a clearer referent for what rationality might entail on a day-to-day basis and on the importance of rationality not as a broad issue of overarching structure, but as one that involves the bits and pieces of information that become part of the broader structure. The transition from the grander notions of governmental rationality to the events of daily organizational life is sometimes a difficult one, both for those looking at government and for those doing its work.

Abridged from *Public Integrity*, vol. 6, no. 1 (2003-04): 5-23. Copyright © 2004 by American Society for Public Administration (ASPA). Reprinted with permission of M. E. Sharpe, Inc.

Deceit

A good place to begin is with the most elementary assault on the rationality of an organization: the creation of falsehood rather than truth, deception rather than accuracy. People make things up. Sometimes they do so willfully, with premeditation and considerable craft. Sometimes they make things up spontaneously and perhaps even unconsciously. In some cases people are misguided about events and report them inaccurately. Such reporting lacks the willfulness of other misinformation but can be just as damaging. From the organizational point of view, the intentionality of misinformation may be less important than the effects. Both the willful lie and the misguided misinterpretation create a deviation from accuracy. Such deceptions come in a variety of forms, but, as in Bok's (1999/1978) classic analysis, are most easily considered in the rawer form of stated lies. In the general course of human life, Bok would hold out the possibility of some deceit for some purposes, and others have stressed the inevitability of deceit (Sullivan 2001)—and perhaps even its creative human value (Nyberg 1993). Despite these broader arguments, lies would seem to have little place in government. But they occur, they have consequences, and their general dynamics deserve consideration.

First-party lies

Perhaps the simplest lie that one may commit in an organization is about oneself. The standard format is "No, I didn't do that" for something one should not have done. This is the basic weapon in the personal cover-up. It is surprisingly and wonderfully effective. If someone denies that something happened, and does so with some discretion, it is usually difficult to establish the inaccuracy of the statement. In one case, a budget officer had agreed that a project would only cost $2,000 and then went out and purchased the services for $3,000. He simply denied that he had increased the cost. Nobody else was very clear about the facts of the case, and therefore it was assumed that he was telling the truth, or was at least immune from any charge of untruthfulness. The simple "I didn't do it," in cases of desperation after contrary evidence appears, can extend into the "I'm sorry, I forgot" defense. Thus if the lie itself does not work, the immediate cover-up is simply that the error was accidental. Misinformation is transformed into simple miscommunication. It is also a good idea to elaborate a little more along the lines of "I forgot, there was a lot of confusion on that" or "I forgot, you know I've been so overloaded." Some people invoke personal and family problems that lend the explanation greater force.

The other standard first-party lie is "Yes, I did it" for things that should have been done. It is the ideal response to "Did you get that job done?" Usually, there is still sufficient time to actually get the job done. If not, there are all kinds of possibilities for explaining away the lie: "I lost the report," "Somebody borrowed it," or—in a more desperate situation—"I'm sorry, I thought you meant the other project" (and a repeat of the apology for being confused what with everything else going on). Again misinformation is passed off as miscommunication. Another even easier version of this is the promise "I'll take care of it this afternoon" (or tomorrow or next week or as soon as I get back to the office). If it does not get done, of course, the existing stock of first-party lies comes in handy: "Yes, I got it done," "Okay, I'll go find it," or "Sorry, I thought you meant that other project." The mark of true masters at this is that one tends to believe them even when one knows they are making it up.

Second-party lies

Second-party lies are trickier than first-party lies because they involve convincing other people that they did something they did not do. For example, a subordinate can tell a boss, "I thought you told me you wanted it done that way." The boss, with more raw power to draw on, might dispense with actual words said and move to intentions: "You implied that you were going to get this done right away. I'm very disappointed in you." Since discussions about what people said, thought, and intended in the past are subject to much confusion anyway, a cleverly inserted lie has a very good chance of succeeding because—barring a transcript—nobody can be proved to be wrong or right. Further, the social costs of implying that someone is being deceitful are high.

Second-party lies are interesting because they involve direct interaction between two persons who both have independent access to the same information about the events. Thus they highlight intersecting dimensions of power, authenticity, and salesmanship. In terms of power, when there is a great hierarchical difference between the two parties, the superordinate can impose a vision of reality whether or not the statement is believed by either of the two. Alternatively, one person may well have the upper edge in terms of memory—either through ability to focus or through supplementary materials. Notes are a good source of support, but of course they are written by one of the involved parties and therefore subject to *cui bono* questions (i.e., whose interests do they serve?). Yet the statement "My notes indicate..." often carries great weight. The lack of contravening evidence or witnesses is vital. Finally, salesmanship is crucial. Lacking clear documentation or sharp memory, a creative, energetic recreation of how events should have been may well carry the day: "No, no, we wouldn't have done that because..."

Third-party lies

Third-party lies are in many ways the easiest. One person tells another person something about a third person. Since the third party is not there, the issue of corroboration may never be addressed. One agency head, for example, had a meeting with two staff people who reported to a manager who, in turn, reported to her. She told the staff people that the manager had not attended the meeting because he (the manager) did not want to be bothered with personnel issues. The manager only accidentally found out that the meeting had taken place, and then he told the staff people that his one rule was that he was *always* available for personnel issues. If such a third-party lie comes to light, it is time for either more third-party lies ("Well, that's what John told me") or perhaps a quick jump to the classic first-party lie ("I never told them anything of the kind"), or better yet, to turn misinformation into miscommunication with something like "Well, that wasn't my understanding."

The situation is more complex when many people are involved as the targets of misinformation and more people are privy to the misinformation. More people then have their own independent information and there is a greater chance that at least one of them will have a connection to those who are negatively affected by the misinformation. Third-party lies in such situations are best structured as in-group lies about out-group people. Even if there is a break in the boundaries between the groups, the testimony of each group will tend to be automatically discounted by the other. Such lies can stand almost as easily as a basic third-party lie of which the third party never hears. Lack of communication remains, however, the best solution because it avoids even the need to create a miscommunication excuse.

For organizations, the problem is not that misinformation exists, but that it often bears directly on the work to be done. The work of the organization—most especially of public sector organizations—must be out in the open and must be accurate. If the work is hidden, or the information about it inaccurate, it will be unanalyzable, unevaluatable, and unreportable. In most organizations there are occasions for missing or incorrect information to come out in the open: in formal meetings, in informal groups, and over time cumulatively in one-on-one discussions. Piece by piece, at different times with different people, or all at once in a large meeting, the possibility exists to untangle what has become tangled. Collectively, the organization can begin to assess the problem and triangulate where the source of the tangle might lie. It is at this point that the organization faces a crucial decision: Will the unclear be made clear and the inaccurate accurate? Or will the more convenient option of covering up the problem be chosen?

As an example, consider a personnel situation involving three key employees: a unit supervisor (Clarice), her boss (Jill), and Jill's boss (Hank). Several accusations were made both personally by Clarice and anonymously (possibly also by Clarice) that employees had been submitting inaccurate travel vouchers. Clarice said that Jill had actively encouraged her to do this. An ombudsperson in another part of the agency contacted Hank about this, and the two of them began talking to Clarice and her staff. They learned from staff that there had indeed been tampering with travel vouchers. In particular, it became clear that Jill had approved an unofficial system of extra travel benefits for two employees. Hank knew he had discussed this issue with Jill and that Jill had indicated that nothing of the kind was going on. Jill had clearly not only flouted the agency's regulations to help particular employees, but in the process had lied to Hank, her direct supervisor.

Since the issue came to light with such clarity and documentation, the ombudsperson and Hank decided to pursue disciplinary action and wrote a detailed report on the incident to the agency head. At this point, Jill refused to discuss the issue further without the presence of an attorney. The agency head, for a mix of reasons, including personal friendship with Jill and fear about her potential retention of counsel, ignored the report and its recommendations. Instead, the agency head wrote a letter of warning to Jill about the issue and placed a copy of the letter in her personnel file. When Jill pointed out that an informal letter violated personnel policy, it was removed from her file and destroyed. The agency head made the choice that it was better to smooth over the issue than to take the opportunity to bring a problem to light. An important precedent had been set. Here, as in Bok's classic analysis, a relatively innocuous lie—perhaps excusable if not justifiable— was transformed into a part of broader organizational practice, mirroring her concern about the "great susceptibility of deception to spread, to be abused, and to give rise to even more undesirable practices" (Bok 1999/1978, 104).

Incompetence

A second problem area involves incompetence. The lore of incompetence in government is extensive: from cost overruns in contracts, to systems that do not work, to bureaucrats who do not know their own regulations, to senior managers who rotate in and out of jobs so fast that they only learn their job by the time they leave it. When the government is out of favor, the incompetent bureaucrat becomes its emblem, castigated on one side by the public and on the other by elected officials who themselves are often lambasted as yet more incompetent at the actual work of government than even the maligned bureaucrats.

Incompetence comes in all shapes and sizes—some people cannot deal with computers; others have limited writing skills, do not do well in interpersonal situations, have difficulty making decisions, are poor analysts, or simply cannot follow through on tasks. Everyone is, after all, certifiably and predictably incompetent in at least some tasks some of the time, exactly as everyone is certifiably and predictably competent at other tasks (or even the same tasks) at other times. Managers sometimes regard certain employees as incompetent in some overall sense; more seasoned managers understand that people have a range of areas in which they are more or less competent. The package of competencies and incompetencies can vary greatly, from the relatively uncommon person who deals ably with people, ideas, and technology, to the even more uncommon person who is poor in all these areas.

The management issue is not incompetence per se, but the allocation of different levels and types of competence to the tasks for which they are needed. The central managerial task is to put employees where their competencies are most useful and their incompetencies are least damaging. Recruitment, retention, promotion, and sanctions are all part of this overall competency-allocation responsibility. With luck, this managerial responsibility will be shared by the employees, because they too are trying to match their competencies against the job. Over time, one hopes to limit the effects of incompetencies and maximize those of competencies. In an organizational utopia, management of the employee and self-management by the employee would be fully consonant.

Assessing competence and incompetence requires accurate information. The organization and the employee must both know where competence and incompetence lie and how the one can be fostered and the other minimized. If some people are poor analysts who simply cannot think abstractly, they should not be doing analysis. This is perhaps the most elementary functional application of reason at the organizational level. There are many dangers: that there will be no information, that the information will not be accurate, that the information will be anti-accurate in that it actually undermines accuracy, as when the competent are termed incompetent, and the incompetent, competent. With a reminder that the issue here is not incompetence but how an organization manages incompetence, several examples follow dealing sequentially with work not getting done at all, work not getting done well, and work getting done in a way that undermines other work.

Not getting things done

Surprisingly often, work does not get done or gets done breathtakingly late.

> Bill was doing a small follow-up study on a government agency. Previous studies by his colleagues indicated that the agency should add staff, but now Bill was suggesting that it needed to reduce staff. Bill's boss was more than a little embarrassed about the change. This permitted Bill to dig in his heels and extend what was probably a one-month project for nearly a year.

> John was a senior manager who publicly excoriated staff to do their performance evaluations on time, but for many years he himself never did such evaluations at all. When he finally did them one year, he was months late and did not follow the agency guidelines. His failure to do evaluations was noted in a public audit report, but this did not ensure that the work got done.

Jane was a supervisor and had agreed with her boss and staff to make some changes in how a certain policy was handled: specifically, which clients would have to fill out a particular form. However, she never implemented the change. Nearly two years later, her boss discovered this. Once Jane found out that her boss had discovered this, she immediately made the change. However, since the discussion had taken place so long before, she had forgotten the details. The change was thus made incorrectly. This, in turn, aggravated the agency's clients, embarrassed the organization, and required yet another round of procedural change.

Knowing the people in these examples, it is hard to resist some comment on the personal dynamics involved. Bill, it seemed, could not give up the limelight of the "burr under the saddle" role he had stumbled into; John was frightened of conflict and uncertain of his own competence, and thus putting evaluative comments in writing was to be avoided; and Jane was so intimidated by her supervisor that she could not communicate with anybody about the procedural issues involved. However, the important issue is not the dynamic underlying the events but whether the events were taken as information, and thus as the basis for improved management. In all these cases the answer was no. Bill was never reined in, John was coddled and eventually promoted, and Jane was further removed from exactly the policy issues in which she needed to be directly involved.

Not getting things done well

In addition to work not getting done—or getting done very late—work is often not done well.

Sarah was providing energetic oversight of a service contract. She was newly trained and, with a fresh psychology degree, intent on making this project work. However, her constant tinkering with the project increasingly threw it off schedule. The result was a 20 percent overrun in the project's already publicized high cost.

Harry was rising to the top of the organization and wanted to bring more of it under his direct control. He intervened to axe a carefully budgeted plan to replace some of the agency's equipment. As complaints subsequently grew over the increasingly outdated equipment, he reinstituted the plan for upgrading equipment but ended up doing so at a sharply increased cost—even though equipment prices were falling.

Charley decided to oppose a plan to revise some of the forms his department used. He suggested an alternative plan that would involve serious procedural changes. He indicated that he would outline the changes so that everyone could see what they looked like. A year later, nothing concrete had been done: only some general ideas that brought the changes no closer.

Again, it is possible to see personal dynamics in each of these situations. Sarah was intent on project control yet was working with people far senior to her in educational credentials. Harry also wanted control and was willing to override the department and division managers to have it—even in areas where he had little background or competence. Charley effectively defended his turf, but having done so, slid back into his usual non-productive activities of socializing with other staff during work hours—for which he was notorious.

The issue here, however, is not such personal inferences, even though such inferences were consistently used. Instead, the issue is how the organizations responded to these cases of incompetence. Once again, the response was to avoid dealing with the specific issue in favor of mollifying the people and sometimes even effectively rewarding them.

Sarah was promoted to have more influence over exactly the kinds of projects she had mishandled. Harry solidified his position. Charley maintained the status quo and his ability to avoid changes being forced on him. Since the revision process was contingent on his initial work, and that work had not produced anything concrete, he was entirely free from *any* revision process.

Counter-productivity

Incompetence often goes beyond the failure to get work done, or to get it done well, into actual destruction of existing work. Counter-productivity is seen in many of the examples already given. For example, Jane's inability to remember the policy change led to confusion among the agency's clients and some measure of embarrassment. Harry's version of the equipment upgrade caused delay, increased costs, alienated technical staff, and undercut the agency's attempt to develop a more open budgeting process. Charley's defense of the status quo delayed changes that would have prevented some heated public complaints.

A more detailed example may be of use. A senior manager had taken a particular fondness to George, one of his temporary support staff, bringing him into a full-time position and then increasing his rank and salary to the point at which he was the highest-ranked person in the organization who lacked any specific area of responsibility. The manager assigned George to various special projects that were then used to increase his status. (This was partially explained on the basis of his graduate degree in finance.) One of these projects was a manual telling the agency's lower-income clients how to apply for special seasonal assistance. George was a somewhat ironic choice for this because his written work tended to be erratic—largely because no one had ever reviewed it or imposed editorial control. The manual was meant to be a short-term project, but George was well known for not getting projects done. The project's completion date indeed began to drag out from "this spring" to "next fall" and finally all the way around to "next spring." George's efforts to enlist the assistance of the staff members who actually processed the materials and knew the relevant policy (and indeed had written a manual themselves) caused considerable aggravation.

The net effect was delay. This increased the scale of the project, since there now had to be a reason for the delay. No longer was the manual to be simply an overview of existing procedures—instead it was to be the mechanism for a new set of procedures that would redefine the client population. This caused even more aggravation among staff as George went into departments where he had no formal role with this new and more intimidating project. At least one manager made a formal request of the agency head to clarify—and limit—George's role. There was no response to that request, leading to confusion on top of the aggravation. At the same time, rumors began to circulate that the agency head had plans to make George a formal manager of the unit with responsibility for the program of special seasonal assistance.

Ultimately, the sheer complexity and weight of the proposals caused their collapse, and there was a return to the original idea of a manual documenting current application procedures. In the process, however, the organization and several of its people suffered damage. Formal complaints had been made against George. His reputation and that of the agency head had been compromised. Comments on favoritism and secret personal networks circulated throughout the agency, fueling an atmosphere of distrust. Perhaps more telling, the idea of a formal manual for the public, which everybody had originally supported, had become a point of such irritation (eyes rolling heavenward at the mention of "George's manual") that it no longer provided a point of forward movement for the agency.

None of these examples of work not done, work done poorly, or work that was counter-productive is very horrifying. The people served by these agencies may not have been well served, but they were not terribly ill-served either. The effects on them were more annoying than damaging. What these examples illustrate is wasted effort and lost morale. In every instance, the organization let standards lapse, instead acting to tolerate incompetence and mollify incompetents. In George's case, the organization failed to monitor his work and to keep issues of work separate from personal interests. This failure was sufficiently public that not only a disavowal was needed, but an active cover-up. George's boss would ultimately claim with utter inaccuracy that "George does great work. He gets along well with everybody." Here then is a different variant of Bok's (1999/1978) concern about the implications of the individual case for the broader social practice. A situation ("case" in her terms) of incompetence created not only a continuing pattern ("practice" in her terms) of incompetence, but also one of misrepresentation.

Corruption

As acceptance of misinformation and incompetence grows, an organization moves further from an ability to assess itself internally and to make corrections when needed. It is not just that the organization ceases to maintain any standards for its conduct, but that it loses the ability to think because there is no longer any accountable standard of truth. The organization is corrupted not only in a moral sense, but in the technical sense in which "corruption" is used in talking about databases. There corruption goes beyond the accuracy of information to whether it even conforms to its proper structure. What is corrupt by this definition is not just incorrect but unprocessable. It may make other information unprocessable as well.

Corruption also has a clear moral meaning in government. There are, after all, individual acts of criminal corruption: graft and bribery, for example. In the relatively open environment of American government, this kind of corruption has a more discreet face: The cooperation of a government official, for instance, may result in a handsome post-government job offer. Some useful legislative votes may translate into a later judgeship for that "retirement thing." These forms of corruption are "civilized," because they require discretion and the restraint necessary to wait a bit before the rewards roll in. However, there is also a more mundane form of corruption that runs more pervasively through organizations. Often petty in substance, it is nevertheless profound in its implications for the overall functioning of the organization. The problem with such corruption, to continue the theme of this discussion, involves not the episodic failings per se, but the failure to disavow them and sometimes even the act of rewarding them. Several examples follow involving routine handling of funds, management of personnel issues, and the reporting of agency work. Deviations often occur in each of these areas. The crucial issue is how the agency responds.

The abuse of money

In most organizations, there is a fair amount of petty pilfering—pens and pencils disappear, travel vouchers are rearranged (sometimes simply to get costs into a reimbursable category), photocopiers are used for personal purposes, secretaries type their boss's personal correspondence or papers, personal faxes go out on the agency machines. It is difficult to completely rule out such activities, since people's schedules may make it nonsensical to do so: taking a lunch hour, for example, to photocopy or fax a letter. Attempts to reimburse for the use of office equipment raise difficult problems.

Petty pilfering, however, often grows. In one organization, for example, the agency head used to require staff to come out and do occasional painting at his house. In another case, an agency head would give himself whatever new computer equipment became available. He even had office staff program his home computers so that his children could play the latest video games. In such cases, the pilfering remains relatively modest in total cost. Its greater effect is the indirect one of misallocation of staff time. But the implications of such a sloppy moral standard—considering that public funds are involved—are more serious. It sets a standard of conduct that outrages some employees, induces others to seek similar special consideration for themselves, and leaves yet others caught between these two positions. Those who seek similar preferential treatment can do so with a relatively clear conscience because they are only emulating authority. Those who do not seek such special treatment will be doubly outraged by seeing the self-aggrandizement replicated in the behavior of others around them, and sometimes even by employees who report to them. For managers, the only objection to such activity by subordinates can be that they are not yet high enough in the organization to benefit from unofficial perquisites. Most administrators are likely to find this an unsatisfying position and instead ignore the issue entirely.

The serious problem, then, is not the pilfering but what it does to the organization. There may be a hardening divide between staff who seek proper use of public funds and equipment and those who mimic the attempt to feed more greedily—and more openly—at their portion of the public trough. The individual case would be only a routine personnel problem, but the acceptance of such self-aggrandizement signals a more pervasive corruption. This is a moral problem, but also a practical one. One consequence, for example, is a ruined budget process. Even a good and necessary budget decision will be tainted by the distrust arising from previous misallocations of funds.

Twisting personnel policy

Governmental organizations are in a unique position when they recruit, retain, and compensate employees. Since their employees work for the public and are themselves part of the citizenry, they are, to a certain extent, working for themselves. Thus it is essential that management of personnel policies be both equitable and effective. Deviations from proper and equitable policies reverberate throughout the organization and are quickly woven into its unofficial history. They challenge the very heart of the enterprise, for the covenant between government and citizen is also a covenant between employer and employee.

Deviations from proper personnel policy are matters of great concern. Sometimes deviations are simply matters of rewarding personal favorites:

The agency head believed that Sally was just the right person for the new job. He insisted that she be given the job—and quickly. Sally was probably the best qualified candidate and would almost inevitably have been awarded the position through an open process, but as a result, she was installed in the position by fiat instead. This seriously damaged her reputation, which was already somewhat tarnished by rumors of an affair with another senior manager. It also reinforced the existing view in the organization that advancement was based on personal connections.

A department manager insisted from the beginning that he did not want to even consider one of the candidates (Hannah) because he did not like her—based on very limited professional contact. Hannah turned out to be technically the best candidate for the job, but because of the department manager's attitude, she was ruled out of contention and another person was selected. Hannah subsequently applied for another job, for which she was the final selection. She was far less suited for this job, however, and ended up causing a variety of work problems.

Preferential hiring and non-hiring are routine, but the costs can be significant. Sally did a good job; Hannah did not. In both cases, however, the willful imposition of personal preferences explicitly placed the formal process in a secondary position and served to undermine any sense that such practices would be handled fairly and "by the book."

A more extended example shows how convoluted personnel issues can be. The example returns to the story of Clarice, Jill, Hank, and the travel vouchers. Jill had, in fact, admitted that she had condoned some fudging of the reporting, and it was only after this partial admission that she indicated she would seek representation by an attorney. The personnel manual was clear that this violation was subject to formal action, and that is what Hank subsequently recommended against both Clarice and Jill. The action would not have caused either Clarice or Jill any actual loss, but it would have put both of them on very clear warning about tampering with travel documents.

Since the agency head and Jill were friends, and there was a general fear of people contacting attorneys, the issue was, as noted, completely dropped. In the process, however, outside authorities were at least partially misinformed about the formal complaints that had been made. In addition, Hank had previously written up another staff member for related problems. He felt obliged to rescind this because he was not willing to take action against one staff member but not against the agency head's personal friend. Jill ended up effectively immune from managerial direction thereafter. With the dual strategies of personal connection to the agency head and the threat of retaining a lawyer, no real standards could be imposed on her. Furthermore, no one involved was ever likely to believe again that the personnel system could be applied without calculating who was personal friends with whom. The initial issue was a minor one: No one was under any threat of serious disciplinary action, although two employees would have been formally put on notice. However, something far more serious happened. As a careful investigation of one incident of wrong-doing was thrown out, so also was the very possibility that the organization's rules for its own self-conduct would ever be followed.

Such issues of personnel management are particularly good ones through which to consider how organizations do or do not use rationality in Dewey's broad sense as a tool and process focused on both means and ends (on "moral goods" and "natural goods") within their internal environments (Evans 2001, 267-268). But organizations also have external environments. One key element in an organization's relationship to its external environments is how it represents its work to them. Much of any organization's work can be described in numbers, and numbers can be manipulated. The next—and final—case example concerns the corruption of an organization's representation of itself.

Faking the numbers

Faking the numbers is a well-established craft in most organizations. There are always reasons to count things in the most favorable light, to obscure the less favorable numbers, and to devise new ways of counting things that would be advantageous. This in itself has dangers. But even more dangerous is the likelihood that the faked numbers will be formally released and thus become unretractable. The organization will then not only have engaged in petty tinkering with numbers, but will have embarked inexorably on a never-ending cover-up.

The efforts of an enterprising manager at one agency provide an example:

> Gerry was intent on advancing, and in order to do so, he had to show that what he was doing was working. He began to play with the numbers. In one case, he did not like what the numbers showed, and asked people to recount their work in a different way to get the numbers higher. In another case, he put out a report that bunched duplicative work counts together to show a greater increase in workload than had actually occurred. On another occasion, he found a junior staff person to do a chart for him that a senior staff person would not do because it was misleading. On yet another occasion, he concocted a different reporting period so the data would show what he wanted.

Although this example shows unusual creativity in finding alternative numbers, such tinkering is not uncommon. Gerry prospered from his misreporting, but the organization had established a pattern of duplicity that put it perpetually in cover-up mode. When a public sector organization, as in this case, tampers with its own numbers, it has taken a fatal step away from its responsibilities to the public and to itself. Turning back will be very difficult. Yet the effect may be worse at the practical than the moral level. In effect, the organization can no longer see its own work because it must try to shade parts of its work from the view of outsiders, disavow that it is shading the work, and substitute fabricated alternative images of its work that it must then certify as authentic. No longer can the issue even be discussed openly.

Despite the effects, much corruption of this kind is often very undramatic at its inception—people "go with the flow," they "let them [upper management] decide." Staff may complain, but this only tightens the cover-up. No standard need apply as the organization forfeits its moral structure, retaining only the ability to react to political pressures from outside and the social pressures within. No standard need apply even on the pragmatics of daily operations. Instead, the organization's acquiescence in incompetence and corruption is enwrapped and shielded by that most useful of organizational tools: the cover-up. It is time for the grand collective first-person lies: "We didn't do it" for the things that should not have happened, and "We did do it" for the things that should have been done.

...These cases suggest that an agency may profit in vital ways from dealing with—even experimenting with—relatively minor issues that can be resolved with little threat to the organization or its people. The crux is not scale but timing. Modest self-discipline on modest issues with modest inconvenience *now* may well yield great benefits in the long term. The counter-case—an inexorable and corrosive loss of faith in government's ability to govern itself—is a harrowing one.

References

Bok, Sissela. 1999/1978. *Lying: Moral Choice in Public and Private Life*. New York: Vintage Books.

Evans, Karen G. 2001. "More Democracy, Not Less, in Twenty-First Century Governance: Dewey's Ethics and the New Public Management." *Public Integrity* 3:262-276.

Nyberg, David. 1993. *The Varnished Truth: Truth Telling and Deceiving in Ordinary Life*. Chicago: University of Chicago Press.

Sullivan, Evelin. 2001. *The Concise Book of Lying*. New York: Farrar, Straus & Giroux.

Building a Strong Local Government Ethics Program

Michael W. Manske and H. George Frederickson

On April 1, 1997, when the citizens of Wyandotte County and Kansas City, Kansas, voted to merge and consolidate their county and city governments, there were only 31 such consolidations in the United States. The citizens voted not only to reconstruct their local government but also to do away with a long history of political corruption and employee misconduct.

The consolidation referendum called for the establishment of an ethics commission with teeth in it, as well as a jurisdiction-wide ethics program. Mayor Carol Marinovich put it this way: "Elected officials of the newly consolidated city and county governments recognized that the success of any form of government would depend largely upon the trust established between the government and the citizens of the community. They also understood that trust would not evolve without the absolute expectation and enforcement of high ethical standards of conduct for every elected official, administrative official, and employee."

The newly elected mayor and county commission decided on an ethics program designed to stamp out corruption, bolster public trust in government, and improve public service to the citizens. The foundation of the ethics program was a new ordinance, adopted in May 1998. But a code of ethics would not achieve all the leadership goals that the unified government wanted.

The code was augmented by a multifaceted and comprehensive program that featured a unique method of code administration, as well as a comprehensive education program, complaint hotline, investigation protocol, and independent oversight function. It was believed that this combination of interrelated and supporting functions would work in harmony to promote ethical conduct.

Reprinted with permission from *Public Management* magazine, June 2004. Copyright © 2004 by the International City/County Management Association, Suite 500, 777 N. Capitol St., N.E., Washington, DC 20002.

The comprehensive ethics program rests on four pillars: 1) the code of ethics, 2) the ethics education program, 3) the oversight of the ethics commission, and 4) the office of the ethics administrator. Each pillar plays an equal part in the ethics program, and each depends upon the others for reinforcement and support. An ethics education program, for example, supports the code by giving each elected official and employee the needed instruction in the code of ethics, as well as in the policy rationale behind the rules. Even the finest code of ethics would be rendered ineffective if government officials did not understand its provisions or why those provisions were there and what their importance was.

An independent ethics commission continually monitors the activities of government, recommending amendments to the code when appropriate and advising on policy matters, as well as ruling on ethics complaints. And finally, the ethics administrator supports the ethics commission as its executive agent and is responsible for comprehensive ethics education and for engaging in ethics investigations and preparing advisory opinions.

Implementation of the Unified Government Code of Ethics and management of the jurisdiction's comprehensive ethics program are contracted out. This contract calls for the appointment of a part-time ethics administrator, an extensive ethics education program for all jurisdiction officials and employees, an ethics complaint hotline, and staff support for the ethics commission. Subcontractual work is directed by a team from the University of Kansas.

Over the past five years, this interdependent combination of functions has proven worthwhile. County Administrator Dennis Hays says: "There has been a huge impact on the unified government organization since the consolidation of governments in 1997. Prior to consolidation, there was great discontent among the citizens with the ethics of political leadership and with jurisdiction employees regarding propriety.

"Through the establishment of the ethics administrator and ethics commission, and with the development of the code of ethics, there is a much greater sense of trust and confidence in the government and within the organization. This confidence and trust is further regarded as a high standard by the public, as there has been no public outcry regarding a public official."

Code of ethics

The code of ethics was adopted by the unified government as an ordinance, which set clear rules of ethical conduct in government and the mechanisms for enforcing these rules. The code includes many rules of conduct common to governmental ethics, such as prohibitions against conflicts of interest, gratuities and kickbacks, nepotism, and objectionable outside employment. It sets clearly defined rules for the acceptance of gifts, handling of confidential information, and appropriate exercise of official duties.

These standard provisions are joined by a comprehensive statement of both permitted and prohibited political activities. The code includes a whistle-blower protection provision and provides for confidential communication of ethics complaints through several "hotline" vehicles. It both prohibits retaliation against officials and governmental employees who make complaints and provides redress. Constant review and refinement have kept the code relevant and timely through a series of amendments recommended by the ethics commission.

Ethics commission

The presence of an authoritative body of citizens who can exercise independent oversight is essential to promoting public integrity in government. In the unified government, this function is the responsibility of the commission and established by ordinance. The five-citizen panel is charged with monitoring governmental activities, recommending code amendments, and issuing advisory opinions.

The commission is responsible for important policy debates that affect the overall ethical environment of the government. It also reviews and recommends discipline on ethics complaint cases and responds to inquiries from officials and administrators on the ethical review of proposed policies and activities.

Ethics commissioners are not appointed by the mayor or by the county commission but by three "politically insulated" and independent officers in the government: the chief judge of the district court, the district attorney, and the legislative auditor. The important point is that neither the mayor nor the commission of the unified government appoints the members of the ethics commission. The ethics commission, which is therefore independent of jurisdictional politics, is able to advise the mayor and commission objectively on matters of ethics and, should it be necessary, even to oversee investigations of elected officials.

Ethics commissioners are chosen by region, serving voluntarily and without compensation in staggered four-year terms. With a previously published agenda, commissioners meet once a month in regular sessions open to the public. A typical meeting agenda includes a review of contemporary ethics issues, complaints suitable for investigation and disposition, and inquiries from the government that have been resolved through advisory opinions.

In the past three years, the commission has advised the board of commissioners or the county administrator to adopt a whistle-blower protection amendment to the code of ethics. The commission also has led the following six initiatives: 1) to standardize appointment procedures for appointed boards and commissions; 2) to make vendor lists more generally available to the public; 3) to allow employees of the unified government to run for elected office without the requirement of prior resignation or termination; 4) to set policies and procedures for the receipt, acceptance, and distribution of complimentary tickets to Kansas Speedway races; 5) to supervise more closely the electronic mail of individuals using unified-government computers; and 6) to monitor the pressure put on employees concerning the amount and character of their charitable giving.

These initiatives illustrate the capacity of the commission to keep the code current and to keep ethics matters part of the public dialogue. By virtue of its leadership and autonomy, it has been instrumental in bolstering public trust in the ethics program.

Ethics administrator

The office of the ethics administrator was established in the code of ethics ordinance. Like commission members, the administrator is an outsider independent of jurisdictional politics and, also like the ethics commission, the administrator is selected by the same three-person committee. This is done to ensure the highest credentials and independence. Ethics administrator is a part-time position, provided under a contract overseen by the legislative auditor.

The administrator serves as the executive agent of the commission, preparing meeting agendas and minutes and support materials for commission meetings. He or she operates the ethics hotline, conducts ethics training, investigates allegations of misconduct, and recommends disciplinary measures, should they be called for.

Ethics education

After the code of ethics became effective on January 1, 1999, the office of the ethics administrator began an aggressive ethics education program designed to train every official, administrator, and employee of the unified government. These introductory training sessions began with the newly elected mayor and the members of the board of commissioners.

Ethics training then branched out to include more than 2,200 senior administrators, supervisors, and employees of the departments and agencies within the government. Each introductory session consists of a two-hour block of instruction in which the provisions and policies of the code are presented, together with spirited discussions of ethics dilemmas wherein the rules of conduct are tested, validated, and given practical meaning and effect.

Training sessions also include an overview of the components of the ethics program and their respective functions, as well as a thorough review of the complaint and investigation processes. At the end of each introductory session, trainees are asked to take an ethics pledge as their commitment to ethical conduct; then they receive certificates of completion, to be annotated in their personnel files.

The education component of the ethics program proceeds along a two-pronged track. Not only does it include introductory sessions for existing officials, administrators, and employees but also it requires sessions for each newly elected official or recently hired employee (within his or her first 90 days of service).

After successfully completing the introductory session, each official, administrator, and employee receives a "training anniversary date." Three years after their introductory training, all elected officials and employees participate in a continuing education session to review and refresh their commitment to ethical conduct.

Continuing education sessions consist of a one-hour block of instruction in which trainees again work through a series of ethical dilemmas. But unlike the introductory sessions, the ethical-dilemma cases in the continuing education sessions involve the most frequent ethical challenges encountered in the unified government during the past three years. Completion of a continuing education session is noted in the personnel file, and the employee's training anniversary date is reset for another three years.

The curriculum for the ethics education program has been carefully constructed to facilitate meaningful instruction in ethical conduct. The formal language of the code of ethics has been restated in an easy-to-understand format, and ethical-dilemma cases have been developed to present clear—yet challenging—vehicles through which practical application may be enhanced.

Two sets of scenarios have been written: a set of general principles to be used in the introductory sessions, and a focused and timely set to be used in the continuing education session. Employees do not simply relearn the previous lessons; they benefit from topical treatment of current issues. In almost all training sessions, there is a lively discussion and an in-depth analysis of ethical issues faced by employees.

Hotline and investigations

The ethics hotline is actually one of five confidential mediums continually monitored to ensure responsiveness both to complaints and to inquiries: the telephone hotline itself, e-mail messages, United States Mail service, telefax letter transmission, and a verbal complaint process. The hotline telephone number, e-mail address, and fax numbers are prominent parts of all ethics training and are posted widely in jurisdiction buildings and offices.

The first and most important purpose of the ethics hotline is to provide unified government officials and employees with a reliable source of advice on ethical dilemmas. The second purpose is to report allegations of ethical misconduct.

All hotline complaints are guaranteed confidential handling so that citizens, elected officials, and employees can make an ethics complaint without fear of reprisal. If there is substance to an ethics complaint or allegation, the administrator works with and through the administration to determine appropriate discipline. Cases involving serious breaches of the code, other ordinances of the unified government, or the laws of the state of Kansas are turned over to the district attorney.

Complaints and allegations involving possible code violations by elected officials are handled directly by the ethics administrator. Should the course of action recommended by the administrator, based on the facts of the allegation, not be agreed to by an elected official, the administrator can take the matter to the ethics commission, and the commission, in open meeting with the media present, can recommend a course of action.

The telephone hotline is the most popular communication method through which contacts are made. The hotline is a confidential answering machine remotely accessed every 48 hours (necessary because the office is not otherwise staffed, nor is telephone reception available outside normal working hours). The answering-machine message advises callers about the confidentiality of their calls and provides the assistant director's home telephone number, in case the call is not returned within 48 hours.

A response is made to all contacts received, and in the case of requests for advisory opinions or other information, 100 percent of contacts receive favorable resolution. A little more than half (almost 54 percent) of the contacts alleging an ethics violation have concerned, in fact, not violations of the code of ethics but important complaints all the same.

Resolved through an appropriate referral are: reports such as complaints by employees against their supervisors (purely personnel issues properly handled by management), complaints for which only a private remedy exists (subject to private litigation), complaints of a political nature (campaign conduct and the like), and general complaints about government (problems with services or benefits provided by local, state, or federal government). All other contacts result in either informal or formal resolution.

Making progress

In the five years since unification and the adoption of the ethics program, the Unified Government of Wyandotte County and Kansas City, Kansas, has made considerable progress. Property values have increased sharply, population decline has stopped, new housing developments are springing up, and large commercial development with hotels, theaters, a NASCAR track, and large regional "destination" stores like Cabela's and Nebraska Furniture Mart have been built.

The ethical climate of the unified government is now high, and there have been no political scandals. Mayor Marinovich describes progress in this way: "Since the city and county governments were consolidated and the ethics program was established, a significantly positive change has occurred in the growth, economy, and political atmosphere of Wyandotte County. Property values are increasing, delivery of services has improved at lower cost, neighborhoods have started working together to increase quality of life, and major reinvestment is being made in the community. The county is experiencing new life and new hope for the future.

"Of course, the ethics program is not [alone] responsible for the resurgence of governmental effectiveness, but it did play a part. Through the establishment of the ethics program and the priority placed on public integrity, trust in honest and effective governance is being reestablished in our community. Public integrity breeds trust, trust breeds partnerships, partnerships breed action, and action breeds progress. One cannot be done without the other."

"In my opinion," says County Administrator Dennis Hays, "since the consolidation of governments in 1997, the public's trust and confidence in the government have increased dramatically. I am proud that there has been no public wrongdoing; however, should something arise, with the proactive avoidance through the ethics program, a swift and unbiased judgment will be made."

District Attorney Nick Tomasic is of the opinion that "the extensive ethics training sessions for all elected officials and employees of the unified government have produced visible changes in the conduct of local government employees. The continuing training teaches new public servants a keen awareness of ethical behavior and the rules they are expected to follow, as well as reinforcing these expectations in veteran employees.

"The ethics program has been instrumental in promoting good government and reassuring public trust. While there have been isolated incidents of misconduct, they have been quickly identified and dealt with swiftly and openly. The ethics commission meets regularly in open sessions and allows citizens and employees the opportunity to report misconduct. This transparency and accessibility in the process has built trust among members of the public, who too often are skeptical and mistrustful of government."

Finally, former Kansas Lieutenant Governor Gary Sherrer says: "Throughout my public life and private life, I have never been part of such a dramatic political, social, and economical change as what has occurred in Wyandotte County. While ethics alone would not have produced all that has been achieved, all that has been achieved would not have been accomplished without the strong emphasis on ethical behavior."

Building a successful local government ethics program is not unlike most other aspects of good management and leadership. Here are some lessons learned from the ethics program experience:

1. A successful ethics program cannot be just a code of ethics or just an ethics-training program or the work of an ethics administrator or a citizens' ethics board. All are necessary, and all must be carefully integrated.

2. Independence and autonomy are essential. An ethics administrator or a citizens' ethics board appointed by elected officials will be reluctant to look at ethical issues associated with these officials.

3. Confidentiality in the treatment of allegations and investigations is vital. Persons with credible claims of misconduct must know that their identity will be protected.

4. Trust is critical. Citizens, elected officials, employees, and employee unions must trust the administrators of the ethics program to be approachable, fair, just, and reasonable.

5. While it is important to find misconduct when it is occurring and to fix it, it is equally important that this discovery not be made with an attitude of "gotcha." The purpose of an ethics program is to promote good and honest local government. It is essential that administrators of the programs understand that their work is part of the general administration of the jurisdiction.

Ethics Management in Cities and Counties

Donald Menzel

This article explores ethics management in U.S. local governments of all sizes, with a particular focus on two cities and two counties—Tampa; Chicago; King County, Washington; and Salt Lake County, Utah. Among America's 84,000 local governments, nearly all large cities and counties have ethics management programs. Los Angeles has one of the most comprehensive programs in the country. Other cities, for example, New York, also have ethics codes and agencies to enforce them, although these may be less ambitious than they sound, as the primary emphasis is placed on managing financial conflicts of interest.

A handful of counties—King County (Washington), Miami-Dade (Florida), Anne Arundel (Maryland), and Cook County (Illinois)—have local ethics commissions armed with substantial investigatory powers. Some cities, like St. Petersburg, Florida, do not have a separate ethics commission but do have an ethics investigatory process. Under these circumstances, when a violation is alleged, city councilmembers put on their hats as members of an ethics commission to investigate the allegations and render a ruling.

Smaller local governments are even less likely to devote resources to ethics. And some experts contend that this is a significant deficiency. Mark Davies, executive director of the New York City Conflicts of Interest Board, asserts that, contrary to what people think, "...small municipalities are most in need of ethics boards because in small municipalities conflicts of interest are absolutely unavoidable" (*Public Integrity*, Fall 1999, 408).

Not all small communities, however, are without ethics management initiatives. Whiting, Indiana, a community of 5,137 people located 20 minutes from Chicago, is an example. In 2004, the city adopted an ethics ordinance that applies to all city officials, elected and appointed, and to the workforce of 150 employees. The ordinance proudly proclaims that public officials shall conduct the government "with loyalty, integrity, and impartiality."

Reprinted with permission from *Public Management* magazine, January/February 2006. Copyright © 2006 by the International City/County Management Association, Suite 500, 777 N. Capitol St., N.E., Washington, DC 20002.

To achieve this lofty goal, the ordinance calls for rules dealing with financial disclosure, the acceptance of gifts, electoral activities, and the use of city property. The ordinance also establishes a three-member ethics commission consisting of the mayor, the chair or president of the board or commission of the alleged noncompliant person (or the head of a city department if the complaint is filed against an employee), and the ethics officer. The ethics officer, who is also the city's water superintendent, was appointed by the board of public works and safety and was charged with the responsibility of overseeing investigations into alleged wrongdoing.

Among the more than 19,000 special districts in the United States, few have launched ethics initiatives. The *2003 Ethics Update* released by the Council on Governmental Ethics Laws identifies only one special district that has an ethics management program—the Los Angeles County Metropolitan Transportation Authority. Ethics management by this authority is directed by a chief ethics officer and five colleagues in a separate ethics department. The ethics staff "educates and advises employees, board members, contractors, and the public about ethics rules and maintains the records concerning lobbyist reports and employee statements of economic interest disclosures" (2003 COGEL Ethics Update). The transit authority has issued three ethics codes: an 11-page code for the 13-member board of directors, a six-page code for contractors, and a 10-page code for the authority's 9,000 employees (view them on the Web site at www.metro.net/about_us/ethics/ codes.htm).

Tampa

Ethics reform in Tampa was set in motion in 2001, with a scandal involving a romantic relationship between the city housing chief and a top aide who had moved rapidly through city ranks. The housing chief and his aide built a 4,200-square-foot house for the bargain basement price of $105,000. Adding more suspicion to the situation, the builder had received more than $1 million in housing contracts through the city's housing department. Along the way, the city began an investigation of the housing director's handling of his office and, in October 2001, placed him on a 90-day paid administrative leave pending the resolution of criminal charges.

The following month, the Florida Ethics Commission reported that the housing director had not violated state ethics laws. Later in the same month, however, the commission repudiated this report, saying that the information submitted by the city and the mayor was unreliable. A year later, the housing director and several others were indicted on fraud and corruption charges. The accusations eventually landed the housing director and his now-wife in court, when the builder confessed to bribing the city housing chief. The couple was tried in 2004 and found guilty of more than 25 counts of conspiracy, wire fraud, and accepting bribes and gratuities.

Not surprisingly, in 2003, the city council began to deliberate the wisdom of a city ethics code that would guide the ethical behavior of its 4,800 employees. In the same year, a new mayor was elected who is a strong advocate of ethics and integrity in city governance. The city promulgated its first-ever code of ethics in November 2003, including a prohibition on "fraternization." Specifically, no city employee or officer shall appoint, employ, advance, recommend, or advocate the appointment, employment, or advancement to any position of "any individual with whom they have a close personal relationship" (Sec. 2-548, Division 2. Conflicts of Interest, City of Tampa Ethics Code). Enforcing this prohibition will be another matter, most likely to be resolved at some future date in a court of law.

Code implementation

The city's new code and its implementation, however, involve many other matters. The department of human resources is designated as the ethics office, and the HR director as the city officer. The ethics office is charged with overseeing the code's implementation, with the ethics officer assigned the task of developing education and training programs for city officers and employees. The officer also is expected to "serve as the liaison between the ethics commission and the officers and employees of the city" (Sec. 2-621, Division 2. Conflicts of Interest, City of Tampa Ethics Code).

Each city department has an ethics liaison person who assists the ethics officer in the formulation of ethics awareness training sessions, conferences, and seminars. Ethics education and training are required of every elected official, who must attend an "Ethics in Government" program within 90 days of taking office. Newly appointed employees must participate in an ethics training program within six months of their employment. The code also mandates that current employees be trained as soon as practicable.

There is no requirement that elected officers or employees attend an Ethics in Government program on a continuing basis. Nor are there whistle-blowing provisions in the code to protect city employees. This measure was omitted because it was seen as unnecessary, as city employees are protected by Florida's whistleblower law.

Ethics commission

The code of ethics also created the City of Tampa Ethics Commission, a five-member body with two members appointed by local universities, two appointed by the chief judge of the 13th Judicial Circuit, and one member (who has held elective office at the local level) appointed by the mayor. One university appointee must be a faculty member who is knowledgeable in legal ethics, while the other is a faculty member with expertise in ethics more broadly defined. Ethics commissioners serve staggered four-year terms and are precluded from partisan political activity or employment by the city. They serve without compensation but are reimbursed for expenses incurred while conducting commission business.

The ethics commission is empowered to "review, interpret, render advisory opinions and letters of instruction, and enforce" the code. Advisory opinions must be requested in writing, with the facts either real or hypothetical. If an advisory opinion is rendered, it is binding on the conduct of the person who sought the opinion. A written, sworn complaint by a citizen submitted to the ethics officer initiates the enforcement process. The complaint is then delivered to the commission for a preliminary investigation. If the commission finds "probable cause" that the code has been violated, it must notify the complainant and the alleged violator in writing.

A public hearing may or may not be called depending on the circumstances. If the commission finds that a violation has occurred, it then recommends to the appropriate party—agency head, council, mayor, chief of staff—that "appropriate action for correction or rectification of that conduct" be taken. The commission has no enforcement power, that is, it cannot impose a disciplinary action on a code violator. Disciplinary measures can range from a verbal admonishment to censure, suspension, or removal from office.

In general the ethics management approach taken in Tampa parallels that found in many other cities: "Know what the city defines as acceptable behavior to stay out of trouble," and, if you land in trouble, here's what can happen to you....

These provisions and others suggest that Tampa is moving forward on its intention "to elevate the level of ethics in local government, to provide honest and responsible service to the citizens of Tampa, and to maintain the confidence and trust of the public that this government serves" (Sec. 2-501, Purpose and Legislative Intent, Division 1. Generally, City of Tampa Ethics Code).

Chicago

Historically, ethics and Chicago have not been known to go together. Norms in the "city of big shoulders," with its industrial, blue-collar past and its hard-nosed machine politics, have often meant that votes and more were up for sale. Happily, this reputation has receded in recent years, thanks in part to the creation of the city's board of ethics in 1987. The seven-member board, whose members are appointed by the mayor and confirmed by the city council, is supported by a nine-member professional staff and is "responsible for helping to ensure public confidence in Chicago government" (Annual Report 2003-2004). The board's activities include education and training, advice and guidance, and regulation and disclosure.

Advice

The board's advice and guidance program consists of two categories of assistance: inquiries and cases. An inquiry is a request for information or professional advice in which the inquiring person does not ask for a written response. In 2003-2004, more than 1,900 inquiries were acted on. A case is a written complaint or a request for an opinion. Fifty-two cases were acted on in 2003-2004, with 140 reports being issued as a result of the investigations. Financial-interest disclosure, gifts, and lobbying were the subjects most often addressed by inquiries and complaints in 2004.

Investigation and enforcement

Regulation and enforcement activities encompass campaign financing, financial disclosure, and registration of lobbyists, as well as investigations, complaints, and preliminary inquiries. The city's campaign financing ordinance limits the amount of money—especially in contributions from lobbyists—that can be given to an individual seeking elected city office.

The 12,000 city employees and officials are required to file statements of financial interest with the board each spring. Failure to file a financial disclosure can result in a fine levied by the board. Lobbyists are required to register with the board, revealing who their clients are and listing all of their lobbying-related compensation and expenditures. Nearly 400 lobbyists were registered in 2004, representing more than 1,000 clients. The board maintains a list of registered lobbyists and their clients on its Web site at www.cityofchicago.org/Ethics.

The board has considerable authority to investigate wrongdoing. Unlike most boards, it can initiate an investigation on its own, though this authority is limited in the case of a complaint against an alderman. A complaint of an alleged violation of the governmental ethics ordinance by an alderman must be signed and sworn. The board also has subpoena power. All investigations are treated as confidential, and results are only made public when the final report of a violation is issued.

For the most recent reporting year, 2003-2004, the board received 15 complaints; three of these claimed violations involving the unauthorized use of city property, and one each made an allegation of post-employment misconduct, conflict of interest, violation of fiduciary duty, and employment of relatives. The board also conducted 107 investigations of city employees who failed to file statements of financial interests within the time prescribed by law. Thirty-five investigations into claims of campaign violations that had been filed in the previous year were closed.

Ethics training

The Governmental Ethics Ordinance (Chapter 2-156, Municipal Code of Chicago) sets forth an ambitious educational requirement that all 50 aldermen, aldermanic staff members, and employees in the senior executive service attend ethics training every four years. The ordinance also requires that all new employees who are subject to mandatory training attend an ethics training program within 120 days of entering city service and again every four years afterward.

Those who fail to attend ethics training are subject to a $500 fine. About 3,800 employees, or approximately 10 percent of the city workforce, are covered by the ordinance. Although the vast majority of the workforce is not subject to mandatory ethics training, a good number of departments routinely provide ethics training for their employees, with the cooperation and support of the board of ethics staff.

King County, Washington

Among America's 3,034 counties that have policies and procedures for dealing with unethical conduct, King County may have the oldest system of this kind.

Ethics code and board

King County (Seattle) enacted a code of ethics in 1972, in response to local government corruption. The code focused on conflicts of interest, placed restrictions on business transactions between former commission members and sitting commissioners, and required financial-disclosure statements by commissioners and senior county managers.

A three-member, appointed ethics board was set up to enforce the code. In its first 17 years of existence, "the board held only one major public hearing [and] very few county employees knew of the code's existence" (J. Patrick Dobel, *The Realpolitik of Ethics Codes: An Implementation Approach to Public Ethics in Ethics and Public Administration*, edited by H. George Frederickson, 1993, Armonk, NY: M. E. Sharpe, Inc., p. 164). After a series of scandals erupted in 1986 through 1987, the code and its enforcement were strengthened. A new ethics code went into effect in 1990 that, unlike its predecessor, presented "a positive vision of public service" and emphasized its role in building legitimacy and respect for government, as well as its support for independent judgment and public trust (Dobel 1993, 171).

The revised code was accompanied by the establishment of an independent ombudsman's office and a fulltime ethics administrator who reports directly to the King County Board of Commissioners. In 1994, the board began an intensive education and training program to familiarize county employees with the code and to "provide them with the decision-making skills necessary to resolve routine ethics issues within the workplace" (www.metrokc.gov/ethics/history.htm).

Effectiveness

How effective has the King County ethics program been over the past decade? A true measure of effectiveness is difficult to construct. Some output data, however, are available and were reported in the 2003 annual report:

- Nearly 1,800 employees received ethics training in 2003, half of whom were new employees. New employees are required to sign a statement that they have received a copy of the summary of the ethics code. Ethics training is mandatory for supervisors every 18 months.
- Post-employment provisions were added that ban a former employee for one year from being a contractor or subcontractor on any county action over which he/she had responsibility as a county employee.
- From 1991 through 1999, the board issued 148 advisory opinions; in contrast, none were issued in 2003.
- Statements of financial disclosure were filed by 1,969 elected officials and employees and by 343 contractors and vendors.

The ethics board has never conducted an ethics audit or an organizational survey to measure the ethical climate of county agencies. The board did initiate an ethical awareness campaign in 2003 that included, among other things, developing a voluntary survey quiz in 2004. The quiz, which went out by e-mail and hard copy to the county's 13,802 employees, was completed by two of every 10 employees. The confidential survey tested employees' knowledge of the county's ethics code.

Ombudsman

Ethics complaints and other complaints about the administrative conduct of King County executive-branch agencies are handled by the office of the ombudsman. Alleged violations of the county's whistleblowing ordinance also fall under the authority of the ombudsman to investigate. The office is staffed by four professionally trained ombudsmen and a support staff of five.

The office of the ombudsman can begin investigations on its own volition. Subpoena power to compel sworn testimony from any person and to retrieve records or material relevant to an investigation is also available to the ombudsman's office. If the ombudsman finds reasonable cause for a violation of the code of ethics, the respondent may appeal the ruling to the board of ethics.

The civil penalty for a violation by one of King County's more than 13,000 officers or employees can range from a slap on the wrist, like suspension without pay for one month, to termination of employment. The criminal penalty is a fine not to exceed $1,000 or imprisonment in the county jail not to exceed 90 days, or both. The ombudsman can recommend disciplinary action but cannot compel an agency to take such measures. The board of ethics is equally lacking in enforcement authority. "The employee's management makes the ultimate determination as to whether disciplinary action will be implemented," says Matthew Conquergood, assistant to the Ombudsman, King County Office of Citizen Complaints–Ombudsman.

The 2004 Triannual Reports of the Ombudsman show that the ombudsman's office received 1,385 inquiries for information, 311 requests for assistance, and 128 complaints.

There were nine complaints alleging violations of the ethics code and 12 complaints of retaliation for reporting improper governmental action, as protected under the whistle-blowing code. Four of the nine cases alleging violations of the ethics code were resolved by the ombudsman, and five were found to be unsupported.

Salt Lake County, Utah

Reform measures to foster ethical governance in Salt Lake County were launched in 2004, when the county mayor was forced from office, accused of felony misuse of public funds. It was alleged in court documents that she had misused health department funds to hire bookkeepers at a boys' and girls' club where her daughter was the chief financial officer. The scandal set in motion a call for ethics reform.

Ethics proposals

The deputy mayor, standing in for the mayor, put together a set of proposals for consideration by the county commission. The opposing mayoral candidate (now mayor) offered a similar list of proposals, with some additions. Combined, these measures urge that Salt Lake County:

- Audit all departments under the county mayor's jurisdiction, to prevent abuse and mismanagement. Salt Lake County is a mayor-council form of government with a nine-member council, three of whose members are elected at large. All elections are partisan. There is one elected constitutional officer, a district attorney, and seven independently elected statutory officers: assessor, auditor, clerk, recorder, sheriff, surveyor, and treasurer.
- Establish a bipartisan ethics panel to review ethics policies and complaints, as well as to assess redistricting proposals.
- Ban all gifts accepted by elected officials and employees unless the donated items are reasonably necessary to perform their duties.
- Prohibit any high-level county employee from accepting employment as an officer or director of a major county vendor or contractor for at least a year after leaving county employment.
- Prohibit county employees from using county facilities or equipment for any personal business or outside employment.
- Require written disclosures of conflicts of interest.
- Publish a list of all county contractors on a citizen-accessible Web site.
- Prohibit cars and car allowances as benefits of employment, and restrict the use of county vehicles to county-business purposes only.
- Require lobbyists to file registration forms and declare their clients.
- Open cabinet meetings of the executive branch to the public.
- Limit campaign-financing contributions from any one donor to $5,000 for countywide races and $2,000 for council-district races.
- Formalize ethics training requirements, and make training a prerequisite to employment. This requirement specifies that all county elected officials, appointed

officers, and employees will attend one hour of training every two years "regarding their ethical duties." Employees are awarded four hours' additional vacation during the year when the training is received.

- Require all county employees to subscribe to the following ethics statement: Employees of Salt Lake County "support, obey, and defend the Constitution of the United States, the Constitution of the state of Utah, the laws of the state of Utah, and the ordinances of Salt Lake County, to the best of my ability and that I will strive always to meet the highest ethical standards implicit in my employment and in furtherance of the best public interest."

State of reform

While not all of these reform measures have been put into place, it is clear that Salt Lake County is on a sound ethics-management path. The reform initiatives (1) acknowledge that ethics and integrity in county governance are important, and (2) require the commitment of county resources to building a strong ethical climate. They do, however, take a legalistic approach to ethical management, while recognizing that this approach is not sufficient as evidenced by the training requirement.

These reforms cover many but not all county officials, inasmuch as the emphasis is placed on employees of the county executive. It is difficult to say with certainty whether county leaders have learned from ethical failure, but the signs are promising, given the strong endorsement of these measures by the newly elected mayor. Will ethics reform be enough to transform the culture of Salt Lake County's governance? Perhaps, but it will take some time, maybe as much as a decade before a firm conclusion can be drawn.

As we have tried to show, ethics management is alive and well in America's cities and counties. Is more activity needed? Most assuredly, but the effort to instill ethics and integrity in city and county governments is an exciting journey that holds great promise for strengthening public confidence and trust in local governance.

Partisan Politics, Ethics, and the Home Rule Charter

A township manager's ethical dilemma

Craig M. Wheeland

Resolving ethical dilemmas successfully is an important skill that can be learned through the analysis of case studies, and through reflection upon the actions taken by the officials featured in cases. The ethical dilemma discussed [here] is an example of how what appears at first glance to be a low-level ethics violation can result in a well-publicized scandal that jeopardizes the careers of elected and appointed officials. A minor mistake became the issue that brought the Home Rule Charter to the public's attention, and raised the kind of questions, such as the proper relationship between elected officials and township employees, that had been dormant for almost two decades.

I tell the story from the different perspectives of the people involved, and ask readers to put themselves in the place of the town manager who must find a way to competently resolve the ethical dilemma. Readers are invited to answer questions before the after the township manager's action to experience the dilemma, and to be able to compare their approaches to that of the township manager....

This case is based on a recent event in a Pennsylvania municipality. All names, places, and dates are altered to provide anonymity to the individuals involved, and especially because the characterization of their thought processes is speculative. I relied on three sources of information: newspaper articles, interviews with five of the individuals involved, and township documents....

The case

Democratic activist Joan Barkley decided to check the "bulletin board" on Channel 22, the Brighton Cable Company's government-access channel, to confirm the date and time

Abridged from *Public Integrity*, vol. 2, no. 4 (2000): 347-362. Copyright © 2000 by American Society for Public Administration (ASPA). Reprinted with permission of M. E. Sharpe, Inc.

of the next township commission meeting. It was the end of September and the election campaign for four seats on the township commission was heating up. A rejuvenated Democratic Party had four excellent candidates and all of them were thought to have a chance to win on November 4. Barkley wanted to attend all the commission's meetings to show her support for the candidates and to gain the kind of knowledge she needed to be able to help them develop campaign strategies.

As she read the announcements, Barkley was surprised to see one for the "Richard C. Bowdler Memorial Golf Tournament." Barkley knew this was a Republican fund-raising event, and did not think it was fair that the announcement appeared with the other official information listed by the Department of Parks and Recreation. That the announcement did not indicate it was a Republican fund-raising event only made Barkley more suspicious of the relationship between township staff and Republican candidates for the commission.

Barkley's decision to pursue this matter initiated what would become one of the most important events in the township's recent history. What appears at first glance to be a relatively low-level mistake became the issue that brought the Home Rule Charter to the public's attention and raised questions such as the proper relationship between elected officials and township employees that had been dormant for almost two decades.

The community context

Goodnow is an upper-income, suburban township in Pennsylvania with a population in 1997 of about 30,000. Goodnow has a commission-manager form of government established by a Home Rule Charter adopted in 1976.

Goodnow has a long history of partisan politics dominated by the Republican Party. Partisan, ward elections are used to elect the seven members of Goodnow's commission. Republicans enjoy a 2 to 1 registration advantage over Democrats across the township, although Democrats are more competitive in some wards, such as Wards 1 and 3. Both political parties are active in many ways: they raise money, use the opinion pages of the local newspapers, hold monthly meetings, mail information to voters regularly, and nominate candidates in primaries.

In the early 1970s, the largest faction of the Republican Party joined with Democrats to support a bipartisan reform effort designed to secure "good" government for the township. The desire to insulate administrative officials and township employees from partisan politics and to insulate township government from the Republican "organization" controlling the county government led Goodnow's Government Study Commission to recommend a Home Rule Charter that included seven prohibitions:

1. no person shall, in employment by the township in any capacity, appointment to any Board, Commission, or Authority, or removal there from, be favored or discriminated against because of.... political or religious opinions...

2. no township official or employee shall utilize township facilities, equipment or supplies, directly or indirectly, in political campaigns, or to the benefit of any political candidate;

3. no township employee shall during working hours or when on township business take part in any political activity or solicit any contribution or subscription to any political party or candidate;

4. no official or employee, whether elected or appointed, shall promise an appointment to any municipal position as a reward for any political activity;

5. no township official elected under this charter, no appointed official, and no full-time township employee shall hold any elected or appointed political party office;

6. no elected or appointed township official and no employee of the township shall request any township employee to make a political contribution or engage in political activity; and

7. no township official elected or appointed to an elective office under this charter and no full-time township employee shall hold any other township employment or any other elective or appointive township position. No township official elected or appointed to an elective office under this charter and no full-time township employee shall hold any full-time employment, or any other elective position, with [Baker] County or the Commonwealth of Pennsylvania. This provision does not apply to employees of school districts or other educational institutions.

The reformers believed the Home Rule Charter, especially these seven provisions, would preserve and nurture openness, independence, and professionalism in township government, and also permit the vigorous contesting of elections by political parties. Violation of any seven of these provisions "shall constitute grounds for forfeiture of office, termination of appointment, or dismissal."

The event

In 1997 there were five Republican and two Democratic commissioners. Four seats on the commission were up for election in 1997: both Democratic commissioners (Wards 1 and 3) and one Republican commissioner (Ward 7) sought reelection, and the other incumbent Republican (Ward 5) retired. This case involves the actions of the Republican commissioner from Ward 7 seeking a third term.

The Ward 7 commissioner, Thomas Daley, was a leader of a faction of the Republican Party that wanted to alter the charter to permit closer ties with the county Republican "organization" and to permit partisan considerations to guide appointments of township officials and employees. Indeed, rumors circulated and concern was expressed in letters to the editors of local newspapers, that the current township manager, Frank White, who enjoyed a reputation in the township, the metropolitan region and across the state for being a "real professional," did not have the support of Daley and his faction of the Republican Party. During the fall campaign, Daley organized the annual "Richard C. Bowdler Memorial Golf Tournament" in order to raise money for Republican candidates. Daley placed an ad in the local newspapers during the month of September hoping to attract participants.

About two weeks before the golf outing, an announcement appeared on Channel 22 inviting citizens to participate in the outing (this is the announcement that Joan Barkley saw). The announcement ran about one hundred times from September 19 through September 26. Unlike the newspaper ad, this announcement did not indicate that it was a Republican fund-raising event. Furthermore, it appeared in a format used to announce the Department of Parks and Recreation's events.

The information appearing on Channel 22 is prepared by employees of the Department of Parks and Recreation. The director of this department happens to be Daley's son-in-law, Robert Marconi. Marconi is rumored to be the next township manager if Daley and other "organization" supporters can gain control of the commission.

The Democrats reacted quickly to what they charged was a clear violation of the Home Rule Charter. The evening after first seeing the announcement, Joan Barkley discussed the incident with Sarah Downs, the Democratic candidate running against Daley. Downs informed Barkley that not only was running the announcement "unfair," airing it on Channel 22 violated the provisions of the charter. Rather than file the complaint, Downs thought Democratic chair Elizabeth Hall would be the best person to file it, because it might otherwise be perceived to be "just another campaign tactic" if she made the allegation. On October 9, Elizabeth Hall filed the ethics complaint with the Ethics Board against Daley and Marconi, and called for a full investigation of this incident before the election in November. Hall specifically complained that prohibitions (2) and (3) (see above) had been violated. Hall also sent a copy of the complaint to the local newspapers.

In response to questions from reporters, Marconi denied he placed the announcement and also denied any knowledge of the incident, including how the announcement appeared on Channel 22. Marconi reported that as soon as he found out about the announcement he removed it.

Daley responded to reporters by initially accepting responsibility for broadcasting the announcement on Channel 22. Daley claimed he made a simple mistake and that he did not intend to violate the charter; he only wanted to increase participation in the event to raise money for Republican candidates. When the issue would not go away, Daley defended his actions, suggesting the Democrats were exaggerating the importance of the incident to help their candidate run against him in the November election. Daley said his son-in-law, Marconi, was not involved, but he also would not say who put the announcement on Channel 22, other than that a township employee did it.

The decision problem

Township manager Frank White had to define his role in the investigation of this incident. He decided immediately that he would not comment to the press about the incident other than to say that he did not know who put the announcement on Channel 22. Beyond this decision, he was unsure how to proceed. He knew the Ethics Board had not met regularly during his time as township manager, in part because no cases had been brought to the board. Further, he did not know much about Peter Byrd, the chair of the Ethics Board, other than that he was a lawyer and a Republican. Could he rely on Byrd and the other members of the Ethics Board? Should he take charge of the investigation?

As a first step to determine how to proceed, White decided to identify some of the obligations influencing his decision. As township manager he must enforce the provisions in the charter. As a professional he should follow the provisions in the International City/County Management Association's (ICMA) Code of Ethics (2000). [The ICMA Code of Ethics is reprinted as Appendix C in this book.] As township manager he must consider the impact this incident, and his response to it, would have on all township employees. He also recognized the personal dimension this kind of incident can have, especially the stress on his family, who had heard the rumors about Daley's faction in the Republican

Party wanting to appoint Marconi township manager. Finally, beyond the legal require-ments in the charter, White recognized his obligation to be responsive and fair to the entire community. Having identified various obligations, White next struggled with how to prioritize and/or balance these competing obligations. With more than twenty-five years' work experience as a local government manager and ten years as Goodnow's township manager, White had encountered a variety of ethical challenges, but none of the previous dilemmas had this volatile mix of personal, political, professional, and public pressures.

Questions to guide the analysis

1. Should Frank White lead this investigation to fulfill his obligation to uphold and enforce the Home Rule Charter?

2. What should be the relationship between the Ethics Board and Frank White in investi-gating and resolving this incident?

3. Should Frank White suspend the director of Parks and Recreation, Robert Marconi, pending the outcome of the investigation?

4. What weight should the seriousness of the action have in the way the incident is handled? Is this alleged violation a minor transgression or is it symptomatic of a more concerted effort to change the Home Rule Charter informally by undermining the pro-fessional integrity of the township staff?

5. Does Tenet No. 7 in the ICMA Code of Ethics prohibiting managers from participating in the election of the members of the council (commission) restrict Frank White's role in investigating this incident? [See the ICMA Code of Ethics in Appendix C.]

6. Given the rumors circulating among leaders in the community and in the press about his status as township manager, how can Frank White avoid the appearance of protect-ing his self-interest in the way he manages this incident?

7. Should Frank White adopt a pragmatic approach to guide his actions in this dispute?

8. Should White focus on the spirit of the law and choose a course of action based on what he thinks is morally right regardless of the consequences?

The investigation

Rather than lead the investigation, White decided he could best fulfill his obligations, especially to his profession and to the charter, by assisting the Ethics Board in its investi-gation. White reasoned that the charter established an Ethics Board as the proper insti-tution to investigate and recommend actions to the township commission. White also scheduled a special meeting of department heads to review the ethics provisions in the charter, as well as the ICMA Code of Ethics. He reminded them that as "professionals and senior leaders they have an obligation to uphold both codes." White decided not to suspend Marconi pending the outcome of the investigation, because of the nature of the alleged infraction, which White did not think reached the level of misconduct warranting a temporary removal from office. By working with the Ethics Board, talking with depart-ment heads, and allowing Marconi to continue to work, White also thought he could avoid appearing to try to influence the reelection of Daley, an official who had a reputa-tion for wanting to replace him with Marconi.

The Ethics Board's investigation did not begin smoothly. Hall's complaint was the first one ever filed under the Home Rule Charter. Indeed, the Ethics Board never adopted rules of procedure to guide them in handling an ethics complaint, so it had to decide how to proceed with an investigation before they could begin the actual investigation of Hill's complaint. The chair of Goodnow's Ethics Board, Peter Byrd, promised a fair investigation just as soon as rules of procedure were adopted, but Democrats were skeptical.

Byrd asked White and Goodnow's solicitor, Ronald Kingman, to develop written rules of procedure. Initially, Kingman advised Byrd to use provisions in the state's Sunshine Act, which would permit closed meetings because this case involves personnel matters. The idea of closed meetings did not please the Democrats or the press, but eventually it became part of the rules of procedure.

After further investigation of the board's files, White found a 1977 draft of rules of procedure. White and Kingman used this draft as a basis for preparing the rules of procedure and they both added ideas of their own. White adopted ideas from his conversations with other township managers as well as his personal experiences in a previous job and from the procedures used by ethics boards in other municipalities. Kingman turned to the procedures used by the state's Ethics Commission.

While the rules of procedure were being researched, Daley canceled the golf event because of a lack of participants. Daley also won reelection on November 4; only one of the two incumbent Democrats won reelection. The Township Commission in January 1998 would now have six Republicans and one Democrat.

After the Ethics Board adopted the rules of procedure recommended by White and Kingman, Byrd stated emphatically that the Ethics Board would be fair. He explained that "If anybody who is a Republican thinks they are going to get a break, they are kidding themselves. We will treat Democrats and Republicans as equal. If they don't believe it they will find out." Byrd's serious approach to the case and his consistent support for an impartial investigation began to reassure Hall and other Democrats that he could be trusted. Indeed. once the rules of procedure were sent to the Township Commission for approval, the Democratic Party's solicitor, Ben Caldwell, praised the rules and Byrd's leadership.

Under the rules, the Ethics Board permitted Daley and Marconi to respond in writing to Hall's complaint and, as the defendants, to determine if they wanted a closed meeting or a public meeting. In early January 1998 both responded in writing to the allegations. In his letter, Marconi steadfastly maintained his innocence. In a strange twist, Daley defended his actions by claiming "he was not acting as a township official when he requested the announcement be put on Channel 22," and that his "actions did not violate the Cable Franchise Agreement with Brighton Cable Company." Marconi and Daley also sent copies of their letters to local newspapers.

In comments to the press, Byrd expressed his anger at both Daley and Marconi for not honoring the Ethics Board's rules regarding the confidentiality of the investigation. Daley and Marconi claimed they did not know their letters were to be confidential reports to the Ethics Board, and they simply wanted the public to see their side of the story. In addition to Byrd's comments, columnists in the local newspapers criticized, even ridiculed, Daley for claiming he was not acting as township official and for his irrelevant reference to the franchise agreement.

At the end of January, two new members of the Ethics Board were appointed to replace a member whose term had expired and another member who had resigned. The press revealed that one of the new members, Marion Tasker, had served as a Republican committeewoman in Daley's ward. Tasker claimed that she had been asked by friends and neighbors to apply for the position. She also defended her independence by stating that she would not allow her past connections to Daley to affect her judgment about this case or any other one. In comments to the press, Byrd said he did not know of Tasker's political connection to Daley, but suggested that Tasker may need to recuse herself from the Daley/Marconi case (note: she did not do so). Democrats expressed concern about Tasker's appointment, and the fact that Daley voted on both appointments. Daley defended his votes by arguing that "the 7th Ward voters expect their commissioner to vote on all matters." Daley did not think voting on the appointments to a board investigating him presented a conflict of interest.

Throughout this period of time, White maintained a low profile. He did not comment publicly on aspects of the ongoing investigation, the Tasker appointment, or Daley and Marconi's use of the local newspapers to publicize their responses. He continued to work on routine township business and to assist the Ethics Board, especially in drafting a new ethics awareness program for township employees.

The aftermath

In early February, Daley submitted to the Ethics Board a revised letter in which he took full responsibility for having the announcement broadcast on Channel 22. He also included an apology and claimed he did not know about the provisions in the Home Rule Charter. Daley promised to abide by those provisions in the future. Daley would not comment to the press about his reasons for submitting a revised letter.

Byrd announced that the Ethics Board accepted Daley's admission, apology, and claim about not intentionally violating the charter. Under the rules of procedure, the board did not need to proceed since Daley admitted to the violation, and the preliminary investigation had cleared Marconi, because he was not present "at the moment" the announcement was put on Channel 22. Without explanation to the public, the board agreed to Daley's request to keep secret the name of the township employee who put the announcement on Channel 22. In its final report to the township commission, the Ethics Board offered a set of recommendations designed to avoid problems with Channel 22 programming and with the charter's ethics provisions in the future:

1. before any notice is broadcast on Channel 22, it should be first submitted to the Township Manager, or in his absence, to the Assistant Manager for review and approval;

2. only those township employees specifically designated by the Township Manager shall be authorized to enter broadcast notices;

3. all political announcements of any type are prohibited; and

4. a Township Ethics Awareness Program should be started that would include (a) distributing the ethics provisions to all employees and elected officials, (b) having the Township Manager meet with all department heads to review the ethics provisions and impress upon them the need to have them and personnel they supervise comply with

the ethics provisions, (c) informing employees that the Ethics Board may offer advisory opinions on matters that may give rise to an ethics complaint, and (d) circulating a directive to all employees advising them that the Home Rule Charter prohibits individual commissioners from directing an employee's action, and they should report any incidents to the Township Manager.

Byrd believed a "golden opportunity to 'set the ethics' tone for the Township" existed if the Township Commission adopted these recommendations. White joined Byrd in strongly endorsing the recommendations in the Ethics Board's final report during a public meeting of the township commission. On June 15, 1998, the Goodnow Township Commission adopted the resolution to implement the Ethics Board's recommendations.

■ Final questions

1. Did White's approach meet his obligations to the ICMA's Code of Ethics? to the Home Rule Charter? to all township employees? to the entire community? to his family?

2. Will the Ethics Board's recommendations prevent Channel 22 from being used for political announcements in the future?

3. Will the Ethics Board's recommendations making the township manager the primary person responsible for upholding the ethics provisions make it more likely that township employees will be insulated from partisan political influences/activities in the future?

4. How should the publicity of this case, especially regarding the Daley faction's interest in making Marconi the next township manager, affect how White manages Marconi in the future? Will White be able to hold Marconi accountable to the ethics provisions?

5. Should the Ethics Board have recommended that Daley be removed from office?

6. How important will the composition of the Ethics Board's membership be in determining the township manager's ability to hold elected officials and township staff accountable to the ethics provisions in the charter?

■ Epilogue

Frank White continues to serve with distinction as Goodnow's manager. Indeed, White's approach to resolving this ethical dilemma enhanced his reputation for being a man of integrity, fair judgment, and professionalism. White balanced his various obligations found in the ICMA Code of Ethics (especially Tenets 2, 3, 7, and 11) and in Goodnow's charter (especially Prohibitions 2 and 3), with his obligations to township employees (e.g., to protect them from partisan interference in the conduct of their official duties), to the entire community (e.g., Democrats could trust him and the Ethics Board), and to his family (his job is more secure because of his exemplary conduct, an increased community awareness of ethical obligations, and the precedent set by the Ethics Board's successful effort).

In resolving this ethical dilemma, White avoided being trapped by what Gawthrop (1998) labeled "the bondage of habit." His decision not to suspend Marconi and to immediately remind all employees of their ethical obligations reveals a personal commitment to ethical action. He acted with fairness toward both Daley and Marconi by allowing the board to conduct the investigation and to recommend a resolution to this short-term aspect of the dilemma. White's effort to prepare rules of procedures for the Ethics Board, an ethics awareness program for township officials and employees, and requiring that notices to be broadcast on Channel 22 receive the township manager's approval indicates a wise focus on the long-term prospects for ethical government in Goodnow. This institution-building effort and his own exemplary conduct reveal White's primary concern with achieving what Dobel (1998) calls an "excellent political achievement" White understood that "excellent political achievements do not stand in isolation but sustain the legitimacy of institutions and build community" (Dobel 1998, p. 79).

The moral qualities advocated by Bailey (optimism, courage, and fairness tempered by charity) sustained White through this dispute, and he will need to draw on these qualities in the future. As Dobel (1993) suggests, the "politics of ethics" makes the implementation of codes difficult. Managing Marconi and working with Daley will continue be a challenge for White, but he is now in a better position. His prudential leadership contributed to an outcome that affirmed community support for the ethical provisions in Goodnow's charter, increased the awareness of ethical obligations among township employees, the press, township officials and Goodnow's residents, and revitalized the Ethics Board. White has demonstrated how through skillful ethical reasoning and action local government managers can help resolve ethical dilemmas in their communities.

References

Bailey, S. K. (December 1964). "Ethics and the Public Service." *Public Administration Review* 23: 234-243.

Dobel, J. P. (1993). "The Realpolitik of Ethics Codes: An Implementation Approach to Public Ethics." In H. George Frederickson, ed., *Ethics and Public Administration,* 158-174. Armonk, NY: M. E. Sharpe.

Dobel, J. P. (January/February 1998). "Political Prudence and the Ethics of Leadership." *Public Administration Review* 58 (1): 74-81.

Gawthrop, L. C. (1998). *Public Service and Democracy: Ethical Imperatives for the 21st Century.* New York: Chatham.

International City/County Management Association (2000) *Code of Ethics.* Retrieved March 1, 2000, from the World Wide Web: http://www.icma.org/resources/index.htm. [The Code of Ethics is reprinted as Appendix C in this book.]

Ethics Training in U.S. Cities
Content, pedagogy, and impact

Jonathan P. West and Evan M. Berman

Interest in ethics has grown in recent decades, fueled by political corruption cases in cities like Miami and Providence, and debacles at Enron, WorldCom, and elsewhere (Menzel with Carson 1999; Petrick and Quinn 1997; Weaver, Treviño, and Cochran 1999a, 1999b). Ethics training has become a centerpiece of corporate and government compliance and values-oriented initiatives, along with the adoption of codes of ethics and the review of managers' ethical conduct (Berman, West, and Cava 1994; Bruce 1996; Wells and Schminke 2001; West et al. 1998). Ethics training sharpens participants' awareness and competence in dealing with the myriad issues that often arise in the work life of employees and managers. It is one way to reduce risk and control present or future ethics problems, thereby increasing stakeholder confidence in organizations.

Although both the public and the private sectors have devoted increased attention to ethics training, most of the relevant academic literature on ethics training is based on private sector data. Less is known about the nature, extent, and delivery of ethics training in the public sector, especially at the local level. This study first considers the use of training as an integral part of ethics management efforts during the last decade. It then explores in detail current reasons for using ethics training, and its content, duration, and pedagogy. A model is then presented of the impact of ethics training and ethics management strategies on organizational culture, labor-management relations, and performance. Data for this study were drawn from a national survey of all cities with population over 50,000.

Framework

Ethics training is a form of workforce training, and the questions that it poses are similar. Specifically, we ask:

1. What are the stated purposes of ethics training? How do they relate to organizational efforts to improve ethical conduct and to achieve other objectives?

From *Public Integrity*, vol. 6, no. 3 (Summer 2004): 189-206. Copyright © 2004 by American Society for Public Administration (ASPA). Reprinted with permission of M. E. Sharpe, Inc.

2. What topics are covered by ethics training, what are the pedagogical and the delivery mechanisms, and how are the lessons of training reinforced?

3. What are some correlates of ethics training regarding both workforce performance and the conditions affecting the use of such training?

Purposes of ethics training

The purposes of ethics training are now widely accepted to include a "high" road and a "low" road (Paine 1994). The low road (which is also sometimes referred to as "defensive") involves efforts to help organizations avoid the embarrassment associated with allegations of legal wrongdoing. Recent ethics scandals have increased the salience of this approach. The high road (which is sometimes called "aspirational") includes efforts to develop employees' capacity to identify, articulate, and resolve issues. This is sometimes complemented by additional efforts to increase openness, communication, and accountability, which some authors view as a desired state of workplace relations, and others as a way to increase organizational productivity.

Ethics training is one of several strategies through which organizations pursue their ethics objectives. The integration of ethics training with other ethics efforts may include such actions as demonstrated top management interest in ethics (e.g., making ethics a criterion in hiring and promotion) as well as on-the-job application and reinforcement (e.g., ensuring that lower managers identify ethical issues and assist employees in clarifying them). Ethics training augments and bolsters these other activities. For example, although top managers are important in setting the tone of the organization, training reinforces their commitment (e.g., it operationalizes managerial priorities by giving training on specific procedures). Ethics training, in turn, is buttressed by top management commitment, which signals to employees the extent to which they should take the training seriously. Likewise, on-the-job application of what is learned in ethics training fosters ethical awareness and ability to make decisions, which then reinforces the need for training. Thus, training is best considered as part of the system of ethics activities that seeks to achieve the above purposes.

Training form and content

The "form" of ethics training can vary widely. In some jurisdictions, training is offered only sporadically, whereas in others it is a routine occurrence. In some cities, ethics training involves a series of progressive learning modules, emphasizing higher levels of awareness and problem-solving abilities. Participation may also vary. In some organizations it is entirely voluntary, whereas in others it is mandatory for all members or only for selected members (e.g., managers, new staff, those who have committed ethical offenses). Ethics training can be offered as a separate activity or integrated with other activities, thereby focusing more specifically on applications in different areas, such as law enforcement or budgeting. To date, little is known about how it varies across jurisdictions, and a reasonable hypothesis is that more frequent and integrated efforts have greater impact on the above-stated purposes.

Trainers can choose from an ethical smorgasbord of general and specific topics when designing the content of training sessions. Payne (1996, 313) distinguishes between training focused on "knowing" and training emphasizing "knowing how": "ethical knowledge is not only 'knowing that' a particular conduct is wrong but also 'knowing how' to cope with one's responsibility in regard to such conduct." Training in coping strategies and the rationale behind ethics goes beyond mere cognition—teaching the "rules" or "principles" alone neglects the panoply of ethical dilemmas confronting government employees as well as the spirit of public service. Thus, the content of such training can range from general knowledge (e.g., ethical principles) to specific desirable or undesirable behaviors (moral exemplars, codes). In some instances particular tools and problems are identified and discussed (guidelines for ethical decision-making, the consequences of misdeeds), and often these are applied to specific operational settings (Bonczek 1998; Jones 1988-89; Rice and Dreilinger 1990; Sims 1991).[1]

Pedagogical approaches

Because in-service training involves adult learners, adapting training to adult learning styles is important. Several learning considerations and instructional methods need to be considered in designing an effective program. Best practices for ethics training have been summarized by Ponemon and Felo (1996), who identify twelve features crucial to success:

- live instruction
- use of a professional trainer
- a powerful message from the manager
- small class size
- at least four hours of training
- a decision-based focus
- significant group interaction
- realistic case materials
- comprehensive employee involvement
- separate course for compliance areas
- follow-up communications
- new-employee programs.

Although authors may differ in their assessments of what features are essential, the literature reflects a clear preference for reality-based, varied, active learning adapted to the needs of adult trainees. This entails, among other things, allowing sufficient time for digesting information, encouraging trainee participation, using experiential teaching techniques to supplement traditional lecture methods, and emphasizing competency-based learning applicable to workplace decisions (Knowles 1973; LeClair and Ferrell, 2000; Van Wart, Cayer, and Cook 1993).

Correlates of training

The broad interest in ethics also prompts inquiry into factors associated with the use of training, the extent of its use (e.g., is it voluntary or mandatory?), and its impact. One can readily hypothesize that ethics training is associated with ethical leadership by top management when such managers view it as an implementation strategy for their ethics concerns. Another plausible hypothesis about associations with ethics training is related to the "teabag test" of ethical convictions, "You never know how strong they are until they are in hot water." Following this logic, it is expected that jurisdictions experiencing heightened levels of litigation or grievances will be more likely to increase their use of ethics training. Insofar as the reasons for litigation and grievances are ethical in nature, these factors can be the "hot water" that spurs ethics training. Other characteristics of jurisdictions that have a stronger commitment to ethics training are also examined, such as general orientation to provide extensive employee training and resources for training.

This study, however, highlights the correlates of ethics training, as a form of workplace training, with perceptions of workforce productivity as a measure of impact. Until now, very little evidence has been provided about the productivity-improvement impact of ethics training. Is it associated with a perceived increase in openness, accountability, and productivity in organizations? The tenets of ethics typically emphasize these orientations and outcomes, which, in turn, are thought to be associated with perceptions of employee productivity and even citizen trust. It matters that empirical evidence is brought to bear on these questions because training needs to be shown to have positive impacts on the organization.

Methods

Data were collected as part of a 2002 questionnaire mailed to city managers and chief administrative officers (CAOs) in all 544 U.S. cities with populations over 50,000. Two hundred usable responses were received after three rounds of mailing, for a response rate of 36.8 percent. This is similar to the rates reported in other studies (e.g., Hays and Kearney 2001). Survey respondents, by and large, had extensive government experience: an average of twenty years in all, eleven with their current jurisdiction. With few exceptions, respondents stated that they were familiar or very familiar with workplace relations in their municipality (94.7%). Since the respondents held a variety of very senior positions, the response groups are referred to as "senior managers."[2]

Analysis of the sample indicates that it is broadly representative by city size, form of government, and geographical region. A smaller subset of the sample indicating use of ethics training ($N = 125$) was contacted for telephone interviews. Written responses to open-ended survey items provided additional qualitative information. Tests for sample bias were conducted by examining whether addressees differed from other respondents in answering specific questions. Despite a few exceptions, the responses did not differ significantly. Other background characteristics of respondents were examined to see whether they affected the findings, but it was determined that the mix of respondents did not affect results. In addition, forty-four telephone interviews were conducted among a random group of non-respondents to test for non-response bias (i.e., did non-respondents differ in their views from respondents?). They answered a shorter list of questions extracted from the larger mail survey, but no evidence of non-response bias was found.

Findings

How much ethics training?

Table 1 shows the use of ethics training in U.S. cities. After reviewing the definition of ethics training shown in the table, 64.1 percent of respondents stated that their jurisdiction offered training that meets the definition as "activities that increase participants' knowledge of the standards of conduct within an organization (and) deals with what is right and wrong, giving both guidelines and specific examples for identifying and addressing issues of ethical concern." However, only 36.8 percent of respondents stated that their training was called "ethics training." Usage did not vary significantly by region or form of government, but large cities were more likely to offer ethics training. Respectively, 81.5 percent of cities with populations of 250,000 and over used ethics training, compared to

---

Table 1. Ethics training (*N* = 195).

Definition: "Ethics training" is defined as activities that increase participants' knowledge of the standards of conduct within an organization. Ethics training deals with what is right and wrong, giving both guidelines and specific examples for identifying and addressing issues of ethical concern.

Providing ethics training	Percent
We offer ethics training that meets the above definition	64.1
We offer ethics training that meets the above definition and it is called "ethics training"	36.8
Nature of ethics training*	
Providing an overview of ethics practices for all new staff	64.0
Ethics training is offered as a separate activity	61.0
Mandatory ethics training for all managers	50.9
Voluntary ethics training for employees	43.5
Voluntary ethics training for managers	42.6
Mandatory ethics training for all employees	37.3
Mandatory ethics training for violators	25.3
Related ethics activities*	
Regular communication to employees about ethics	50.4
Making counselors available for ethical issues	37.2
Surveying employees about ethics issues	14.6
Establishing an ethics hotline	11.6
Ethics audits	9.2
Ethics focus groups	6.9

*Among jurisdictions that provide ethics training only (*N* = 125).

71.4 percent of those between 100,000 and 250,000 and 58.5 percent of those from 50,000 up to 100,000. Among those that offered training, about one-third (37.3%) offered it as mandatory for all employees, and 43.5 percent offered it as voluntary. Most of the remainder included training only offered to managers, new staff, or violators. The mean duration of voluntary ethics training for employees was 5.77 hours per year (*Mdn* = 4 hours), and for mandatory employee ethics training it was 4.14 (*Mdn* = 3 hours).[3] In more than half of the jurisdictions (61.0%) ethics training was offered as a separate activity.

Although this is a modest amount of training (about two half-mornings a year), it frequently occurs in conjunction with other forms of ethics activities. For example, among those that provided ethics training, 82.8 percent also stated that "exemplary moral leadership" by senior managers was used as a strategy for ensuring an ethical climate. Similarly, 58.3 percent stated that they also monitored adherence to a code of ethics, 51.3 percent also used ethics as a criterion in hiring and promotion, 52.5 percent regularly communicated with employees on matters of ethics, and 57.5 percent required financial disclosure. Indeed, jurisdictions that used training were also more likely to use other ethics management strategies. Of the five ethics strategies listed in this paragraph, three were used by jurisdictions that offered ethics training, whereas only 1.8 were adopted by those that did

Table 2. Use of ethics management strategies, 1992 and 2002 (in %).

	(*N* = 427) 1992 (A)	(*N* = 129) 2002 (B)	Change from 1992 to 2002
Exemplary moral leadership by senior management	73	81.3	8.3
Adopting a standard of conduct	41	68.2	27.2
Exemplary moral leadership by elected officials	57	62.5	5.5
Adopting a code of ethics	41	60.0	19.0
Requiring financial disclosure	53	55.9	2.9
Monitoring adherence to a code of ethics	29	55.5	26.5
Requiring approval of outside activities	56	53.9	−2.1
Requiring familiarity with code of ethics	29	53.5	24.5
Regular communication to employees about ethics	29	50.4	21.4
Using ethics as a criterion in hiring and promotion	27	48.4	21.4
Voluntary ethics training for employees	41	43.5	2.5
Making counselors available for ethical issues	22	37.2	15.2
Mandatory ethics training for all employees	29	37.2	8.2
Mandatory ethics training for violators	6	25.3	19.3
Surveying opinions about ethics issues	7	14.6	7.6
Establishing an ethics hotline	3	11.6	8.6

not use ethics training ($\tau = 0.153$, $p < 0.05$). This suggests that, consistent with the above framework, training is often one of several activities in an overall ethics strategy.

Table 2 compares the use of training and other activities over the last decade, as reported earlier by West, Berman, and Cava (1993). Although voluntary and mandatory ethics training for employees has not much increased in the last decade (respectively, the increases are only 2.5% and 8.2%), other forms of ethics management have increased. Mandatory training for violators has greatly increased from a mere 6 percent to 25.3 percent, the availability of ethics counselors has almost doubled from 22 percent to 37.2 percent, and regular communication about ethics has increased from 29 percent to 50.4 percent. The use of codes of ethics has also increased, from 41 percent to 60 percent, as have "enforcement" activities, such as monitoring adherence to a code of ethics (from 29% to 55.5%) and using ethics as a criterion in hiring and promotion (from 27% to 48.4%). Overall, it is concluded that ethics activities, during the last decade, have proliferated considerably *within* jurisdictions, and that some broader diffusion *across* jurisdictions has also occurred, at least as measured by the number of jurisdictions that have adopted a code of ethics.

Purposes and content of training

Table 3 shows that training serves a broad range of "defensive" purposes (avoiding embarrassment, "low road") and aspirational purposes ("high road," see framework). Regarding the former, reducing the frequency of misconduct was widely mentioned by 82.5 percent of respondents, as was heightening familiarity with key legal requirements (77.3%), avoiding litigation (75.2%), and reducing the legal liability of the jurisdiction (74.6%). Among cities that used training, 84.8 percent mentioned at least one of these defensive purposes. Training also serves aspirational purposes, or at least aims for a behavioral impact beyond narrow but important legal concerns. Two-thirds of respondents said that a

Table 3. Purposes of ethics training (*N* = 123).

	Very important or important (%)
Reduce the frequency of unethical conduct	82.5
Use ethics training as a means of reinforcing the organizational culture	82.5
Heighten familiarity with key legal requirements	77.3
Communicate and discuss ethical standards and expectations	77.0
Offer practical guidance decision-making on ethical issues	75.4
Avoid litigation	75.2
Reduce legal liability to the jurisdiction	74.6
Encourage critical thinking about ethics	66.7
Use ethics training as a means of transforming the organizational culture	43.4

purpose of ethics training is to encourage critical thinking about ethics, and three-fourths mentioned that a purpose is to offer practical guidance. Also, 43.3 percent used training as a means of transforming the organizational culture, and 82.5 percent viewed it as a means of reinforcing the organizational culture. Eight in ten respondents mentioned at least one of these purposes. Also, 77 percent used training to communicate and discuss ethical standards and expectations, which could be used for either reinforcing or transforming organizational culture.

Ethics training covers a variety of topics. Table 4 shows a list of fifteen general topics and eleven specific issues, and reports the percentage of items that, according to respondents, were covered in depth or adequately (other response categories were "somewhat" or "not/almost not" covered). With the exception of ethics audits, a significant omission (White and Lam, 2000), a majority of cities covered each of the items mentioned. The most frequently covered items on the "general" list related to key principles: justice, individual rights, due process. A series of more practical process-oriented "how" and "why" issues stressed by Payne (1996) were also covered (although to a lesser extent), including "*why* ethics is important," "*how* to address complaints," "*how* to decide what is unethical," "*how* to cope with ethical dilemmas," and "*how* to deal with ethical violations." Even less frequently addressed were potentially perplexing problems for busy public managers: detecting warning signs of unethical behavior, dealing with inadvertent mistakes, balancing legal and ethical considerations.

With so few hours devoted to ethics training, a reasonable question is the depth of coverage. Jurisdictions that offered two or more hours of mandatory training agreed more often than jurisdictions that provided less than two hours that these topics were covered thoroughly or in-depth. For example, whereas 44.8 percent of respondents with two or more hours of mandatory training agreed that "warning signs of unethical behavior" were covered thoroughly or in depth, only 15 percent of those that offered less than two hours of mandatory training agreed. Likewise, the percentages regarding "how to deal with inadvertent mistakes and missteps" were 25 percent and 5 percent; "explains what 'conflict of interest' is in operational terms," 41.4 percent versus 17.9 percent; and "examples of standards of professional conduct," 42.9 percent versus 22.5 percent. In short, respondents reported that more training allowed for a more thorough (deeper) coverage of the topics, and still more training would presumably allow for even better coverage. It is important to note that ethics training is not the only source of information on these topics in organizations (e.g., inter-departmental memos, presentations by top managers, on-the-job discussion, hiring/promotion decisions). In this sense, the purpose of training is to clarify and strengthen ethics expectations and procedures established by managers and their organizations.

Also, as might be expected, jurisdictions that emphasized aspirational purposes were more likely to thoroughly cover such topics as "transparency," "why ethics is important," and "balancing law and ethics," than those that did not. By contrast, jurisdictions that emphasized defensive purposes were more likely to thoroughly cover such topics as explaining what "conflict of interest" and "having financial interest" mean in operational terms.[4]

Table 4. Topics covered in ethics training (*N* = 123).

	Covered in depth or covered adequately (%)
Ethics in general	
Making decisions that are fair and just	84.8
Due process	80.7
Respect for individual rights	80.4
Why ethics is important	76.8
Consequences of ethical violations	74.1
How to decide whether something is "unethical"	73.2
How to address ethics complaints	72.1
Coping with ethical dilemmas	71.7
The importance of getting the facts before jumping to a conclusion	71.2
Balancing law and ethics	67.9
Warning signs of unethical behavior	63.4
Doing what is best for the majority of people	60.4
Evaluating ethical options	58.6
How to deal with inadvertent mistakes and missteps	53.2
Ethics audits	11.7
Specific issues of ethics	
Ethics issues in specific areas (e.g., law enforcement)	82.7
The importance of being a good role model	82.1
Legal requirements	80.0
Diversity	79.1
Explains what "conflict of interest" is in operational terms	79.1
Examples of standards of professional conduct	78.5
Explains what "having financial interests" means in operational terms	68.5
Dealing with elected officials	65.8
Explains "personal honesty" in operational terms	65.1
Disclosure of financial interests	62.7
The importance of transparency	49.5

Pedagogy

Respondents were provided with a list of twenty-two items and asked which methods of instruction were used for ethics training in their jurisdiction. The responses in Table 5 show that most training was offered in the form of live instruction with very limited use of Web-based or other forms of electronic instruction. Instruction was often reality-based and practical, involving hypothetical scenarios (82.5%), case materials (80.9%), or role-plays or short exercises (67.89%), and had a decision-based focus (57.5%). These methods are consistent with most descriptions of best training practices (see Ponemon and Felo 1996) and with knowledge concerning adult learning styles. The schedule for training often involved different points in time (84.1%), and training was delivered with optimal class sizes (81.7% had thirty or fewer trainees). The training was tailored to the needs of

Table 5. Methods of instruction for ethics training (*N* = 123).

	% answering yes
Is offered in the form of live instruction	94.6
Training occurs at different points in time	84.1
Includes hypothetical scenarios	82.5
Is delivered with class sizes or 30 or fewer trainees	81.7
Is designed so that time away from the job is minimized	81.6
Includes materials for later reference	81.4
Includes realistic case materials	80.9
Is specifically tailored to the needs of our jurisdiction	79.6
Includes in-class evaluation of training	72.3
Includes role plays or short exercises	67.8
Involves the use of a professional trainer or outside consultant	64.3
Is delivered primarily in lecture format	61.4
Has a decision-based focus	57.5
Is part of our new-employee initiation program	56.6
Is one of a series of training modules for all employees	53.1
Includes self-assessment instruments	42.9
Includes a powerful message from the city manager or CAO	42.5
Includes a "how to" checklist for ethical decision-making	42.5
Includes follow-up communications	34.2
Includes separate courses for compliance areas	28.3
Uses Web-based or other electronic means	9.6
Includes an ethics audit survey	8.8

the jurisdiction (79.6%) and delivered in ways that minimized time away from the job (81.6%). Professional trainers or outside consultants were used in most cities (64.3%), and the lecture format was the primary means of delivery (61.4%). Post-training materials were provided for later reference (81.4%), and in-class evaluation of training was conducted (72.3%). These results clearly reflect that ethics training has become, in many ways, "professionalized."

Some less favorable findings are also evident in the data. As mentioned, ethics audit surveys, which provide the basis for needs assessment and ongoing monitoring, were seldom used (8.8%). Furthermore, top-level support can be signaled by a powerful message from the city manager or chief executive officer endorsing ethics training (Moeller 1988; Rice and Dreilinger 1990; Weaver, Treviño and Cochran 1999a). Such a message was provided in only 42 percent of cities. Also, socialization of new employees into an organization is the ideal time to signal the importance the employer attaches to ethical behavior (West 2003). However, a bare majority of cities (53.8%) capitalized on this opportunity by providing ethics training at the time of new-employee initiation. Finally, only a third of cities included follow-up communications after the completion of ethics training to provide additional support and determine the long-range effects of training. Thus, some need for further improvement was clearly indicated.

Correlates of ethics training

Why do some cities provide broad coverage and use numerous methods of ethics training, while others do not? To examine this question, some factors mentioned in the framework above are considered. Having adequate resources for training is associated with use of more ethics training (τ = .182, $p < 0.05$), even controlling for the size of the jurisdiction. Training was also associated with respondents' perceptions that their jurisdiction frequently developed new, innovative programs (τ = 0.208, $p < 0.01$). However, perceptions of the amount of litigation or employee grievances were not associated with the use of ethics training. Such perceptions may be related to other, non-ethics factors. Training was also (weakly) associated with using ethics as a criterion in hiring and promotion (τ = 0.103, $p < 0.05$): It stands to reason that employees need to be informed and trained in that for which they are held accountable.

The above associations were stronger for more targeted ethics training efforts. Consistent with the model of adult learning, a six-item index variable was made of training whose content (see Table 4) emphasized warning signs of unethical behavior, the importance of getting facts, dealing with inadvertent ethical missteps, addressing ethical complaints, consequences of ethical violations, and ethical issues in specific areas (e.g., law enforcement). These are among the more applications-focused items (hereafter referred to as "targeted" items) in Table 4, and the index variable has an appropriate level of internal reliability (α = 0.84). This measure is more strongly associated with using ethics as a criterion in hiring and promotion (τ = 0.330, $p < 0.01$), and it is also associated with monitoring adherence to the code of ethics (τ = .240, $p < 0.05$), although it is less strongly associated with frequently developing new, innovative programs (τ = 0.160, $p < 0.05$).[5]

To examine the impact of training, an index variable of revitalized "organizational culture" was developed, here measured as a construct of the following items (α = 0.83):

Table 6. Correlates of ethics.

	Organizational culture	Labor-management relations correlations (τ - c)	Employee productivity
Ethics training–general			
We offer ethics training	.301**	.173*	.149*
Ethics training is a separate activity	.113	.109	.157
Ethics training is part of other training activities	.228*	.353**	.183*
We provide an overview of ethics practices for all new staff	.222	.190*	.163
Mandatory ethics training for all employees	.139	.031	.050
Voluntary ethics training for employees	.146	−.020	−.001
Ethics training–content			
Why ethics is important	.044	.120	.018
Warning signs of unethical behavior	.130	.158*	.169*
Respect for individual rights	.151	.072	.061
Importance of getting the facts before jumping to a conclusion	.292**	.191*	.120
How to decide whether something is unethical	.103	.032	.012
How to deal with inadvertent ethical mistakes	.180*	.153	.185*
Consequences of ethical violations	.149	.271**	.153
Ethics issues in specific areas (e.g., law enforcement)	.240**	.146*	.250**
Code-based strategies			
Adopting a code of ethics	.067	.145	.004
Adopting a standard of conduct	.199*	.143	.077
Requiring familiarity with code of ethics	.199*	.208*	.153
Monitoring adherence to a code of ethics	.257**	.123	.160
Leadership strategies (non-training)			
Exemplary moral leadership by senior management	.147*	.146*	.032
Using ethics as a criterion in hiring and promotion	.393**	.263**	.226*
Requiring approval of outside activities	.192**	.204**	.334**

$* p < .05.$ $** p < .01.$

"in our city, people are strongly supported to put forth their best effort," "our organizational culture encourages creativity and new ideas," "our organization encourages open and constructive dialogue," "our organization rewards passionate commitments to accomplishment," and "in our city, people are encouraged to take on rather than avoid new challenges." In the sample, 51.8 percent agreed or strongly agreed with these statements.[6] Table 6 shows that ethics training was significantly associated with improvements in the organizational culture. Indeed, among jurisdictions offering training, 67.2 percent reported having a revitalized organizational culture, compared to only 29 percent of those that did not do ethics training. Similarly, among jurisdictions that had targeted (applications-oriented) ethics training discussed above, 79.6 percent reported having a revitalized organizational culture, compared to only 25 percent of those that did not do such training.

Table 6 also shows that ethics training was associated with perceived improvements in labor-management relations and even with employee productivity. Among jurisdictions that offered ethics training, 51.2 percent agreed or strongly agreed that employee productivity was high, compared to 39.1 percent of jurisdictions that did not offer ethics training. Among jurisdictions that offered targeted training, 67.3 percent agreed or strongly agreed that employee productivity was high, compared to 40.3 percent of jurisdictions that did not offer targeted ethics training. The table further indicates that training was more effective when it was part of other training activities. Items of ethics training content that were most significant are included, along with a few others of interest. Table 6 also shows that adopting a code of ethics is associated with improvements in the organizational culture, as are various leadership-based strategies.

These associations invite questions of causality. For example, does ethics training cause improvements in the organizational culture, or are cities with revitalized organizational cultures more likely to use ethics training? Moreover, are the impacts, direct or indirect, caused by other intervening variables? Such questions of causation and immediacy are explored in Figure 1, a Structural Equation Model (SEM) of the impact of ethics training and the factors affecting its use. This technique provides a more rigorous test of the above associations. Although path analysis can also be used to estimate this recursive model, the approach used here includes additional tests for the appropriateness (specification) of the overall model. Figure 1 satisfies the usual goodness-of-fit standards ($\chi^2 = 13.28$, $p > 0.05$).[7] Effect sizes of the four managerial strategies and other variables are indicated along the arrows; only significant relationships are shown.[8]

Figure 1 shows a variety of effects. First, the model uses the targeted measure of ethics training (the six-item index variable discussed above). The general measure of ethics training is often not associated with the following paths that are significant for the measure of targeted ethics training efforts. Thus, this corroborates the above emphases on targeted measures of training. Second, the model shows that although the relationship of ethics training to citizen trust and employee productivity is complex, training is significantly associated with improvements in the organizational culture and positive labor-management relations. The direct relationship between ethics training and employee productivity (and even citizen trust) is not significant, and is therefore not shown. The impact of training on these latter outcomes is indirect.

Third, the total effect on perceptions of employee productivity (as defined by the sum of all paths from ethics training to employee productivity) is of about the same magnitude as moral leadership by senior managers (respectively, 0.208 and 0.191), both of which are

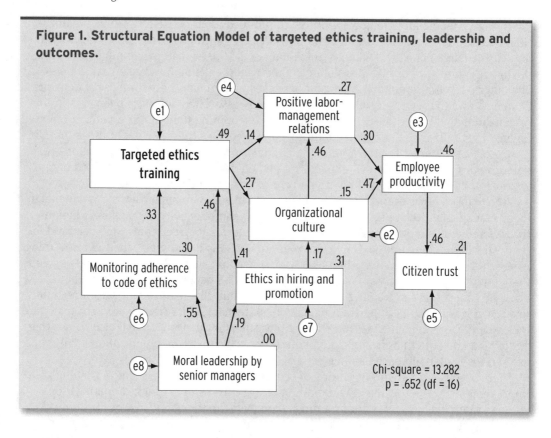

Figure 1. Structural Equation Model of targeted ethics training, leadership and outcomes.

less than the direct effects of organizational culture (0.608) and positive labor-management relations (0.304). Nonetheless, the model shows that ethics training has an effect on important concerns of public administration. Fourth, the figure also shows that ethics training is one of three strategies affected by the moral leadership of senior managers.[9] Interestingly, the moral leadership of senior managers does not directly affect perceptions of employee productivity and citizen trust (these paths are not shown because they are insignificant), but it does affect other factors that affect these outcomes. Specifically, the moral leadership of senior managers affects the use of ethics training, as well as the monitoring of employee adherence to the code of ethics (if an organization has one) and using ethics as a criterion in hiring and promotion. Overall, Figure 1 clearly shows the relationship of ethics training to other ethics activities, leadership, and important organizational outcomes.

■ Conclusion

About 64 percent of cities offer some form of ethics training, although only 36 percent call it "ethics training." Comparison of data from 2002 and 1992 shows little increase in ethics training, but substantial increase in other activities, such as regular communication about ethics and adopting codes of ethics. Training is part of a jurisdiction's ethics management practices, and the results indicate that it provides managers with leverage as they seek to attain their ethics goals. Indeed, this research finds that training is associated with fostering organizational cultures of openness, accountability, and performance that, in turn, are associated with increased employee productivity. The study further reveals considerable variation in the extent of ethics training and in the depth with which different topics are covered. The results also suggest that the perceived effectiveness of training is greatest when it is applied to specific problems and when managers monitor ethics implementation.

In many cities where ethics training is conducted, the form and content as well as the pedagogy is consistent with features recommended in the "best practice" literature. Recall Payne's (1996) admonition stressing the importance of "knowing how" (not just "knowing that") as well as understanding the "why" of ethics training. The program design in most cities that conduct ethics training incorporates these ideas, albeit to a lesser extent than other training content. In addition, a combination of what Paine (1994) refers to as "low" road and "high" road strategies are being employed. Similarly, the pedagogical features stressed by Ponemon and Felo (1996) and those found in the adult learning literature are evident in most of the municipal ethics training efforts described here. The subject matter content covered suggests that training heightens employees' awareness of ethical issues and provides them with tools for better identifying, clarifying, and resolving these issues.

While ethics training has been substantially professionalized in the last decade, further progress is needed. The depth of training is still modest at best, about a half-day or so a year. Although not the only source of ethics-related information and priorities in organizations, it is important from the perspective of reinforcing management priorities. Why is more not being done? The usual reasons still exist in some organizations, such as managers considering ethics to be a private or confidential matter for individuals to resolve, or perceiving that addressing ethics can be construed as an affront suggesting that coworkers are deficient in some way. Although these reasons are hardly new, they persist. Another plausible explanation is linked to what Gueras and Garofalo (2002) refer to as Ethics Aversion Syndrome (EAS): the discomfort experienced by some who believe that fully ethical behavior is unattainable in flawed organizations, that addressing ethical concerns through training unnecessarily complicates the manager's job, that purported experts who conduct training often lack crucial job-related knowledge, and that training may reveal individual or organizational wrongdoing that requires unwelcome action to correct.

Those who view ethics training as a passing fad that will soon disappear may resist it, and those who see it as a palliative required as penance for past wrongdoing may resent it. Others may object if they think the organization is espousing good ethics but failing to live up to its rhetoric. Those who think the ideals conveyed are good in theory but impractical to apply in their workplace setting may question the value of ethics training. As Rice and Dreilinger (1990) have noted, managers need to be prepared to deal with such objections.

Yet another reason that more is not being done may be the lack of an integrative ethics strategy that links all of an organization's ethics efforts to intended outcomes. Indeed, substantively, the absence of training on conducting ethical audits suggests that cities may be designing ethics management initiatives without first conducting a thorough needs assessment and then installing a monitoring mechanism to identify and ensure the most appropriate strategic response. Likewise, this study finds that ethics training is most effective when it is applied to specific problems and settings. This, too, requires some preliminary decisions with regard to which areas to target, and which issues to raise. Such forethought and strategic integration may be among the most important frontiers in ethics training today.

One implication of this study is that more research is needed on ethics training, particularly the factors causing organizations to pursue it, and issues associated with the effectiveness of the training material, especially from the trainees' perspective. Was the material covered relevant to their jobs? Were the analytic tools useful in resolving day-to-day ethical dilemmas? Was the mode of instruction sufficiently engaging to capture their interest? Was the time allocated sufficient to accomplish the learning objectives of the training program? To what extent was organizational behavior influenced by the insights provided in ethics training sessions? How was this assessed? Perhaps most important, is a training emphasis on ethics compliance activities associated with more ethical organizations?

The increased use of ethics management strategies in the past decade indicates the growing salience of ethical issues. The relatively modest use of ethics training suggests a strategic opportunity to improve performance and increase public trust. A challenge for future public managers is to give more balanced attention (and resources) to the development of the ethical competencies of their workforce to match the attention and resources given to cultivating technical and leadership competencies. Ethics training is an appropriate vehicle for achieving this needed balance.

Notes

1. There are a number of valuable ethics training resources that can complement instructional activities, including ASPA (1998), Berman et al. (1998), Brattebo and Malone (2002), Cooper (2001), Gueras and Garofalo (2002), Kazman and Bonczek (1998), LGI (1995-98), NCSL (2003), Pasquerella et al. (1996), and www.aspanet.org/ethics community/compendium.

2. Respondents were demographically diverse: about half were female (51.3%); most were between forty-five and fifty-four years (52.8%), some were younger than forty-five years (28.0%), and others over fifty-four years (19.2%); most had post-graduate degrees (67.2% with M.A. degrees, 3.7 percent with J.D.s, and 3.2 percent with Ph.D.s), 23.8 percent had a B.A., and only three respondents had less than a B.A. Public administration (or related) was the primary field of study of their highest degree for most respondents (50.55%), followed by business (20.1%), and others majoring in social science, education, and counseling. Respondents were also very senior. They were initially identified from the directory of municipal officials under the "appointed administrator" category in *The Municipal Year Book 2002*, published by the International City/County Management Association. Cities were then called to verify the accuracy of the list and the address

of the appointed administrator. Respondents included city managers and chief administrative officers (26.2%), assistant city managers (22%), and human resource directors or respondents with similar titles (19.9%). Almost all of the remaining respondents had such titles as manager of employee development, director of budget, director of administrative services, city clerk, director of organizational effectiveness, and so on.

3. The duration of training for managers was 4.64 hours per year for voluntary ethics training (Mdn = 4 hours) and 4.92 hours per year for mandatory training (Mdn = 4 hours). The survey did not include any further descriptors of the type of managers or employees who attended the training or the proportion of the organization's employees or managers attending ethics training.

4. The respective percentages of the five items mentioned are 22.6 percent vs. 9.6 percent, 40.7 percent vs. 19.0 percent, 23.6 percent vs. 8.8 percent (all aspirational), 34.1 percent vs. 10.7 percent, and 28 percent vs. 6.9 percent (both defensive).

5. Following a reviewer's suggestion, an index of aspirational items was added to Table 4, specifically, "doing what is best for the majority of people," "respect for individual rights," "making decisions that are fair and just," and "the importance of transparency" (α = .079). However, these items are much less strongly associated with the items

mentioned in the text paragraph: using ethics as a criterion in hiring and promotion ($\tau = .194$, $p < .05$), and they are also associated with monitoring adherence to the code of ethics ($\tau = .196$, $p < .05$), although they are less strongly associated with frequently developing new, innovative programs ($\tau = .168$, not significant). Therefore, this measure is not pursued further in this study. Other measures were also tried.

6. Here defined as an average score of 2.5 or higher on the index variable scale of 1 = strongly agree to 7 = strongly disagree.

7. Other measures indicating acceptable fit are the RMSEA of 0.056 (under the norm 0.08), the Goodness of Fit Index of 0.983, the NFI of 0.975 and AGFI of 0.961 (all above 0.9, and close to 1.0), the RMR of 0.028 (under 0.05), and the maximum Modification Index is 2.55. The PNFI value of 0.557 compares favorably with other valid, competing models. Although this is not statistically the most parsimonious model, it does show the theoretically relevant linkages.

8. Shown are the standardized (beta) coefficients. The beta coefficients can be compared against each. For example, a standardized coefficient of, say .50 suggests an effect that is twice as much as a variable with a coefficient of 0.25 in the model. Standardized coefficients should not be confused with the squared multiple correlations shown in the upper-right corners of the endogenous variables (e.g., 0.49 in "ethics training").

9. One reviewer speculated that the "positive correlations found (between moral leadership by top managers and targeted ethics training) may indicate that the relatively unusual absence of moral leadership is related to lots of other shortcoming in an organization. I fear that moral leadership, since it is so commonly reported by cities, may be a necessary but not sufficient condition for other positive characteristics." The results of the SEM analysis in Figure 1 certainly support this view.

References

ASPA. 1998. *Applying Standards and Ethics in the 21st Century*. Washington, D.C.: American Society for Public Administration.

Berman, Evan M., Jonathan P. West, and Anita Cava. 1994. "Ethics Management in Municipal Government and Large Firms: Exploring Similarities and Differences." *Administration & Society* 26, no. 2:185-203.

Berman, Evan M., Jonathan P. West, and Stephen J. Bonczek, eds. 1998. *The Ethics Edge*. Washington, D.C.: International City/County Management Association.

Bonczek, Stephen J. 1998. "Creating an Ethical Work Environment." In *The Ethics Edge*, edited by Evan M. Berman, Jonathan P. West, and Stephen J. Bonczek, pp. 77-79. Washington, D.C.: International City/County Management Association.

Brattebo, Douglas M., and Eloise F. Malone, eds. 2002. *The Lanahan Cases in Leadership Ethics & Decision Making*. Baltimore: Lanahan.

Bruce, Willa M. 1996. "Codes of Ethics and Codes of Conduct: Perceived Contribution to the Practice of Ethics in Local Government." *Public Integrity Annual* 1:23-29.

Cooper, Terry L. 2001. *Handbook of Administrative Ethics*. New York: Marcel Dekker.

Gueras, Dean, and Charles Garofalo. 2002. *Practical Ethics in Public Administration*. Vienna, Va.: Management Concepts.

Hays, Stephen W., and Richard Kearney, eds. 2001. "Anticipated Changes in Human Resource Management: Views from the Field." *Public Administration Review* 61, no. 5:585-597.

Jones, T. M. 1988-89. "Ethics Education in Business: Theoretical Considerations." *Organizational Behavior and Teaching Review* 13, no. 4:1-18.

Kazman, Jane, and Stephen J. Bonczek. 1998. *Ethics in Action*. Washington, D.C.: International City/County Management Association.

Knowles, Malcolm. 1973. *The Adult Learner: A Neglected Species*. Houston: Gulf Publishing.

LeClair, D. Thorne, and Linda Ferrell. 2000. "Innovation in Experiential Business Ethics Training." *Journal of Business Ethics* 23:313-322.

LGI. 1995-1998. *Honesty and Fairness in the Public Service*. Tacoma: Local Government Institute.

Menzel, Donald C., with Kathleen J. Carson. 1999. "A Review and Assessment of Empirical Research on Public Administration Ethics: Implications for Scholars and Managers." *Public Integrity* 1, no. 3:239-264.

Moeller, Clark. 1988. "Ethics Training." In *Ethical Insight, Ethical Action*, ed. Elizabeth Kellar, pp. 116-130. Washington, D.C.: International City/County Management Association.

NCSL. 2003. *The State of State Legislative Ethics*. Denver: National Conference of State Legislatures.

Paine, Lynn Sharp. 1994. "Managing for Organizational Integrity." *Harvard Business Review* March-April:106-117.

Pasquerella, Lynn, Alfred G. Killilea, and Michael Vocino, eds. 1996. *Ethical Dilemmas in Public Administration*. Westport, Conn.: Praeger.

Payne, S. L. 1996. "Ethical Skill Development as an Imperative for Emancipatory Practice." *Systems Practice* 9, no. 4: 307-316.

Petrick, Joseph A., and John F. Quinn. 1997. *Management Ethics: Integrity at Work*. Thousand Oaks, Calif.: Sage.

Ponemon, Larry, and Andrew J. Felo. 1996. Key Features of an Effective Ethics Training Program." *Management Accounting* 78:66-67.

Rice, D., and C. Dreilinger. 1990. "Rights and Wrongs in Ethics Training." *Training and Development Journal* 44:103-109.

Sims, Ronald R. 1991. "The Institutionalization of Organizational Ethics." *Journal of Business Ethics* 10:493-506.

Van Wart, Montgomery, N. Joseph Cayer, and Steve Cook. 1993. *Handbook of Training and Development*. San Francisco: Jossey-Bass.

Weaver, Gary R., Linda Treviño, and Philip L. Cochran. 1999a. "Corporate Ethics Programs as Control Systems: Influences of Executive Commitment and Environmental Factors." *Academy of Management Journal* 42:41-57.

———. 1999b. "Corporate Ethics Practices in the Mid-1990s: An Empirical Study of Fortune 1000." *Journal of Business Ethics* 18:283-294.

Wells, Deborah, and Marshall Schminke. 2001. "Ethical Development and Human Resources Training: An Integrative Framework." *Human Resources Management Review* 11:135-158.

West, Jonathan P. 2003. "Ethics and Human Resource Management." In *Public Personnel Management: Problems and Prospects*, edited by Stephen W. Hays and Richard C. Kearney, pp. 301-316. Upper Saddle River, N.J.: Prentice Hall.

———, Evan M. Berman, Stephen J. Bonczek, and Elizabeth Kellar. 1998. "Frontiers of Ethics Training." *Public Management* 80, no. 6:4-9.

———, Evan M. Berman, and Anita Cava. 1993. "Ethics in the Municipal Workplace." In *Municipal Year Book 1993*, pp. 3-16. Washington, D.C.: International City/County Management Association.

White, Louis, and Long Lam. 2000. "A Proposed Infrastructural Model for the Establishment of Organizational Ethical Systems." *Journal of Business Ethics* 28:35-42.

www.aspanet.org/ethicscommunity/compendium.

Part 4

Ethical Challenges

Ethical Challenges in Privatizing Government Services

Wendell C. Lawther

The trend variously known as reinventing government and as new public management, which began in the early 1990s, has had a significant impact on the structure and values of public administrators (Van Wart and Denhardt 2002). The great flexibility, innovation, and responsiveness that characterize today's work environment have produced values conflicts for responsible administrators who wish to support and maintain an ethical work environment. Privatization of government services is a significant aspect of the new public management trend that remains attractive to officials. Few authors have espoused ethical guidelines or principles, however, that would clarify the values conflicts that arise in implementing contracting out or other forms of privatization (Menzel 2001).[1]

Public managers facing the ethical challenge of privatization are called upon to apply existing ethical principles in adopting policies that were not needed prior to privatization. The issue of fairness takes on a different form because the decision to privatize government services should include supporting and encouraging in-house employees to compete against private-sector organizations. Increased privatization increases the number and size of contracts, thereby increasing the potential for "cozy politics" or conflicts of interest, corruption, and violations of professional ethics. To maintain and increase service quality, the government must be committed to appropriate contract-administration activities, entailing costs and levels of effort that are often unanticipated and for which government expertise may be limited.

A basis for recognizing values conflicts and making ethical decisions is provided by Cooper's *Responsible Administrator* (1998). This framework will be reviewed briefly below, followed by an analysis of the most significant risks inherent in privatization. A more specific discussion then presents three major areas in which ethical challenges arise after a decision to privatize is made: fairness to government employees, opportunities for violations of professional ethics, and commitment to contract administration reflected by a valid assessment of service quality.

From *Public Integrity*, vol. 6, no. 2 (Spring 2004): 141-153. Copyright © 2004 by American Society for Public Administration (ASPA). Reprinted with permission of M. E. Sharpe, Inc.

An ethical framework

Cooper (1998, 69) furnishes a basic ethical framework:

> Generally, we should assume that an administrator will be expected to explain actions from
> a practical perspective in terms such as cost-effectiveness, efficiency, economy, feasibility,
> and productivity, and from an ethical perspective according to values and principles such as
> equity, equality, freedom, truthfulness, beneficence, human dignity, privacy, and democracy.

He also suggests there are four levels of ethical guidance or behavior that can guide the
responsible administrator in making decisions. Two are relevant here:

- Moral Rules: rules and "proverbs" shaped by experiences with family, work, and
  organizational culture.
- Ethical Analysis: used when moral rules are ineffective, or "when values come into
  conflict."

The decision to privatize creates situations in which the practical and ethical perspectives come into conflict. These situations require ethical analysis because they mandate
the application of moral rules in ways unfamiliar to public managers. First, there should
be a commitment to thoroughly analyze the costs and benefits of privatizing a specific service, as opposed to privatizing primarily in response to lobbying pressure from a potential
private contractor. Once that is completed, and the decision to privatize is made, public
managers are faced with a series of decisions regarding the affected employees. Assisting
these employees to respond to a Request for Proposal (RFP) or deciding what salaries
and benefits should be provided by any private contractor who hires them are examples
of decisions reflecting values that can come into direct conflict. The higher the level of
salary the winning private contractor is required to pay, the lower the cost savings by the
government.

Employing a traditional procurement process to identify private or nonprofit contractors may also require ethical analysis. If procurement managers and elected officials are
to achieve the "best value," then retaining a contractor who will maintain or raise service
quality at a reasonable cost over the life of a contract may mean choosing one who did
not offer the lowest bid. Procurement officials charged with achieving the ethical value of
equity and the practical goal of determining the best value in the case of complex services
should proactively seek out the requisite knowledge and education that will enable them
to make the most responsible decisions.

Maintaining service quality may mean a larger commitment of resources to contract
administration than was initially anticipated. Data collection, monitoring and review,
and the imposition of sanctions (and incentives) require skills and expertise that public
employees do not have prior to privatization. Ethically, a responsible administrator is
required to exercise the best technical judgment possible (Cooper 1998). Without this
commitment, the values of equal access to the same level of service may lessen for some
citizens.

The risks of privatization

The trend toward privatization or outsourcing of government services has been growing at
every level of government (GAO 2001a; Greene 1996). Driving this trend is an assumption,
sometimes correct, that a private or nonprofit agency can provide the same if not better
services at a lower cost than its public-sector counterpart.

Not immediately apparent or often ignored are the risks involved in making this assumption. The assumption of greater efficiency and increased service quality may prove invalid for several reasons:

- The expected lower costs may not materialize because the government has not performed adequate comparative analysis between public and private sector costs (see Martin 1993b).

- The cost savings in the first few years of a contract may disappear upon the renewal or renegotiation of the contract (Kettl 1993; Lavery 1999).

- Service quality may deteriorate after privatization because of poor private-sector managerial practices (e.g., Bennett 2002), failure to deliver promised services, or biased delivery practices.

- The most significant risk or problem is the lack of adequate governmental contract management or administration.[2] Government officials may assume that there is little need for contract administration because the private agency can and will deliver the service more efficiently and effectively. Sufficient institutional or in-house knowledge may be lost as managers who retire or leave are not replaced. Penalties or sanctions for poor performance may be poorly written in the contract or may not be enforced. The officials who administer contracts may not be adequately trained (Romzek and Johnston 2002).

Maintaining ethical standards after privatization may be a much more difficult challenge for government officials than if the service were still under government control. Performing appropriate contract administration activities, such as visually observing the results or surveying citizens/customers, may require greater resources and policy changes not fully implemented prior to privatization. This difficulty is illustrated when responsible administrators apply the concept of fairness.

Fairness

In a survey of forty-two senior or retired federal public managers, fairness was one of three concepts mentioned as a "rule of thumb" that most related to "philosophical and cultural underpinnings of public life" (Gortner 1991, 42). Fairness has often meant providing due process rights to those affected by government policies or service delivery. Persons adversely affected by a government decision have the right to protest or file grievances if they feel wronged by the decision or policy.

Fairness also means equal treatment: that is to say, treatment falling in a "range of morally justified outcomes." It is closely related to the concept of equity in at least two respects: correcting mistakes when they are made, and not taking advantage of the weakness of others (Josephson 1998, 19). Employees and citizens who feel they have been treated differently from other employees and citizens have the right to point out the differences to an official with authority to correct errors or misjudgments.

The complexity of determining fair treatment includes an assessment of the degree to which all citizens or employees have the capability to effectively participate in the implementation of a government policy or process. If some are less capable, then fair treatment means government must provide additional resources or training so as to create a "level playing field" that allows everyone an equal or fair chance to benefit from the government policy or decision.

The growing acceptance and popularity of public-private competition for the right to deliver services furnishes a prime example of fair treatment (Martin 1993a; O'Leary and Eggers 1993). In-house government employees are given the right to bid to keep their jobs in the public sector by creating a response to an Invitation to Bid in competition with private organizations. Alternatively, public employees work to change policies and procedures to make their programs and departments more efficient. If they are successful in doing so, an RFP is not issued (Martin 1993a).

Other stakeholders, such as private or nonprofit businesses, may not favor this type of fair treatment, arguing that it creates a bias against contracting out a government service. In contrast, public employees in areas not privatized will be monitoring the privatization process very carefully. Instances of what seems to be unfair treatment may lower the morale of remaining public employees (Denhardt et al. 1995).

Another set of stakeholders are the politicians, legislators, and executives who may fear adverse publicity if they are portrayed as "cold and heartless" by the media. They may prefer, at a minimum, that no public employee lose a job because of privatization. Ultimately the common interest is well served if service quality is maintained or increased while costs decline, whether the service is performed by governmental employees or private contractors.

In many cases, though, the government officials in charge of making a privatization decision pay only lip service to the principle of allowing public-private competition. They assume that the private sector can provide better service at lower costs because they feel that current employees are not as capable as private-sector counterparts (Martin 1993a). In doing so, they provide little assistance to public employees to help them assess how to make processes more efficient and respond effectively to an RFP.

As a result, there are several potentially adverse consequences for the employees whose positions will be replaced by privatization. These include lower morale and productivity, career disruption, relocation and reciprocity, and undermining of trust and credibility (Timmins 1990).

To a certain extent, government officials can minimize these consequences by ethical action. When a decision to privatize is being considered, they should inform employees of all their actions and discussions. Officials can maintain an "open door" policy, answering questions, allaying concerns about future employment status, and even inviting participation in the decision to privatize. Once the decision is made, and a private organization is awarded a contract, public employees can be assisted to find positions elsewhere in the government (Denhardt et al. 1995).

The impact on careers can be lessened by a choice of requirements that can appear in the RFP and subsequent contract. These include giving public employees "right of first refusal" for all positions with the private contractor, guaranteeing that salaries will be not be reduced, and requiring a minimum employment period for public employees who agree to work for the contractor (Lawther 1999).

Of particular complexity is the issue of the pension rights of public employees when they are employed by a private contractor.[3] Since the laws governing such rights vary from state to state, there is often no clear guideline for public officials. The most ethical approach, short of requiring an equal level of pension benefits, is to provide compensation to unvested public employees when they become private-contractor employees (Ravitch and Lawther 1999).

Fairness to public employees when their positions are privatized requires the responsible administrator to:

- Assist employees to prepare a response to an RFP or to improve existing processes and procedures to gain efficiencies.
- Preserve employee morale by communicating frequently throughout the privatization process if a private contractor is chosen.
- Ensure that productive public employees do not lose substantial salary and/or benefits if they choose to work for the contractor.

Treating public employees fairly when privatizing, whether in providing appropriate pension benefits or career opportunities, is one of several concerns that are also influenced by professional standards of conduct.

Standards of conduct and professional behavior

Once a decision to privatize has been made, the process of obtaining a private or non-profit contractor can begin. This process is influenced ethically by several concerns. Public procurement efforts are governed by state and local laws, the *2000 Model Procurement Code for State and Local Governments* (ABA 2000), and the Federal Acquisition Regulations (FAR) Standards of Conduct. Corruption, taking bribes or kickbacks, and all other conflicts of interest that are illegal or prohibited by regulations are clearly unethical.

Other forms of unethical behavior are less apparent. Kobrak (1998, 181) identifies what he terms "cozy politics": "Cozy political arrangements enable companies or nonprofit agencies to win public agency contracts through political influence rather than through technical core competency."

Cozy politics may begin, for example, when a city council member is contacted by an executive of a national waste-management company. Conversations focus on how much could be saved if the city's garbage were collected by the private firm rather than a government agency. These are followed by a well-polished presentation to the city council. The suggestion is then made to the city manager that contracting out is worth serious investigation. What may follow may be one or more of several types of cozy politics, many of which result in misuse of the procurement process. If the normal procurement process is bypassed entirely, and contracts are awarded without any Request for Proposal or Invitation to Bid, then unethical and probably illegal behavior has occurred.

A second category reflecting the possibility of cozy politics, a deliberate choice to award a contract on a sole-source basis, is permissible when only one contractor has been found that can perform the contract, or "one source among others...for justifiable reasons, is found to be most advantageous for the purpose of the contract award" (Nash et al. 1998, 481). Political considerations may influence the definition of the "justifiable reasons" that determine which private or nonprofit agency receives an award. Smith and Lipsky (1993) claim that political influence frequently occurs in choosing nonprofit agencies to provide social services. By implication, these same agencies will benefit from continued funding through such methods as placing prominent politicians and citizens on their boards of directors.

Politics may also influence the outcome of a procurement process that follows all government regulations until final approval is obtained from the city council or other legislative body. In some jurisdictions, private and nonprofit organizations are allowed to lobby the local legislative body for a contract award. The council may then award a contract to an organization that was not the recommended first choice of local procurement officials.[4]

The ethical issues become more complex and unclear with more complex government services. Two themes are especially relevant: (1) awarding a contract to an organization that is not the lowest bidder; and (2) gaining a sufficient understanding of the service-delivery process so that the contract can be validly awarded to the most technically competent contractor.

Traditionally, governments purchasing goods and equipment have used standardized, clear specifications that identify what is needed. A two-step bidding process, in which price is the primary criterion for awarding a contract, is the traditional means of acquiring standardized goods. In many cases, state or local law requires that contracts must be awarded to the bidder who offers the lowest price. These laws are supported by standards of conduct that define any other decision as unethical or biased.

With the purchase of services, however, there is often a need for a more customized approach. Unlike the situation with routine services, such as refuse collection, lawn services, and building maintenance, each potential contractor may offer a different service-delivery process that has to be customized, or "tailor made," to more completely meet the goals reflected in the RFP and ultimately the contract. Negotiations are likely with all the bidders placed on a short list or found to be in a "competitive range."[5] Ideally, a bidder whose bid and proposal constitute the "best value" will be awarded the contract at the end of this process.

In making this determination, cost should be secondary to considerations of service quality, projected citizen satisfaction, and overall effectiveness. This decision may cause negative reactions. If the bidder with the lowest cost is not awarded the contract, it is likely that an appeal will be filed. At a minimum, perceptions of bias or favoritism will occur. The responsible administrator must realize that it is unethical to award a contract to a private or nonprofit firm that does not provide the highest-quality service, and therefore must be fully prepared to explain and justify the contract-award decision.

For the most complex services, such as the purchase of information technology software and hardware systems, it becomes more difficult to act ethically. Government officials charged with committing often substantial financial resources and time to such purchases must make a concurrent investment in obtaining requisite knowledge and education. Agency program managers are often heavily influenced by salespeople and other representatives of one company. They become biased toward buying a proprietary system without fully investigating and understanding similar systems from other companies.

For the most complex purchases of equipment and services, it is vital that the government form a team of evaluators that includes procurement officials, agency program managers, and even key stakeholders. When such a team is not formed, cost overruns and system failures (e.g., software programs that cannot process data as promised) are all too often the consequence. The most ethical decision, one that adheres to professional standards and reflects a commitment to service quality, requires that the government officials proactively obtain sufficient knowledge to make the most accurate and fair decision.

In summary, "cozy politics" may appear in one or more of the following forms:

- "Well-polished" presentations to legislators.
- Illegal bypassing of procurement regulations.
- Sole-sourcing contracts without sufficient justification.
- Legislators overturning contract choices recommended by procurement professionals.
- Awarding contracts to the lowest bidder without determination of which bidder offers the best value.
- Insufficient understanding of service-delivery issues, which results in inappropriate biases toward specific contractors.

The responsible administrator must be vigilant in preventing such political relationships from forming. The result can be a decrease in service quality after privatization.

▪ Service quality

Service quality is seen as an ethical principle that is part of an ethics culture or work environment (Bonczek 1991; Van Wart 1995). It also appears as an element in professional codes of ethics. The International City/County Management Association Code of Ethics indicates that the professional city or county manager should seek to "improve the quality of public service" (ICMA 1998). This ethical commitment to maintaining and improving service quality remains after privatization. As suggested by Auger (1997), transfer of services to a private provider does not reduce government's responsibility to provide high-quality service. What is challenging for the responsible administrator is to validly measure and assess the extent to which service quality is maintained.

Contract administration is a function performed in a variety of ways. An assistant public works director can administer a contract for refuse collection in addition to a myriad of other duties. More complex contracts require a full-time contract administrator. For the most complex services, a team of agency personnel, procurement professionals, and other key administrators perform contract-administration duties.

Too often, the contracting government fails to commit sufficient resources to contract administration, assigning this function to an already overworked public manager. If a contract is not given an appropriate level of attention, service quality may soon deteriorate. For example, to expedite clean-up activities at the Oak Ridge (Tennessee) National Laboratory, in 1997 the U.S. Department of Energy (DOE) issued a performance-based management and integration contract to Bechtel Jacobs LLC. A DOE Inspector General audit, reviewing contract actions undertaken during 1999 and 2000, revealed that annual performance standards were lowered each year to meet the actual work performed by Bechtel Jacobs. In addition, performance incentives were paid for work completed almost two years after the date established by the initial performance standards (DOE 2001).

The Inspector General's Office of the Department of Defense reviewed 105 contract actions (contracts and task orders) related to professional, administrative, and managerial services for the time period 1992-1999. In 67 percent of the cases, there was inadequate contract administration. For all cases, there were no performance measures used to judge service quality (DOD 2000). Poor professional management—the lack of appropriate contract administration efforts to observe operations, collect data, and enforce service quality—is a major ethical violation of privatization efforts.

Deciding what contract administration efforts are necessary depends upon a variety of factors, including the complexity of the service provided and the definition and acceptance of service quality. To simply assume that the private firm will always maintain the same levels of service quality or work to improve existing levels in the absence of government oversight is naive and ultimately unethical.

It must be recognized that maintaining service quality may be more difficult for a privatized service than for a public agency. Since the terms of a contract are the primary means of controlling and influencing the efforts of a private organization, they must be clearly and objectively specified as much as possible, taking into account all possible influences beyond the control of the contractor that could influence performance. If a state agency contracts with a nonprofit firm to place foster children, for example, and the number of children in need of placements increases, there should be contract provisions that allow for higher payment because of the unexpected increase in workload (Damron 2002).

The decision to privatize existing services is often made on grounds of efficiency or a reduction in overall service-delivery costs. As has been documented elsewhere, efficiency and cost reduction can be achieved in privatization for several reasons. Private management has substantial flexibility to implement efficient procedures; the opportunity for incentives leading to higher productivity is present in the private sector; there is potential for lower unit costs because a private firm can provide services for more than one public agency; and the greater use of more up-to-date equipment can lower unit costs and preclude the need for government to purchase the equipment (Morgan and England 1988).

Efficiency and service quality

The argument that privatization leads to improved service quality is difficult to make. A review of the various definitions of service quality will help clarify this causal linkage. Service quality can be defined or measured by:

- The amount of time needed for the service-delivery process.
- The number or amount of errors in the service-delivery process.
- The percentage of the population served.[6]
- Quality as measured by professional standards, established performance measures, or other, more subjective means, such as observation (Ammons 1996).
- Degree of satisfaction with the service as expressed by the service recipients.
- Consistency and timeliness of access to the service by all citizens.

The likelihood that a privatized process will improve service quality ranges from high for the definitions that head this list, to much lower for the latter definitions. Increased efficiency can lead to improved service by reducing the amount of time needed to provide the service. This is especially true for the least complex services, because both service providers and recipients have the same clear understanding and agreement concerning the definition of service quality. Consider this example from the Department of Housing and Urban Development: If, after privatization, the process of approving mortgages for single-family home ownership takes less time, then service quality has increased (GAO 2001c). In this case, the desired outcome of approval is well understood: the mortgage application is either approved or not approved. Increased efficiency can also reduce the number of errors in the process. If there are more Revenue Service agents with appropriate expertise to answer questions by citizens, fewer errors in information will be passed along to callers (GAO 2001b). Changing the schedules for garbage collectors may lead to faster collections and fewer missed pickups. Fewer complaints result, leading to better service quality. Again, this latter example stresses the lack of complexity of the service and the easily apparent determination that errors have occurred.

Greater efficiency can produce an expanded service base, especially if the need for a service is great or is growing. If the amount of time per client in providing job placement services can be reduced through greater efficiencies, such as better scheduling of appointments with caseworkers, then service quality is increased because more clients can be served. This definition assumes that service delivery by a public agency has not sufficiently met all of the demand. The private or nonprofit organization can serve more because of greater efficiencies.

The latter three definitions of service quality assume that greater efficiency may not lead to improved service quality, and rely on measurements that may or may not be related to efficiency. The issue of quality standards is closely related to how performance is measured. Ideally, public agencies have collected data concerning these standards prior to privatization. Examples refer to response time, percentage of clients served who have expressed satisfaction with the service, and results of observations made (Ammons 1996). In some cases, such as road construction or repaving sidewalks, there may be professional or "industry wide" standards that can be used.

The data collected using these measures are often of low validity and reliability. Response time for a fire department, for example, may be influenced by the distance of a fire station from buildings that are likely to burn, or from residences that are likely to require the need of paramedic response. Other influencing factors may include time of year, weather conditions, and workload.

A typical quality measure, citizen or client satisfaction, is often measured by a complaint log. Complaints related to service are logged, with further tallying of whether the complaint was resolved. Yet the validity of this measure can be questioned, as only a small percentage of those who are unhappy with a service may register a complaint. Likewise, the lack of complaints may be interpreted as reflecting a high degree of satisfaction. This assumption may not be accurate, because there may be a wide range of satisfaction among those who do not complain (Hatry 1999).

The final definition is the most significant in assessing service quality from private or nonprofit agencies. Public officials must guard against "creaming": providing the highest priority to clients or tasks that are easiest to serve or complete. Creaming implies that access to service by those who are the most difficult to serve will be limited (Morgan and England 1988).

No matter how difficult it is to evaluate service quality, public agencies have an ethical duty to do so. Determinations of quality should be made prior to privatization so that standards exist to which private agency service delivery can be compared. Commitments should be made to collect and evaluate service-delivery data as part of ongoing contract-administration efforts. Rehfuss (1989), for example, suggests that contract administration should include analysis of data that come from a variety of sources, including contractor reports, inspections and observations, and citizen complaints. The choice of what data to collect should be based on the extent to which the data add to the understanding of service quality.

Conclusion

Privatization means that public managers must adopt new roles to remain ethically and technically proficient. The decision to privatize should take place only after the completion of a thorough study identifying potential cost savings. Existing public employees should be assisted in efforts to increase efficiency and service quality as part of this decision. When a government service is privatized, there is a concurrent loss of control over the everyday delivery of that service. The change from managing employees within a public agency to administering a contract may require monitoring and review techniques, data collection, and efforts to resolve new kinds of problems. If a government agency does not recognize the need to change the tasks and activities of the remaining managers, and to provide appropriate training to ensure that they perform at the highest technical level, then ethical commitment is lessened, and a decrease in service quality is the likely result.

Notes

1. One exception can be found in Amado, Auerbach, and Sharkansky (2002).

2. Contract administration can be defined as "the management of all actions that must be taken to assure compliance with the terms of the contract after the award of the contract" (NIGP 1998).

3. This complexity is increased if the public pension system is a defined benefit type, while the private contractor system is a defined contribution type. See Ravitch and Lawther (1999) for more discussion.

4. Orlando, Florida, adopted stricter lobbying rules to prevent lobbying from the time the city ranks bids to the time the city council awards the contract (Steinman 2002).

5. The competitive range is defined as "the range of proposals that are the most highly rated" (Nash, Schooner, and O'Brien 1998, 108).

6. Population is defined here as the number who need to receive the service (Rossi, Freeman, and Lipsey 1999).

References

ABA. 2002. The 2000 Model Procurement Code for State and Local Governments. American Bar Association, Section of Public Contract Law and Section of State and Local Government Law.

Amado, Rivka, Gedalia Auerbach, and Ira Sharkansky. 2002. "Privatization and Ethics: The Israeli Telecommunications Company." *Public Integrity* 4, no. 1: 81-94.

Ammons, David N. 1996. *Municipal Benchmarks: Assessing Local Performance and Establishing Community Standards.* Thousand Oaks, Calif.: Sage.

Auger, Deborah A. 1997. "Privatization and State and Local Government in the 1990's." In *Competition and Privatization Options: Enhancing Efficiency and Effectiveness in State Government*, edited by Jeffrey A. Raffel, Deborah A. Auger, and Kathryn G. Denhardt, pp. 23-29. Newark: University of Delaware, Institute for Public Administration.

Bennett, David L. 2002. "City May Pull Plug on Water Firm." *Atlanta Constitution*, December 15, D8.

Bonczek, Stephen. 1991. "Creating an Ethical Work Environment." *Public Management*: 19-23.

Cooper, Terry. 1998. *The Responsible Administrator.* San Francisco: Jossey-Bass.

Damron, David. 2002. "Glitches Haunt Foster Care." *Orlando Sentinel*, October 20, B1.

Denhardt, Kathryn, Jeffrey Raffel, Eric Jacobson, Megan Manlove, D. Auger, and Jerome Lewis. 1995. "Employee Issues in Privatization." *MIS Report* 27, no. 10: 1-12.

DOD. 2000. *Audit Report on Contracts for Professional, Administrative, and Managerial Support Services.* Washington, D.C.: U.S. Department of Defense, Inspector General, Report No. D-2000-100.

DOE. 2001. *Audit Report: Incentive Fees for Bechtel Jacobs LLC.* Washington, D.C.: U.S. Department of Energy, Office of Inspector General/IG-0503.

GAO. 2001a. *Contract Management: Trends and Challenges in Acquiring Services, Statement of David E. Cooper, Director, Acquisition and Sourcing of Management, May 22.* Washington, D.C.: General Accounting Office, GAO-01-753T.

———. 2001b. *IRS Telephone Assistance: Opportunities to Improve Human Capital Management.* Washington, D.C.: General Accounting Office, GAO-01-144.

———. 2001c. *Single Family Housing: Better Human Capital Management Needed at HUD's Homeownership Centers*. Washington, D.C.: General Accounting Office, GAO-01-590.

Gortner, Harold F. 1991. "How Public Managers View Their Environment: Balancing Organizational Demands, Political Realities, and Personal Values." In *Ethical Frontiers in Public Management*, edited by James S. Bowman, pp. 34-63. San Francisco: Jossey-Bass.

Greene, Jeffrey D. 1996. "How Much Privatization? A Research Note Examining the Use of Privatization by Cities in 1982 and 1992." *Policy Studies Journal*: 24, no. 4:632-640.

Hatry, Harry P. 1999. *Performance Measurement: Getting Results*. Washington, D.C.: Urban Institute Press.

ICMA. 1998. "ICMA Code of Ethics with Guidelines." In *The Ethics Edge*, edited by Evan M. Berman, Jonathan P. West, and Stephen J. Bonczek, pp. 237-246. Washington, D.C.: International City/County Management Association.

Josephson, Michael. 1998. "The Six Pillars of Character." In *The Ethics Edge*, edited by Evan M. Berman, Jonathan P. West, and Stephen J. Bonczek, pp. 13-21. Washington, D.C.: International City/County Management Association.

Kettl, Donald F. 1993. *Sharing Power: Public Governance and Private Markets*. Washington, D.C.: Brookings Institution Press.

Kobrak, Peter. 1998. "Privatization and Cozy Politics." In *The Ethics Edge*, edited by Evan M. Berman, Jonathan P. West, and Stephen J. Bonczek, pp. 178-193. Washington, D.C.: International City/County Management Association.

Lavery, Kevin. 1999. *Smart Contracting for Local Government Services: Processes and Experiences*. Westport, Conn.: Praeger.

Lawther, Wendell C. 1999. "The Role of Public Employees in the Privatization Process." *Review of Public Personnel Administration* 19, no. 1:28-40.

Martin, Lawrence. 1993a. "Bidding on Service Delivery: Public-Private Competition." *MIS Report* 25, no. 3:1-14.

———. 1993b. *How to Compare Costs Between In-House and Contracted Services*. Los Angeles: Reason Foundation.

Menzel, Donald. 2001. "Ethics and Public Management." In *Handbook of Public Management Practice and Reform*, edited by Koutsai Tom Liou, pp. 349-364. New York: Marcel Dekker.

Morgan, David R., and Robert E. England. 1988. "The Two Faces of Privatization." *Public Administration Review* 48, no. 6:979-987.

Nash, Ralph C., Jr., Steven L. Schooner, and Karen R. O'Brien. 1998. *The Government Contracts Reference Book: A Comprehensive Guide to the Language of Procurement*. Washington, D.C.: George Washington University Law School, Government Contracts Program.

NIGP. 1998. *Dictionary of Purchasing Terms*. Herndon, Va.: National Institute of Government Purchasing.

O'Leary, John, and William D. Eggers. 1993. *Privatization and Public Employees: Guidelines for Fair Treatment*. Los Angeles: Reason Foundation.

Ravitch, Frank S., and Wendell C. Lawther. 1999. "Privatization and Public Employee Pension Rights: Treading in Unexplored Territory." *Review of Public Personnel Administration* 19, no.1:41-58.

Rehfuss, John A. 1989. *Contracting Out in Government*. San Francisco: Jossey-Bass.

Romzek, Barbara, and Jocelyn Johnston. 2002. "Effective Contract Implementation and Management: A Preliminary Model." *Journal of Public Administration Research and Theory* 12, no. 3:423-454.

Rossi, Peter, Howard Freeman, and Mark Lipsey. 1999. *Evaluation: A Systematic Approach*. Thousand Oaks, Calif.: Sage.

Smith, Steven Rathgeb, and Michael Lipsky. 1993. *NonProfits for Hire: The Welfare State in the Age of Contracting*. Cambridge, Mass.: Harvard University Press.

Steinman, John. 2002. "He Now Embraces Lobbying Rules." *Orlando Sentinel*, October 2, B3.

Van Wart, Montgomery. 1995. "The First Step in the Reinvention Process: Assessment." *Public Administration Review* 55:429-438.

Van Wart, Montgomery, and Kathryn Denhardt. 2002. "Organizational Structure: A Reflection of Society's Values and a Context for Individual Ethics." In *Handbook of Administrative Ethics*, edited by Terry L. Cooper, pp. 227-241. New York: Marcel Dekker.

West, Jonathan P. 2003. "Ethics and Human Resource Management." In *Public Personnel Administration: Problems and Prospects*, edited by Steven W. Hays and Richard C. Kearney, pp. 301-316. Upper Saddle River, N.J.: Prentice-Hall.

Private Life and Public Office

Dennis F. Thompson

Private vice may not be a public virtue, but the preoccupation with private vice has certainly become a public vice. Debate about the personal lives of public officials has not replaced debate about substantive issues of public policy, but it is capturing a disproportionate share of public attention and is distorting the character of public discussion. The various social and political causes of this preoccupation have been frequently discussed, but the underlying moral assumptions that support it have been less often analyzed. The increased attention to private lives gains legitimacy from mistaken moral assumptions concerning the nature of political ethics, the basis of privacy of public officials, and the criteria that justify publicizing their personal lives. To begin to restore discursive balance in our politics, we need to understand more clearly how personal and political ethics differ, and why the claims of privacy of public officials and the criteria that justify publicizing their personal lives should rest on the needs of the democratic process.

The differences between personal and political ethics

Political ethics prescribes principles for action in public institutions, and in a democracy its foundation lies in the principles governing the democratic process. It differs from personal ethics in origin, function, and content. Personal ethics originates in face-to-face relations among individuals. It fulfills a social need for principles to guide actions toward other individuals across the familiar range of personal relations. Political ethics originates in institutional circumstances. It arises from the need to set standards for impersonal relations among people who may never meet and must judge one another at a distance.

The function of personal ethics is to make people morally better or, more modestly, to make the relations among people morally tolerable. Political ethics also serves to guide the actions of individuals, but only in their institutional roles and only insofar as necessary for the good of an institution. Political ethics uses personal ethics only as a means—not even the most important means—to the end of institutional integrity, specifically the needs of the democratic process.

From *Public Integrity*, vol. 3, no. 2 (2001): 163-175. Copyright © 2001 by American Society for Public Administration (ASPA). Reprinted with permission of M. E. Sharpe, Inc.

In their most general form, the content of the ethical principles of public and private life have a common foundation. Certainly, one wishes both friends and officials to respect the rights of others, to fulfill their obligations to their communities, to act fairly and speak truthfully. But in this form the principles are too general to guide conduct in the complex circumstances of political life. Once the principles are translated into the particular standards suitable for public institutions, they often recommend conduct that is distinct from, and sometimes even contrary to, the conduct appropriate for private life. As a result, the content of political ethics differs from that of personal ethics.

For example, some conduct that may be wrong in private life is properly ignored by political ethics. The public may think less of politicians who enjoy hardcore pornography or commit adultery, but as long as they keep these activities private and do not let them affect their public responsibilities, political ethics does not proscribe them. Indeed, it may protect some of them. As I shall indicate below, it should protect conduct that if disclosed could distract public discussion from more important matters of public policy.

Conversely, some conduct that is permissible or even praiseworthy in personal ethics may violate the principles of political ethics. Returning a favor or giving preference to a friend is often admirable in private life but, though occasionally useful in public life, such an act is more often ethically questionable and sometimes criminal. Furthermore, many of the problems of political ethics, such as restrictions on types of employment that officials can follow after the end of their public career, do not arise at all in private life. Others such as conflict of interest do not arise in the same form or to the same extent.

The contrast between the ethical demands of private and public life has never been more plainly put than it was by an anonymous supporter of Grover Cleveland in the presidential campaign of 1884. Cleveland's opponent, James G. Blaine, had corruptly profited from public office but lived an impeccable private life. Cleveland had a reputation for public integrity but had been forced to acknowledge fathering an illegitimate child. "I gather that Mr. Cleveland has shown high character and great capacity in public office," said Cleveland's supporter, "but that in private life his conduct has been open to question, while, on the other hand, Mr. Blaine, in public life has been weak and dishonest, while he seems to have been an admirable husband and father. The conclusion that I draw from these facts is that we should elect Mr. Cleveland to the public office which he is so admirably qualified to fill and remand Mr. Blaine to the private life which he is so eminently fitted to adorn" (Howe 1932, 151).

The separation between private and public life is not, of course, quite so sharp as these observations imply. Some kinds of otherwise private immorality may affect an official's capacity to do a job. As citizens, we may not care if the chair of the House Administration Committee has an affair, but we may legitimately object if he gives his mistress a job on the Committee staff, especially if she says: "I can't type. I can't file. I can't even answer the phone" (*Congressional Ethics* 1992, 89). Even if the member does not misuse the powers of his office, his private life may become so scandalous that it casts doubt on his judgment and undermines his effectiveness on the job. Perhaps the chair of the Ways and Means Committee should be able to date an Argentinean striptease dancer, but when he appears on a Boston burlesque stage to praise her performance, citizens properly take notice.

Sexual conduct that would otherwise be private becomes a legitimate subject for investigation and reporting by the press when it violates the law (provided of course the law itself is morally justified). Sexual conduct that would otherwise be private becomes a legitimate subject for investigation and reporting by the press when it violates the law (provided of course the law itself is morally justified). Sexual harassment is not a private matter. Even some conduct that does not strictly speaking violate the law may still be relevant if it reveals a pattern of unwanted sexual advances to persons in subordinate positions. The press therefore could not be faulted for publicizing Senator Bob Packwood's sexual encounters, which the Senate Ethics Committee found constituted a "pattern of abuse of his position of power and authority" (Senate Ethics Counsel 1995, 125).

The basis of personal privacy of public officials

Just because personal ethics differs from political ethics does not mean the claims of privacy made by public officials can be dismissed. In political ethics itself there are strong reasons to grant public officials some substantial privacy. We can best see what they are by first considering three common but inadequate justifications for the privacy of officials.

Individual rights

In general, privacy may be understood as a claim to protect information about an individual that he or she is entitled to control: personal activities that should not be known, observed, or intruded upon without his or her consent. The most common justification for this claim invokes the right of privacy that all citizens should enjoy. Like all citizens, officials surely have some right to the kind of control implied by this right. No democracy should make the price of public service the sacrifice of all one's rights, especially when the consequences may be permanent and follow the individual long after leaving office.

But citizens become public officials by choice, and they may be assumed to consent to whatever limitations on their privacy are reasonably believed to be necessary for the effective functioning of the democratic process. What their rights are, then, depends on what these limitations are. We have to know what the democratic process requires before we can determine what rights officials have.

Political recruitment

Another (related) justification points to effects on the recruitment of public officials. If the press constantly probes the private lives of public officials, who would want to serve in public office? The prospect of exposing to public scrutiny one's personal finances (even those of one's family) or any past indiscretion (however minor) hardly seems a positive incentive to seek public office.

Although many complain about the glare of publicity, many more continue to seek public office in spite of it. The question is not *whether* some decide not to seek office because of the possibility of public exposure, but *which kinds* of people decide not to seek office because of it. No doubt some admirable citizens who would be fine public servants decline to serve. But certainly some less admirable citizens, who have much to hide, decline to serve because they fear that their past (and present) transgressions may come to light. If the latter group is larger (and the number of quality people who are willing to serve does not decline), we should consider the prospect of public exposure a *favorable* effect on recruitment.

There are at least three reasons to doubt that there is a strong net negative effect. First, some of the most talented citizens may be more attracted to government that maintains higher standards and greater respectability. Second, the decision to seek and hold public office is affected by so many weighty personal and political factors that the burden of public exposure is likely to be a minor consideration. Third, studies of the federal executive branch, where restrictions have been more stringent for a long time, generally find no effect on recruitment. In its study of the problem, the General Accounting Office (1983) concluded that it is "extremely difficult, if not impossible, to attribute any specific degree of federal recruiting difficulty to the Ethics Act or to any of its provisions" (Appendix I, 1).

Moral skepticism

Another justification sometimes given for protecting the privacy of public officials is based on moral skepticism (e.g., Himmelfarb 1998). Who is to say what is right or wrong, moral or immoral? If moral judgments are a matter of personal preference or even individual conscience, then the public has no business judging the private behavior of officials and therefore has no need to know about it (unless of course it is illegal and therefore subject to a more objective standard on which judgments can be made).

But this justification proves too much. If moral judgments are so subjective, then who is to say that the press (or anyone else) is wrong when it publicizes private conduct? Moral skepticism is a double-edged instrument here. If it exempts officials from moral criticism about their private conduct, it also exempts the press from criticism about exposing private conduct.

Nor does this moral skepticism *justify* anyone in exposing whatever he or she wishes about private conduct. Permitting the press to report whatever it thinks the public wants, letting each individual make his or her own moral judgments, is not a neutral default position. This permissive policy also rests on a set of moral judgments about what kind of practices best serve society and protect individuals. Moral skepticism thus does not help either side in this dispute because it treats all moral judgments as equal, when the dispute is about which moral judgments we should accept as right.

Democratic accountability

The common failing of all of these justifications is that they do not connect the rationale for privacy to the needs of the democratic process. As a result, the justifications are incomplete or inadequate. The right to privacy argument, once we recognize that public officials do not have the same rights as ordinary citizens, does not provide much help in determining what the limits on publicity should be. The recruitment argument is inadequate because it seems to presume that the less publicity there is the better (or at least offers no criteria for balancing the desire for privacy and the legitimate demands of office). And the skeptical argument is indeterminate because it supports opposite views of the democratic process equally well.

These failings suggest that any adequate justification for privacy will have to rely on a view about what the democratic process requires. Although there are of course many different conceptions of democracy, we can posit a minimal requirement that should be acceptable on almost any conception. The requirement is *accountability*: citizens should be able to hold public officials accountable for their decisions and policies, and therefore citizens must have information that would enable them to judge how well officials are doing or are likely to do their job.[1]

It is plain enough that the requirement of accountability provides a reason to override or diminish the right of privacy that officials would otherwise have. The requirement would clearly justify making some conduct public that is ordinarily private, such as information about mental or physical health and the finances of family members. It also provides grounds for making conduct *more* public that is partially private (such as old court or employment records).

But the accountability requirement has another implication that is less noticed but no less important. The requirement provides a reason to *limit* publicity about private lives. When such publicity undermines the practice of accountability, it is not justified. How can publicity undermine accountability? The most important way is through the operation of a political version of Gresham's law: Cheap talk drives out quality talk. (Not because people hoard the quality talk in the hope that they might be able to enjoy it later, as Gresham thought people would hoard higher-value currency. Rather, the cheap talk attracts readers and viewers, even those who in their more reflective hours would prefer quality talk.)

Talk about private lives is "cheap" in two ways. First, the information is usually more immediately engaging and more readily comprehensible than information about job performance. Most people (understandably) think they know more about sex than tariffs. Second, the information itself is less reliable because it is usually less accessible and less comprehensive. We usually know less about private life not only in a particular case but also in past cases, and we need information about past cases to establish reliable generalizations about the effects of private conduct on public performance in any present case.

Given these characteristics, information about private life tends to dominate other forms of information and to lower the overall quality of public discourse and democratic accountability. Informing citizens about some matters makes it harder for them to be informed about other matters. To take a random example: Even during the first six months of its public life, the coverage of the Clinton-Lewinsky affair dominated media discussion of not only important new policy proposals on social security, health insurance, and campaign finance reform but also attempts to explain the U.S. position on Iraq in preparation for military action.

Journalists argue that they are only responding to what the public wants, and if the only test is what the public reads or views they may be right. But the considered judgments of most citizens in this and similar cases is that they do not need to know so much about the sexual affairs of their leaders[2] and that the press pays too much attention to their private lives.[3] It is perfectly consistent to believe that the political process would be better with less publicity about such matters, and even to prefer to know less about them, while at the same time eagerly reading whatever the press reports about them.

We do not have to assume that in the absence of the scandals citizens will necessarily pay more attention to the more important issues of the day and the more important qualities of candidates. Some citizens would no doubt simply ignore political reporting completely. And reporting scandals might even sometimes *increase* interest in politics. Some viewers might turn on the news to find out the latest about Clinton and Lewinsky, and then stay to see a report on Iraq that they would have otherwise missed.

What exactly are the effects of the coverage of scandalous private conduct? This is an empirical question that unfortunately has not received much serious investigation by social scientists.[4] But there are plenty of examples to support the plausible assumption that serious issues of public policy and important qualities of candidates and officials are likely to receive less coverage and less discussion when they have to compete with stones about the vices of private life. Even if the tilt of political attention from the public to the private affects only opinion leaders and the political classes, it can still have the effect of weakening the system of accountability.

This tendency to dwell on personal ethics also means that some conduct of legitimate public concern is viewed almost entirely from the perspective of personal ethics. This doubly distorts the problem. First, it gives the transgression of personal ethical standards more prominence than it deserves compared to other problems. The overdrafts by members in the House Bank that caused such a public outcry in 1991 is a case in point. Because the scandal seemed to fit easily into the category of personal ethics, it generated more outrage than more serious problems, such as the failures in the regulation of the savings and loan industry, where individual villains in government were less easy to find. Second, the perspective of personal ethics also distorted the House Bank scandal itself by emphasizing individual greed and arrogance more than institutional negligence and incompetence. It was the institutional faults, the management practices and appointment procedures, that needed attention and represented the more enduring and potentially far-reaching problem. Individuals were to blame for these faults, and individuals could be held accountable for correcting them. The faults also revealed an ethical failure, but it was not the kind usually found in a catalog of personal vices.

The relevance of personal life to public office

Democratic accountability thus permits some exposure of the private lives of officials, when such information is necessary for assessing past or likely future performance in office. This is the basis of a familiar "relevance" standard: Private conduct should be publicized to the extent that it is relevant to the performance in public office. But an essential point, often neglected in applying this standard, is that relevance is a matter of degree. The standard does not draw a bright line between private and public life, which would allow that once the conduct is deemed relevant it may be legitimately publicized without limit. The standard, properly interpreted, seeks a proportionate balance between degree of relevance and extent of publicity. We can see more clearly how this should be understood by considering some of the criteria that should guide judgments about what to publicize about the private lives of public officials.

Publicness of conduct

Consider the case of John Fedders, who in the mid-1980s was forced to resign as chief of the enforcement division of the Securities and Exchange Commission after the *Wall Street Journal* (Jackson 1985) reported that he had repeatedly beaten his wife. Although his wife's charges had appeared in the public record at the start of the divorce proceedings nearly a year and a half earlier, virtually no one had taken notice until the *Journal*'s story appeared. The first justification that almost all editors gave for publicizing this case is that the conduct was already on the public record.[5] Abe Rosenthal, the executive editor of the *New York Times,* took this as a sufficient justification: "When stories of repeated wife-beating by a public official . . . become part of the public record, they must be printed" (Taylor 1985, A 16).

But this justification is not sufficient. We should require some independent test of the plausibility of the charges, beyond the fact that the charges are made in public. This case illustrates clearly that the press itself often determines that what is on the public record is what counts. For John Fedders, the difference between a court record and the front page of the *Journal* was the difference between holding public office or resigning in disgrace. More generally, the fact that conduct comes to light whether as a result of court proceedings or (more commonly) through less reputable means does not automatically justify giving it still more exposure. Just because an activity is public (even legitimately so) does not mean that it should be *more widely publicized*. Failure to make this simple distinction leads to the common mistake that Rosenthal made.

Similarly, the fact that the story is likely to be published elsewhere ("If we don't run it, somebody else will") is not in itself sufficient. With this justification, almost any story can be considered legitimate, whether actually public already or imminently so—if not in the *Wall Street Journal* then in the *Daily News,* or if not in the *Daily News* then in the *Drudge Report.* On the relevance standard, properly interpreted, it makes a difference where the story is published—a difference that is becoming more, not less, important in the era of cyberpublicity. Publication in the *Journal* (or its local counterpart) gives a story more credibility, and has more effect on political discussion and accountability, than does publication in the tabloids or on the Internet.

The respectable press often tries to avoid any dilemma by a technique that may be called *metareporting:* writing about the fact that the less respectable press is writing about private scandals. Thus the *New York Times* (Scott 1998) publishes a story about unsubstantiated rumors that the *Daily News* has published about Clinton and Lewinsky—complete with miniature reproductions of the front pages of the *News.* This technique might be more justifiable if the respectable press were not inclined to engage in metareporting about stories that feature sex so much more than about stories that reveal other failings of their fellow journalists.

Unity of character

A second criterion is that the private conduct reveal important character flaws that are relevant to the job. Citizens may reasonably want to know, for example, about someone's tendency toward domestic violence when he is responsible for enforcing the law and regulating the finances of other people. But the appeal to character must be more-specific than the common use of the character argument, which is undiscriminatingly general. The general claim that private conduct reveals character flaws that are bound eventually to show up on the job is a psychological version of the classical idea of the unity of the virtues: A person who mistreats his wife is likely to mistreat his colleagues; a person who does not control his violent temper is not likely to resist the temptation to lie.

We should be wary of this argument because many people, especially politicians, are quite capable of compartmentalizing their lives in the way that the idea of the unity of virtues denies. Indeed, for some people, private misbehavior may be cathartic, enabling them to behave better in public. And private virtue is no sign of public vice. We should remember that most of the leading Watergate conspirators led impeccable private lives. So did most of the nearly 100 political appointees who were indicted or charged with ethics offenses during the early years of the Reagan administration (Lardner 1988).

More generally, as far as character is concerned, we should be primarily interested in the *political* virtues—respect for the law and Constitution, a sense of fairness, honesty in official dealings. These virtues may not be correlated at all with personal ones. And the vices in which the press seems most interested—the sins of sex—are those that are probably *least* closely connected with the political vices.

Character is sometimes thought to be relevant in a different, more symbolic way. Officials represent us by who they are as much as by what they do. We need to know if they have the character fit for moral leadership—for serving as role models for our youth and virtuous spokespersons for our nation. But this conception of public office is too demanding, as most citizens seem to recognize. They seek leaders whose characters display the political virtues (such as honesty), but most do not believe that even the president should be held to higher moral standards in his private life than are ordinary citizens.[6] The question is not whether it would be desirable to have a leader who is as moral in his private as in his public life, but whether it is worth the sacrifice of privacy and the distortions of public debate that would be required to make private probity a job qualification.

If the character trait is specifically related to the job, the case for considering it relevant is stronger, even if the connection is only symbolic. This is part of the reason that Fedders's domestic violence was relevant to his role as a law enforcement official—not that Fedders might actually condone violence or other lawbreaking on the job, but that his private conduct symbolically repudiated the specific values that an official in his position is sworn to uphold. Even smoking cigarettes in the privacy of one's home may be a legitimate target in the case of some public officials. Responding to stories in the press, William Bennett had to give up smoking when he was head of the Drug Enforcement Agency.

Reactions of the public

Private conduct may affect job performance not only because of what the officials themselves do but also because of the reactions of other people when they find out about the conduct. In the early days of the Clinton-Lewinsky scandal, many people said that although they themselves did not think the conduct was relevant to his performance, the expectation that other people, including foreign leaders, would have less confidence in him made it relevant. But we need to be careful about appealing to these kinds of reactive effects. The anticipated reaction of other people should almost never count as a sufficient reason to publicize further what would otherwise be private. The missing step in the argument—the factor that is so often ignored—is the assumption that the private conduct itself is morally wrong, and that therefore the anticipated reactions of other people are morally justified.

Why this step is essential can be seen more clearly if we consider cases of homosexuals in public office being outed. The fact that constituents will vote against their conservative congressman if they find out he is gay is surely not a reason for publicizing his sexual orientation. The mainstream press was right not to disclose the fact that the chief spokesman for the Pentagon during the Gulf War is gay, even though some opponents of the military's policy of excluding gays from the military sought to publicize the fact. If the congressman had actively opposed gay rights or if the Pentagon spokesman had prominently defended the military's policy, the press would have had a reason to expose their sexual orientation. But justification for the exposure should not be that these officials deserved to be punished for their hypocrisy or even that hypocrisy is in itself always inexcusable, but that their hypocrisy is serving a morally wrong cause.

There is an important qualification to the general rule that public reactions should not count as a reason for exposure unless the reactions are morally justified. If the official flagrantly and for no public purpose disregards moral sensitivities, in effect inviting scrutiny of private conduct that offends many people, the press may be justified in exposing it, whether or not it is in itself wrong. Perhaps the press should not spy on a prominent senator who goes off on a yacht for a rendezvous with his mistress, but when he declares himself a family man and dares the press to prove otherwise, the press has a reason (though not necessarily a sufficient reason) to expose his activities (Dowd 1998).

The senator is guilty of failing to take into account the reasonable reactions of citizens. Officials who behave in such ways display a form of the traditional vice of "giving scandal." In Thomist ethics, "giving scandal" is defined as providing the "occasion for another's fall" (Thomas Aquinas 1972, 109-137). In secular terms, we could say that a public official who fails to take into account the reasonable reactions of citizens fails to fulfill an important public duty, and citizens deserve to know about that failure. In his escapades with Monica Lewinsky, President Clinton was inter alia guilty of "giving scandal." Except for the issues of perjury and obstruction of justice, this ultimately may be the strongest justification for the press's treating his affair differently (in the early phase) from the more discreet relationships that Robert Dole and George Bush were alleged to have had.

If we invoke reactive effects when applying the relevance standard, we cannot escape making substantive moral judgments. Even when editors decide to disclose on the grounds that citizens themselves should decide whether the conduct is justifiable, they are in effect judging that the anticipated reactions are not bad enough to outweigh the value of informing citizens about the conduct. Once the story is out, the decision has been made. Without judging to what extent the reactions they are anticipating are justifiable, editors (and citizens more generally) will not be able to distinguish between outing a homosexual and exposing a wife beater.

Priority of process

The last criterion relates private conduct to other public issues. To what extent does knowing about this conduct help or hinder citizens' knowing about *other* matters they need to know to hold officials accountable? Even when private vices bear some relation to the duties of public office, public discussions of politicians' ethics have an unfortunate tendency to dwell on private conduct to the neglect of conduct more relevant to the office. Senator John Tower's drinking problem may have deserved some discussion during the hearings on his nomination to be secretary of defense, but it surely deserved less than his activities as a consultant for defense contractors (Babcock and Woodward 1989). Yet because of the public preoccupation with private immorality, citizens heard little about these financial dealings, which probably would have revealed much more about his record as a senator and his capacity to head the Department of Defense.

In the confirmation hearings of Clarence Thomas, the press, the public, and the Senate Judiciary Committee paid more attention to Clarence Thomas's relationship with Anita Hill than to his judicial qualifications. The Gresham effects are especially damaging when, as in this case, irreversible decisions are made under tight constraints of time, so that any distortions in the process of accountability cannot be corrected as they might be in the normal course of politics.

The Gresham effects go well beyond particular cases such as Clarence Thomas and Bill Clinton. The cumulative consequences of many cases, as they increase in number and prominence, create a pattern of press coverage that distorts our common practices of deliberation. Habits of discourse—the considerations we easily identify, the distinctions we readily make, the reasons we immediately accept—become better adapted to controversies about private than to public life. The more citizens hone their skills of deliberation on the finer points of sexual encounters (would he have really put her hand there?) the less they are prepared to develop their capacities to deliberate about the nuances of public policy (should he support this revision of social security?). Democratic deliberation gets into a rut—the rut of smut, it might be called. That is not the best place to develop the discourse of democratic accountability

Publicity about the private lives of public officials can damage the democratic process by distracting citizens from more important questions of policy and performance of government. When deciding whether to publicize what would otherwise be private conduct or when judging such decisions made by others, including the press and officials themselves, the key questions concern the effects on accountability. Is the conduct of a type about which citizens generally need to know in order to hold officials in this position accountable? If the conduct is relevant in this sense, is the degree of the publicity proportionate to the relevance? Are the character flaws revealed by the conduct closely and specifically connected to the office (are they political rather than only personal vices)? If negative public reaction to the conduct is part of the reason for publicizing it, is the reaction morally justified? Is the publicity about the conduct unlikely to distract citizens from paying attention to other political matters they need to know to hold officials accountable (will there be no Gresham effects)? If more citizens, journalists, and officials themselves would more often consider these questions seriously, and more regularly restrain their penchant for publicity when they cannot honestly answer them in the affirmative, we might notice some improvement in the quality of democratic discourse. In the meantime, we will remain hostage to the vagaries of the political version of Gresham's law.

Notes

1. For analysis of this principle as part of deliberative democracy, see Gutmann and Thompson 1996, 128-164. Also see the discussion of "publicity" at pp. 95-127. Accountability applies not only retrospectively but also prospectively. Citizens can hold an official accountable for what they reasonably predicted on the basis of what they learned about the official as a candidate for office.

2. Sixty-four percent of respondents in a February 1998 survey (Bennet 1998) said it is not important for the public to know "what the relationship was" between Clinton and Lewinsky. Distinguishing the relationship from legal testimony about it, 61 percent said it is important for the public to know whether Clinton encouraged Lewinsky to lie.

3. In a February 1998 Roper Center national survey, 80 percent of the respondents said they thought the media coverage of the Clinton-Lewinsky story was "excessive" (February 6, 1998). Sixty percent agreed with the more general proposition that the media have "gone too far in disclosing the details of Clinton's private life," while only 9 percent thought the media had not gone "far enough." Even before this scandal, 60 percent of respondents in May 1994 (Roper Center 1994) said that the news media pay too much attention to Clinton's private life. Since the 1980s there has been a steady and substantial increase in the number of people who say that the "increased attention being given to the private lives of public officials and candidates" is a "bad thing" (from 39 percent in 1989 to 47 percent in 1993) (Gallup Organization, June 1989; March 20, 1993).

4. A comparative content analysis (Payne and Mercuri 1993) of the press coverage of Gary Hart in the 1988 campaign and Bill Clinton in 1992 found that the stories of the affairs dominated the coverage of Hart's campaign but "did not fully eclipse" discussion of Clinton's stand on issues because the press "cast more doubt on the accuser, Gennifer Flowers, and the medium, *The Star*" (p. 298).

5. Norman Pearlstine, the *Wall Street Journal* editor, was more careful. For him, Fedders's public admission of guilt, not just the publicness of the proceedings, was essential.

6. About 53 percent of the respondents in a national survey in 1998 (Roper Center, February 23, 1998) in the aftermath of the Lewinsky publicity said that "when it comes to conduct in one's personal life," the president should be held to the same standard you hold yourself, while 44 percent said he should be held to a higher standard. An overwhelming majority, 84 percent, agree that "someone can still be a good President even if they do things in their personal life that you disapprove of."

References

This article draws on some of my previously published work: "Privacy, Politics, and the Press," *Harvard International Journal of Press/Politics* 3 (Fall 1998): 103-113; "Paradoxes of Government Ethics," *Public Administration Review* 52 (May-June 1992): 254-259; and *Ethics in Congress: From Individual to Institutional Corruption* (Washington, D.C.: Brookings Institution, 1995). For an earlier and more comprehensive discussion (written not only before Monica Lewinsky but even before Gary Hart), see "The Private Lives of Public Officials," in Joel Fleishman et al., eds., *Public Duties: The Moral Obligations of Government Officials* (Cambridge, Mass.: Harvard University Press, 1981), pp. 221-247; and a revised version in *Political Ethics and Public Office* (Cambridge, Mass.: Harvard University Press, 1987), pp. 123-147.

Babcock, C. R., and B. Woodward. 1989. "Tower: The Consultant as Advocate." *Washington Post*, February 13, Al, AlO.

Bennet, J., with J. Elder. 1998. "Despite Intern, President Stays in Good Graces." *New York Times*, February 24, Al, A16.

Congressional Ethics: History, Facts, and Controversy. 1992. Washington, D.C.: Congressional Quarterly.

Dowd, M. 1998. "Change of Hart." *New York Times*, March 22, Week in Review, 15.

Gallup Organization. June 1989. *Gallup, Newsweek* (Conducted June 1-2) [Public Opinion Online]. Storrs, Conn.: University of Connecticut.

Gallup Organization. March 20, 1993. *Gallup, Newsweek* (Conducted March 9-10) [Public Opinion On-line]. Storrs, Conn.: Roper Center University of Connecticut.

General Accounting Office. 1983. *Information on Selected Aspects of the Ethics in Government Act of 1978.* Washington, D.C.: U.S. Government Printing Office.

Gutmann, A., and D. Thompson. 1996. *Democracy and Disagreement* Cambridge, Mass. Harvard University Press.

Himmelfarb, G. 1998. "Private Lives, Public Morality." *New York Times*, February 9, A19.

Howe, M. A. D. 1932. Portrait of an Independent: Moorfield Storey, 1845-1929. Boston: Houghton Muffin.

Jackson, B. 1985. "John Fedders of SEC Is Pummeled by Legal and Personal Problems." *Wall Street Journal*, February 25, 1, 22.

Lardner, G., Jr. 1988. "Conduct Unbecoming an Administration." *Washington Post National Weekly Edition*, January 3, 31-32.

Payne, J. G., and K. Mercuri. 1993. "Private Lives, Public Officials: The Challenge to Mainstream Media." *American Behavioral Scientist* 37 (November): 291-301.

Roper Center for Survey Research and Analysis. May 1994. Princeton Survey Research Associates, *Newsweek* (Conducted May 6) [Public Opinion Online]. Storrs, Conn.: University of Connecticut.

———. February 6, 1998. *Clinton-Lewinsky News Coverage* (Conducted January 30-February 4) [Public Opinion Online]. Storrs, Conn.: University of Connecticut.

———. February 23, 1998. CBS News, *New York Times* (Conducted February 19-21) [Public Opinion Online]. Storrs, Conn.: University of Connecticut.

Scott, J. 1998. "Focus Turns Elsewhere in Newspapers and on TV" *New York Times*, February 4, Al9.

Senate Ethics Counsel. 1995. *The Packwood Report.* New York: Times Books.

Taylor, Stuart. 1985. "Life in the Spotlight: Agony of Getting Burned." *New York Times*, February 27, A16.

Thomas Aquinas. 1972. Question 43, "Scandal." In T. C. O'Brien, ed. and trans., *Virtues of Justice in the Human Community*, 35: 109-137. London: Blackfriars.

Public Cynicism

Manifestations and responses

Evan M. Berman

Widespread concern exists about public cynicism toward government.[1] Manifestations of this cynicism include pervasive beliefs that government policies and public officials are corrupt, inept, or out to take advantage of citizens. Such disillusionment causes alienation and disengagement and is therefore of key interest to public administration and processes of democratic governance. Yet little is written about the role of public administrators in shaping public attitudes, and much of what *is* written focuses on administrative processes for managing citizen involvement.[2]

This article provides a theory of citizen cynicism that is relevant to public administration. It also reports the results of a national survey among city managers and chief administrative officers (CAOs) about perceptions of public trust in local government and the efficacy of municipal efforts to increase it.

A theory of cynicism

Cynicism is discussed, in general terms, in the literatures of trust and social capital. Many authors argue that all human relations and exchanges (economic, political, and social) require the trust that promises will be honored and that individuals will not be taken advantage of.[3] Trust is seen as purposive—a lubricant of relations—and also as serving the emotional needs of individuals to belong. Cynicism is defined as low trust—specifically, as a pervasive "disbelief in the possibility of good" in dealing with others. Cynicism increases social distance and diminishes the public spirit.[4]

Cynical attitudes regarding government often concern the integrity, purpose, and effectiveness of government and its officials.[5] Ardently cynical beliefs are usually linked to ideological views that are highly critical of government—for example, "government is always out to get the ordinary citizen." Facts are used selectively to justify claims that "nothing ever changes" and that authorities use "smoke and mirrors" to appease and mis-

Adapted with permission from "Dealing with Citizens' Cynicism," *Public Administration Review* 57 (March/April 1997):105-112.

lead the masses. Milder expressions of cynicism are often characterized by beliefs that are less harsh about government (e.g., "government tries its best, but it just doesn't have the resources") or that give greater weight to facts (e.g., "government doesn't deliver on its promises: the roads are still not fixed"). Because of the greater role of facts, the latter form of cynicism may be more open to persuasion by reason.

Theories of human motivation and behavior suggest that citizens question their relationship with government and feel disenfranchised when they (1) believe that local government is using its power against them (or otherwise not helping them), (2) do not feel part of local government (e.g., they feel misunderstood or ignored), and (3) perceive local government services and policies to be ineffective. When these perceptions and feelings are mild (e.g., when citizens believe that "things aren't done because government doesn't care much about us"), mild forms of cynicism may develop. When these perceptions and feelings are strong (e.g., when citizens believe that government is plotting to exploit and brainwash them), citizens become ardently cynical and withdraw from government.

Analysis suggests that many people develop slightly *negative* orientations about their local governments. They regularly experience government using its power to tax them, charge fees and fines, and cater to special interests. Although citizens often do have positive encounters with agencies, such experiences are incidental and discounted as they do not reflect the full range of citizen contacts that shape public opinions about government power.[6] Thus, because citizens are often less informed about how government helps them through environmental programs, quality education, economic development planning, and so on, negative experiences of government power outweigh positive ones. Citizens also do not normally experience a sense of belonging to government; indeed, many seldom even think of it[7] and usually become aware of local government services only after they fail. Although many services do work, traffic congestion, overcrowded public schools, and a lack of public safety are often cited as evidence of government failure and incompetence. Widespread ideologies favoring privatization also suggest that government is an ineffective service producer. Moreover, citizens frequently discount positive outcomes that are viewed as legal entitlements or as being "due" them in exchange for payment of taxes. Thus, the psychology of citizen satisfaction is stacked against positive public attitudes.

This theory of cynicism suggests three sets of public administration strategies to reduce public cynicism.[8] The goal of the first set of strategies is to show that government uses its power to help citizens rather than to harm them. The above analysis suggests that many citizens are not aware of local government activities and of how these activities help further their own aims. The lack of such awareness reduces trust and suggests a need to reach out to citizens to explain what government does and how it serves the interests of "average" citizens—for example, via communication strategies that involve persistent, diverse, and consistent information campaigns such as mailings.

The second set of strategies aims to incorporate citizen input into public decision making. Traditional public hearings often fail to attract much citizen participation except in unusual, crisis-laden situations. Citizen surveys and panels are two alternative participation strategies.[9] Use of these strategies suggests that frequency and breadth of participation are important conditions, as are the communication and implementation of results and recommendations.

A third set of strategies aims to enhance the reputation of local government as being competent and efficient. Communication is necessary because citizens may be unable to evaluate the cost and quality of government services unless they are provided with information. In this regard, reputational strategies are not a panacea for poor performance; rather, good performance is the foundation of public communication.[10]

Findings

Current levels of cynicism A survey was conducted among city managers and CAOs to assess current levels of citizen cynicism.[11] The results in Table 1 show that, according to city managers, most citizens "agree" or "strongly agree" that services meet their needs (69.7 percent), that local government treats citizens fairly (63.0 percent), and that local government does not take advantage of citizens (59.8 percent). However, according to city managers, fewer citizens believe that local government is competent (56.1 percent), honest (46.3 percent), fulfills its promises (43.0 percent), understands citizen needs (41.6 percent), and can be trusted (41.5 percent). This latter rating reflects negative assessments across different concerns and is therefore lower than specific ratings.[12]

Table 1. Perceptions of citizen trust in local government.

	Percentage of cities responding
Citizens agree or strongly agree[a] that	
Government services meet citizen needs	69.7
Government treats citizens fairly	63.0
Government does not take advantage of citizens	59.8
Government is competent	56.1
Government officials are honest	46.3
Government fulfills its promises	43.0
Government understands citizen needs	41.6
Government can be trusted	41.5
Analysis[b]	
Mean response of "somewhat agree" or less	33.6
(Sub): Mean response of "somewhat disagree" or less	(8.3)
Mean response of between "somewhat agree" and "agree"	43.0
Mean response of "agree" or more	23.4
(Sub): Mean response of three or more "strongly agree" responses	(9.0)
Total	100.0

[a]Responses are based on a seven-point Likert scale, ranging from "strongly agree" to "strongly disagree."

[b]Analysis excludes the general item "government can be trusted." See text for discussion.

One-third of respondents (33.6 percent) have mean responses that fall within the range of "disagree" to "somewhat agree." Their cities are classified in this study as having "cynical" citizen attitudes. The low ratings imply problems of trust because, for example, a city that only "somewhat" meets citizen needs (or less) cannot be viewed as an effective partner in helping citizens to achieve their goals. About one-quarter of cynical cities (or 8.3 percent of all respondents) have average ratings of "somewhat disagree" or less. Citizen attitudes in these cities are considered ardently cynical. Interviews with respondents in ardently cynical cities corroborated the presence of dark attitudes. Specific concerns included the use of government power (e.g., a lack of consideration for minorities), a lack of openness in decision-making processes, a catering to special interests, and the ineffectiveness of local government to solve important community problems such as traffic congestion and crime.

Municipal strategies   Cities use a variety of strategies that affect citizen trust (Table 2). Although information strategies are widely used (group mean = 60.4 percent), the nature of information provided through these strategies varies. Only half of the cities explain how government meets citizen needs (57.1 percent) and the purpose, benefits, and results of taxes (55.1 percent). Even fewer explain how government fairly balances different community interests (34.8 percent). Cities also use a range of reputation strategies (group mean = 49.0 percent). Seeking awards of distinction (76.3 percent) and encouraging managers to make positive statements about the city (70.5 percent) are common. Half of the cities use media campaigns (50.4 percent), although follow-up interviews suggest that many of these campaigns are targeted toward businesses rather than citizens. Few cities respond to negative comments in the media (39.2 percent), and even fewer inform citizens of high ethical standards in municipal government (25.7 percent). Participation strategies are also widely used (group mean = 74.4 percent). Citizen participation through public hearings and open meeting policies is widespread (respectively, 97.5 percent and 94.7 percent), which reflects that such participation is often mandated by law. Other strategies are the use of citizen panels (73.4 percent), which some cities (e.g., Seattle, Washington) use as a principal strategy for engaging citizens at both city and neighborhood levels; citizen surveys (57.8 percent), which many cities (e.g., Memphis, Tennessee; Dallas, Texas; Palo Alto, California) now use to identify citizen preferences, some reporting these poll results and accomplishments through mailings; and voter referenda (50.0 percent).

Public attitudes are shaped by many factors, and it is no surprise that diverse and consistent efforts are needed. Indeed, individual strategies alone are not always associated with lower cynicism. It should be further noted that efforts to reduce cynicism are more effective in cities in which cynicism is high than in those in which high levels of public trust are already present. Thus, as recorded on Table 2, it is important for local governments to use a *range of strategies*. Interviews with respondents in cities with low levels of trust identify the use of public hearings, public-access broadcasts of council meetings, a few citizen advisory panels, annual reports, and sporadic surveys of citizen attitudes as important cynicism-reduction initiatives. By contrast, interviews and survey comments by respondents in "high-trust" cities identify the use of a much broader range of strategies; in addition to the "standard" strategies noted above, these cities use dozens of citizen tasks forces and focus groups, have strategies to respond immediately to citizen queries

Table 2. Municipal strategies in dealing with citizens.

	Use (%)	Association with cynicism[a]
All strategies	61.2	Yes
Two or more strategies from each group	68.9	Yes
Information		
Informing citizens of changes in rules and programs	82.3	No
Using mailings to explain what government does	72.5	Yes
Informing citizens about service performance	63.9	Yes
Using mailings to explain how government meets citizen needs	57.1	No
Using mailings to explain the purposes, benefits, and results of taxes	55.1	No
Using mailings to explain how government fairly balances different interests	34.8	Yes
Group mean	60.4	Yes
Participation		
Conducting public hearings	97.5	No
Adopting open meeting policies	94.7	No
Using citizen panels for controversial issues	73.4	Yes
Using surveys to elicit citizen preferences	57.8	No
Using voter referenda or ballots	50.0	Yes
Group mean	74.4	Yes
Reputation		
Seeking awards of national or regional distinction	76.3	No
Making positive statements	70.5	No
Using campaigns to portray a positive image	50.4	Yes
Responding to negative comments in the media	39.2	No
Demonstrating commitment to ethics through sanctions	32.2	No
Informing citizens regularly of high ethical standards in city	25.7	No
Group mean	49.0	No

[a]All associations are negative and significant at better than the 10 percent level. The associations of "all strategies" and "two or more strategies" with cynicism are significant at the 1 percent level.

and complaints, use surveys to identify citizen preferences (in addition to attitudes), meet regularly with neighborhood activists, prepare bimonthly newsletters, and consistently explain what government does and how it meets citizen needs. Some cities use more than 300 citizen panels and advisory boards, many of which arise from neighborhood activism, and these venues increase the dialogue between city hall and community leaders. In Arvada, Colorado, city officials schedule meetings with residents at their homes. These high-trust cities also often use various reputational strategies. Some have "pride" programs through which local governments increase community awareness among neighborhoods or targeted groups such as children. These and related efforts also help to balance the negative media coverage of local events.

Although performance awards have received much attention in recent years, respondents give mixed assessments regarding their value. In cities such as Phoenix, Glendale, and Scottsdale in Arizona, national and state awards for service excellence are seen as very positive. As one respondent noted, "Before, people did not even acknowledge that we did things like pick up trash until something went wrong. Now, the press gives the city more respect, the neighborhood associations know they are dealing with a competent entity...and people take pride that the city is moving in a positive direction." Respondents in other cities that have also won awards state that "awards are a nice pat on the back, but they have little effect on citizen attitudes.... It is an ongoing helpful attitude from city hall that the citizens value." Another respondent stated that "the thing of importance is having many citizen and neighborhood groups, openness, low crime, and pleasant parks, good services, etc." This ambivalent assessment is consistent with data in Table 2, which show that this strategy of touting awards is not significantly associated with decreasing public cynicism.[13]

Finally, this study also finds that the level of perceived cynicism is greatly affected by economic and social conditions. Well-educated populations and cities with above-average economic growth rates are less cynical toward government; conversely, cities with large poor populations are more cynical. Cities with low crime rates have less public cynicism, as do cities in which citizens take pride and have a historically strong interest in municipal affairs, and in which community groups cooperate well together. Cities where council persons and the media are cynical experience greater levels of public cynicism. These results, such as the association of low crime rates with increased trust, are robust even when controlling for the level of economic growth. Further analysis shows that the efficacy of using a broad range of strategies is also robust even when controlling for these social and economic conditions.

Discussion

Democracy requires a degree of trust that we often take for granted.[14] In this regard, the continuing slide of citizen trust suggests that new approaches are needed to restore public confidence. To this end, manifestations of cynicism should be understood not only as poll statistics, misplaced understandings, or the result of systemic or isolated ethical wrongdoing; rather, as this article suggests, cynicism and trust are deeply rooted in the management of government-citizen relations. That is, public administration matters. To restore trust, citizens must increase their commitment to the purpose of government. Specifically, they must believe that government serves their needs, that they can affect decision making, and that government is able to deliver. Public administration affects these outcomes:

cities that use a number of information, participation, and reputation strategies experience less cynicism, even where there is a broad range of community conditions.

This study finds that cynicism is present in about one-third of all cities with populations above 50,000, and that about one-quarter of these cities have widespread ardently cynical attitudes. Thus, although cynicism about local government is not ubiquitous, it is common. Managers who seek to affect the level of trust might begin by considering how the communications that citizens receive about their agencies and jurisdictions affect their attitudes. In this regard, what do citizens know and believe about the performance and relevance of municipal services? Managers might then use the measures of cynicism reported in Table 1 as an instrument for assessing citizen attitudes in their own jurisdictions. Such surveys provide further evidence for administrators' perceptions, can be linked to local conditions, and identify citizen preferences for information and participation strategies. The strategies reported in Table 2 provide a benchmark of such efforts. Consideration of the latter will lead some jurisdictions to broaden and enhance their efforts, and to develop multifaceted and durable strategies.

This study advances cynicism as a phenomenon that is linked to unsatisfied citizen needs. However, much further research is needed on the subjects of trust and social capital in public administration. Specifically, careful case studies are needed of jurisdictions or agencies that have turned around negative public attitudes. Detailed attention must be paid to the strategies, contexts, and actors' abilities. For example, the role of culture is much understudied as a cause of cynicism, as a barrier to developing anticynicism strategies, and as a self-corrective mechanism against ardent cynicism. The efficacy of different strategies might also be examined in greater detail, focusing, for example, on the psychology of citizen perceptions and on the impact of strategies on the formation of social capital in communities in general. Finally, in public administration, it is often assumed that managers who seek to serve the public interest also develop the skills to ensure trust. It would be useful to know how public administrators perceive their tasks of increasing trust and dealing with cynicism. A role also exists in public administration education to ensure that students have adequate skills and perspectives in this area.

Undoubtedly, in many public settings, greater efforts must be made to combat cynicism. As this study suggests, ensuring the public trust is not a simple task: a broad range of strategies is needed. The time has come to ensure that agencies receive the public support that they deserve.

Notes

1. Gore, Al, 1994. "Cynicism or Faith," *Vital Speeches*, October 1995, 645-649; Dubnick, Mel, and David Rosenbloom, 1995. "Oklahoma City," *Public Administration Review* 55 (September/October):405-406; Greider, William, 1992. *Who Will Tell the People: The Betrayal of American Democracy*. New York, NY: Simon and Schuster; Lipset, Seymour M., and William Schneider, 1987. *The Confidence Gap: Business, Labor and Government in the Public Mind*. Baltimore, MD: The Johns Hopkins University Press; Cisneros, Henry G., and John Parr, 1990. "Reinvigorating Democratic Values: Challenge and Necessity," *National Civic Review* 79 (September/October):408-413.

2. Frederickson, H. George, 1991. "Toward a Theory of the Public for Public Administration," *Administration & Society* 22 (February):395-417; Luton, Larry S., 1993. "Citizen-Administrator Connections," *Administration & Society* 25 (May):114-134; Stivers, Camilla, 1994. "The Listening Bureaucrat: Responsiveness in Public Administration," *Public Administration Review* 54 (July-August):364-369; Box, Richard C., 1992. "The Administrator as Trustee of the Public Interest," *Administration & Society* 24 (November):323-345.

3. Coleman, James S., 1990. *Foundations of Social Theory*. Cambridge, MA: The Belknap Press; Putnam, Robert D., 1993. *Making Democracy Work*. Princeton, NJ: Princeton University Press; Mansbridge, Jane J., ed., 1990. *Beyond Self-Interest*. Chicago, IL: University of Chicago Press.

4. Merton, Robert K., 1957. *Social Theory and Social Structure*. Glencoe, NY: Free Press; Barber, Benjamin, 1983. *The Logic and Limits of Trust*. New Brunswick, NJ: Rutgers University Press. The origin of the word *cynicism* is *canine* or dog. The Greek school of Cynicism believed that to find happiness, people must train their minds to want nothing and, hence, live like dogs. Cynics abandoned most earthly desires and social conventions. The present definition of cynicism shares the belief that the world is a bad place, but it does not adopt the ascetic lifestyle.

5. Starobin, Paul, 1995. "A Generation of Vipers: Journalists and the New Cynicism," *Columbia Journalism Review* 33 (March/April):25-33; Durant, Robert F., 1995. "The Democratic Deficit in America," paper presented at the 56th Annual Research Conference of the American Society for Public Administration, San Antonio, July 22-26.

6. Goodsell, Charles, 1994. *The Case for Bureaucracy*, 3rd ed. Chatham, NJ: Chatham House Publishers.

7. Respondents illustrated this point in various ways. One city manager stated: "Well, there are always folks who don't know in what city they live, but most of the informed ones seem pleased." Another city manager noted: "Most people just aren't interested. After a hard day of work, most people just want to be entertained and many city issues just aren't that exciting. It is hard to compete with *NYPD Blue*."

8. By attempting to reduce the level of citizen cynicism, this study does not imply that cynicism is undesirable; for example, the notion of checks and balances is built around distrust. The present concern is that the level of cynicism is too high. It is unlikely that efforts to reduce cynicism will result in too little cynicism.

9. Giancoli, Donald, 1993. "Citizen Survey Use in Lauderhill, Florida," paper presented at the Southeastern Conference on Public Administration (SECOPA), Cocoa Beach, Florida, October; Glaser, Mark A., and James W. Bardo, 1994. "A Five Stage Approach for Improved Use of Citizen Surveys in Public Investment Decisions," *State and Local Government Review* 26 (Fall):161-172; Bacot, Hunter, Amy S. McCabe, Michael R. Fitzgerald, Terry Bowen, and David H. Folz, 1993. "Practicing the Politics of Inclusion: Citizen Surveys and the Design of Solid Waste Recycling Programs," *American Review of Public Administration* 23 (no.1):29-41.

10. The position adopted here is that advertisement should be informative, not misleading or deceitful. Concerns about government marketing are usually allayed by solely reporting factual data.

11. The survey was sent to all 502 city managers and CAOs in cities with populations above 50,000. A total of 302 useable responses was received (response rate = 62%).

12. These results were compared against the results of other national polls of citizens and found to be consistent with the direct assessments of citizens (ABC/*Washington Post*, January 1990, poll of 1518 citizens; *Changing Public Attitudes on Government and Taxes*, 1993. Washington, DC: Advisory Commission on Intergovernmental Relations; National Opinion Research Center, 1987. *General Social Survey*. Storrs, CT: Roper; Gallup, 1995, monthly poll of citizen attitudes). Table 1 shows that more respondents meet citizen needs than understand citizen needs. This may suggest that although citizens perceive services to be effective, other needs are unaddressed. This analysis also shows the dangers of relying on broad measures of trust.

13. It should be noted, however, that the composite measure of reputation is not associated with cynicism. Two possible explanations are that these efforts are not yet fully developed and that they are targeted at a business audience.

14. Bellah, Robert N., Richard Madsen, William M. Sullivan, Ann Swidler, and Steven M. Tipton, 1991. *The Good Society*. New York, NY: Vintage Press.

Current Ethics Issues for Local Government Managers

Elizabeth K. Kellar

Soon after the first city managers formed the International City/County Management Association (ICMA) in 1914, they felt the need to articulate the standards that communities should expect from them. When they adopted their first code of ethics in 1924, its 12 tenets addressed their aspirations as well as the conduct that was expected.

What ethical issues are ICMA members addressing in the 21st Century? At the top of the list are political activity and issue advocacy. Local government managers have felt a greater obligation to become advocates for their communities as budget pressures increase and governance by initiative grows in some states.

Societal pressures have raised more ethical questions: two-career families, employment matters, private-sector relationships, gifts, and fund-raising expectations. Issues related to workplace diversity also demanded attention.

Some of these issues have led to changes in the guidelines for the ICMA Code of Ethics, while others are part of an ongoing conversation among local government professionals. Against a backdrop of high-profile corporate and government ethical lapses, ICMA members also are giving more attention to the importance of their leadership role in promoting an ethical culture in their organizations.

Political neutrality at the core

A defining element of the city and county management profession is political neutrality. This professional image is so important to the profession that the ICMA Code of Ethics directs members to avoid all political activities that could undermine public confidence in professional administrators. Activities that are specifically cited in the ICMA Code of Ethics as problematic include running for office or supporting any candidate for government office.

After the ICMA Executive Board dealt with troubling cases in the late 1990s involving city managers who were censured for endorsing candidates for office, criticizing certain elected officials in public, running for office, and making contributions to the mayor's legal defense fund, the Board launched a major education effort with the membership. It culminated with a proposed revision to Tenet 7, which was overwhelmingly adopted by the membership in 1998. Despite these efforts, ICMA continued to receive complaints and to hear excuses from the membership that it was not clear what was expected. The Board adopted new guidelines in 2000 to make it explicit that certain political activities are not allowed:

Running for office   *Members shall not run for elected office or become involved in political activities related to running for elected office. They shall not seek political endorsements, financial contributions or engage in other campaign activities.*

Elections   *Members share with their fellow citizens the right and responsibility to vote and to voice their opinion on public issues. However, in order not to impair their effectiveness on behalf of the local governments they serve, they shall not participate in political activities to support the candidacy of individuals running for any city, county, special district, school, state or federal offices. Specifically, they shall not endorse candidates, make financial contributions, sign or circulate petitions, or participate in fund-raising activities for individuals seeking or holding elected office.*

The guidelines were not universally embraced, though most members agreed that the professional standard must be as high as it was in 1924, when one of the tenets read, "No city manager should take an active role in politics." A few members quarreled that they would like to serve on a school board or in other minor elected positions outside of the community they serve as an appointed administrator. Their pleas for exceptions did not prevail. The ICMA Executive Board determined that it was better to have a clear standard than to try to create an exception for certain elected offices.

In Massachusetts, however, some local government managers felt so strongly about the value of running for certain local offices (outside of the jurisdiction that they serve), that they persuaded their state association to break from its tradition to follow the ICMA Code of Ethics in its entirety. The state association adopted a new guideline for the Massachusetts Municipal Management Association (MMMA) Code of Ethics that permits service in a minor elected office as long as it complies with MMMA policy. MMMA policy requires that before running for elected office, the MMMA member obtain approval from his or her employing governing body and consult with the appointed administrator in the jurisdiction where the MMMA member plans to run for office.

Some members expressed concern that the ICMA guidelines are so strong that they should have been incorporated into a tenet and submitted to a vote of the membership. A few individuals said they would prefer that members be permitted to campaign for political candidates *except* those candidates who run for the governing body the member serves.

But most city and county managers went along with the restrictions and supported them without any hesitation. As one ICMA member noted, "I can accept the second class citizenship because of my profession. I understand the need for objectivity." The prevailing view is that the cornerstone of the profession is political neutrality. City and county managers choose to avoid engaging in these election activities because they recognize that neutrality is at the core of their reputation for fairness and impartiality.

Revenue pressures lead to high-profile advocacy

While city and county managers reaffirmed the need to avoid political activities involving candidates, they have become more assertive about other political activities, particularly in states where local revenues have been restricted or raided by higher levels of government.

California has become the poster state for the problems associated with government by initiatives, but it also became the testing ground for an initiative *promoted* by local governments. After enduring years of frustration because the state government had taken local government revenues away, California cities and counties formed a political action committee and persuaded voters to approve a state constitutional amendment (Proposition 1A) in 2004 that they hope will restore predictability and certainty to local government revenues.

Rod Gould, at the time city manager in San Rafael, and former president of the City Managers' Department of the League of California Cities, said that local governments had to resort to the initiative process to restore balance. "Because cities can neither endorse candidates nor provide campaign donations, we are comparative small fry in the sea of interest groups with influence in Sacramento. The initiative process offered cities and counties a way around the legislature directly to the people of California."[1]

Some managers worried that the local government profession would get tarred as too political with high profile advocacy. Fortunately, that did not happen. Tom Mauk, Orange County chief executive officer and former chair of the ICMA Committee on Professional Conduct, attributes the positive outcome to the work that managers did in raising ethical issues before moving into action.

Chris McKenzie, executive director of the League of California Cities (LCC), agrees. The LCC worked with ICMA to develop ethics advice that was tailored to California law and made sure that it was broadly publicized. The advice reminded local government managers that they may not use public materials, equipment, or time to support any ballot measure, even when it is unanimously supported by the governing body.

The advice included an explanation of what an appropriate role would be for an ICMA member with regard to the proposed statewide initiative:

> Tenet 7 deals with political activities, and a guideline on "Presentation of Issues" is the most relevant to this question: "Members may assist the governing body in presenting issues involved in referenda such as bond issues, annexations, and similar matters." In this situation, the League of California Cities has adopted an official position in support of the statewide initiative, and it is appropriate for ICMA members to support those positions when their governing bodies have taken a position supporting the LCC policy. California law allows public resources to be used to objectively evaluate a ballot measure's impact on the city. The results of a fair and impartial analysis may then be made available to the newspapers, advocacy groups, and others who may make use of the information they choose. Public funds may only be used for materials that are strictly informational and not for those that expressly advocate a position.

ICMA Executive Director Bob O'Neill has said that the implications of Proposition 1A are huge. "The real question is how managers can influence decisions in an environment that increasingly is shaped by initiatives. City and county managers can no longer go to the state legislature and make arguments just on the basis of facts. They are looking for a way to have a voice again while taking care not to injure the profession."[2]

As revenue pressures and constraints grow in many other states, local government managers see a growing responsibility to provide leadership in the advocacy area on behalf of their local governments. They take on this responsibility with care, sharing concerns with each other and seeking advice on what is ethical and what is not so that they can maintain their professional reputation and image.

Raising revenues from the private sector

Closely related to managers' expanding role in political advocacy is the pressure they face to raise revenues from private sources on behalf of the community or for professional development events.

Tenet 12 of the ICMA Code of Ethics focuses on the importance of avoiding any impression that a company might believe that it will receive a favor from the manager in exchange for a gift. The guideline on gifts reminds members not to directly or indirectly solicit or accept any gift if it might appear that the gift is intended to be a reward or to influence them in their official duties. The advice on gifts does not answer all of the questions members have today about their role in fund-raising for causes, events, or community activities.

In June 2006, the ICMA Committee on Professional Conduct examined some of the fund-raising questions that had come to its attention and agreed that certain ethical principles should guide local government managers as they consider how to handle the fund-raising expectations that come with their jobs:

- Transparency: Openly disclose the manager's role and activities to the public. Report the amount and sources of contributions regularly.

- Support from the governing body: Whenever city or county managers are expected to raise money on behalf of the community, they should seek a resolution from the governing body that endorses the cause.

- Purpose: The public, professional, or community benefit should be clear.

Beyond these core principles, ICMA members are advised to inform themselves of any laws or local rules that may restrict their role or actions and to avoid any appearance of a conflict of interest. For example, ICMA advises members not to solicit funds from any organization that might come before the local government to request funding or some other consideration. There also may be ways that the local government manager can be effective without making direct solicitations, such as providing advice on fund-raising strategies to others. The Society of Local Authority Chief Executives in the United Kingdom recommends that SOLACE members limit their role to that of an advisor and rely on a fund-raising committee of individuals with broad community representation to handle direct solicitations.

In the advice that ICMA and the League of California Cities prepared to help local government managers avoid ethical missteps in advocating for Proposition 1A, the issue of soliciting funds from employees garnered special attention. Local government managers were reminded that under California law and the ICMA Code of Ethics local officials may not directly or indirectly solicit campaign contributions from other local officials or employees in their city or county unless it is part of a general effort that incidentally includes local officials and employees. City and county managers are advised to avoid any impression that employees are being coerced into making contributions for a particular purpose. At the same time, if local government policy permits payroll deductions, it is appropriate for managers or others to make presentations about a new option to support a cause.[3]

ICMA members are reminded to be careful that their enthusiasm for a ballot measure or cause not be interpreted as putting pressure on employees to make a donation. When employees make financial contributions to a cause that is supported by the local government, the donation should be by check, bank draft, or payroll deduction.

Raising funds for conferences and professional development activities is another expectation for local government managers who seek ways to reduce event costs. While the ICMA staff do much of the fund-raising for the ICMA Conference, local host committees also raise significant funds to enhance the quality of the conference and to reduce costs. Some host committees hire someone to solicit financial contributions, while others ask managers to take on the responsibility personally.

When the Minneapolis Host Committee sought to raise funds for the 2005 ICMA Conference, they organized a fund-raising committee and provided guidelines for making contacts with potential contributors. If a city manager felt it was appropriate, she or he would make an initial contact with a company in the community to encourage that company to meet with someone from the fund-raising committee.

In general, ICMA members are advised not to solicit funds if they feel uncomfortable about it or if a specific issue involving that business will be coming before the local government for action or a decision.

The trend to build stronger relations with the private sector has caused some local government managers to cross an ethical line in offering endorsements, which are prohibited for commercial products.

There have been some discussions about the manager's role in economic development, particularly when an enthusiastic manager crosses into a neighboring jurisdiction to put out the welcome mat for businesses that might want to relocate. While not expressly prohibited by the ICMA Code of Ethics, this competitive behavior runs afoul of the collegial behavior that is part of the professional tradition. Managers expect a phone call from a colleague before hearing about the colleague's activities in their jurisdiction. By having a conversation with colleagues, they say, they might develop a more productive solution, such as a regional strategy for economic development.

■ Employment and job commitment

Personal financial concerns, family considerations, and the changing composition of the governing board are key factors in a manager's decision to accept a job or to look for greener pastures. The manager's credibility with the governing board begins the day the manager agrees to accept that position. Unfortunately, a few managers have not honored that commitment, and their behavior has been a concern to the profession.

From 2002 to 2006, ICMA investigated 15 complaints involving members who left their positions in less than two years. Seven cases were closed because the reasons for the short tenures were due to severe personal problems, illness, or a failure on the part of the employer to honor commitments made to the manager. Eight members received private censures. Most cases involved members who left after serving 10-15 months to accept another position. Two city managers cited difficult political climates as the reason for leaving their positions. The Committee on Professional Conduct advised both members that they had a professional obligation to keep their commitment and to do the hard work required to improve the organization.[4]

Cases that have drawn a public censure have more dramatic facts, such as the city manager who disappeared after he told the city council he was taking a vacation. He later was found to have accepted a higher paying job in another state.

ICMA advises its members that once they accept an offer of employment, they should honor that commitment. ICMA's Code of Ethics stipulates that "oral acceptance of an employment offer is considered binding unless the employer makes fundamental changes in terms of employment." They also are advised that a two-year commitment to the job "generally is considered necessary in order to render a professional service to the local government."

In recent years the Committee on Professional Conduct (CPC) considered whether or not assistant city or county managers have the same obligation to serve a minimum of two years in their position before they move on. The CPC concluded that all members are expected to meet the same standard, including assistants and department directors. One assistant county manager was privately censured for leaving a position after serving a few months to accept a manager position in another community.

At the same time, the CPC agreed that there are exceptions to this guideline. For example, it is appropriate for an ICMA member who has lost his or her job to serve in a job for less than two years if the member has that understanding with the city or county manager who hires them. The local government benefits from having a seasoned manager in an interim assignment and there is a mutual understanding. Local government managers may have similar agreements with assistants who are candid with their bosses about their desire to seek advancement if the right job comes along in less than two years. The CPC found there was no violation of the ICMA Code of Ethics regarding an assistant manager who accepted a manager position, because the assistant had an agreement with the city manager that the tenure might be short.

When members are seeking jobs they can run afoul of the ICMA Code of Ethics, too. To avoid making mistakes in the job-hunting process, ICMA offers these tips:

- Investigate the position and the local political environment and verify that the job is vacant. If the incumbent has not been notified that his or her services are no longer desired, ICMA members may not be candidates. Find out when council elections are held. Some managers accept a position only to discover that the majority that hired them must stand for election in less than a year's time.

- Engage in serious conversations with family members about the community, making sure that it will be a good place for them and fully understanding their feelings about moving.

- Consider all of the factors that are important to salary negotiations, including the cost of housing. Determine which provisions are essential to an employment agreement, including understandings of compensation, severance pay, and benefits, and review the document carefully.[5]

The professional standard is high because the local government management profession is rooted firmly in the reform movement of the early 1900s. From the beginning, city managers have been "dedicated to the highest ideals of honor and integrity." It does not matter whether the acceptance of employment is based on a handshake or a formal employment agreement. The manager's word is what counts.

Personnel and diversity issues

The ICMA Workplace Diversity Task Force made recommendations to the ICMA Executive Board in 2001 to amend the ICMA Code of Ethics to strengthen the profession's commitment to diversity goals in employment practices. In 2004, after giving the issue careful consideration, the ICMA Committee on Professional Conduct (CPC) recommended that ICMA make no changes in Tenet 11 because its broad language is inclusive: "Handle all matters of personnel on the basis of merit so that fairness and impartiality govern a member's decisions pertaining to appointments, pay adjustments, promotions, and discipline."

At the same time, the CPC concluded that changes were needed in the guideline on equal opportunity, which had not been updated since it was created in 1972. The CPC recommended three changes:

1. Replace the term "physical handicap" with "disability" to reflect modern language and sensitivities.

2. Add "sexual orientation" to the list of characteristics of individuals who should be protected from discrimination.

3. Replace the reference to recruiting and hiring "women and minorities" with the phrase "diverse staff."

The new guideline that the ICMA Executive Board adopted in 2004 is shorter and broader than the original 1972 version:

Equal opportunity   *All decisions pertaining to appointments, pay adjustments, promotions, and discipline should prohibit discrimination because of race, color, religion, sex, national origin, sexual orientation, political affiliation, disability, age, or marital status.*

It should be the members' personal and professional responsibility to actively recruit and hire a diverse staff throughout their organizations.

There was a flurry of reactions when ICMA publicized the new guideline, much of it complimentary: "My deepest appreciation and respect go out to...ICMA...for renewing our profession's commitment to equal opportunity and true diversity in our organizations. I have never been more proud than right now to call myself a member of ICMA."

However, other members expressed concerns or misunderstood the intent of the new guideline: "We would all be better served by remaining neutral on this issue [sexual orientation]....Everyone knows what happens when you step out on a slippery slope...you fall and slide to the bottom."

Just as some members felt that political activity guidelines were so strong that they should have been proposed as a Tenet and voted on by the membership, some suggested the need for more membership engagement in considering a new equal opportunity guideline: "The tenets, but not the guidelines, require the approval of the membership. In cases such as this, where the guidelines might appear to have been used to promote a particular social agenda, it is especially important that the entire membership be made part of the decision making process."

In North Carolina, the state leadership took steps to put the new guideline into perspective in its state association newsletter:

> The confusion and questions about this change have focused on the addition of "sexual orientation" to the list of categories upon which discrimination is to be prohibited. Upon hearing of these concerns and discussing it with the North Carolina City and County Association board, President Ed Kitchen, Greensboro city manager, made inquiries to ICMA for clarification. Based on these inquiries it is clear that neither the ICMA Executive Board nor the Committee on Professional Conduct intended for the revised guideline to imply an affirmative duty to recruit, employ, or promote gays or lesbians. Instead, the intention was to prohibit and discourage discrimination based on . . . sexual orientation.[6]

Building an ethical culture

Tenet 8 of the ICMA Code of Ethics focuses on the member's duty to develop the competence of the organization as well as the member's personal competence. City and county managers have been attentive to gaining personal knowledge and understanding of ethical issues. They attend ethics workshops at state and national conferences, and readership surveys show that ICMA's ethics column in *Public Management* magazine is one of its most popular features.

Although ICMA makes ethics training materials available to local governments, and has an electronic library of ethics laws, procedures, and practices on its Web site, increasingly ICMA members see the need to do more to promote an ethical culture. When ICMA conducted an on-line survey of its members in January 2005, 86% of the 692 respondents said they were interested in ethics training or technical assistance for their local governments. Ethics training for elected officials was an area of high interest (453), followed by training for all staff (417) and boards and commissions (323).

To respond to this growing interest, ICMA has expanded its training and peer assistance services for local governments. The core values in ICMA's training programs are Equity, Transparency, Honor, Integrity, Commitment, and Stewardship.

Equity, for example, is a core principle in the ICMA Code of Ethics. Tenet 4 reminds members to "Recognize that the chief function of local government at all times is to serve the best interests of all of the people." It is critical for effective service delivery and important to achieving social justice. Local government managers frequently address equity issues when they examine the needs of particular neighborhoods. In a neighborhood with a high concentration of poverty, it is often necessary to invest more public resources in such programs as early childhood education, childhood immunizations, and after-school tutoring.

Many local government managers take pride in their work with elected leadership to address equity needs in the community. One city manager spoke of the investment that his city made in youth services over time. He, along with the elected and staff leadership, was able to sustain support for the investment by telling stories about the young people who benefited from the city's recreation services.

The value of equity is also imbedded in a guideline for Tenet 7, which exhorts ICMA members to maintain a reputation for serving all members of the governing body equally and impartially. City managers have been censured by ICMA for criticizing one group of elected officials from a particular political party, or for writing letters to the editor criticizing an individual elected official, such as the mayor. What ICMA stresses in its training is the ethical value of serving all of the people in the community while carrying out the employee's responsibilities.

Transparency is another value rooted in the ICMA Code of Ethics. A guideline for Tenet 10 reminds members of the importance of openly sharing information. Accurate financial reporting and open processes for procurement, hiring, and contracting are critical to building trust. Going beyond the legal requirements for transparency is expected in an ethical culture. The higher standard of transparency requires disclosure of any personal relationship or financial matter that could create the appearance of a conflict of interest, found in guidelines for Tenet 12.

Transparency and trust are strengthened by civic engagement with the local government. Local governments that are attentive to civic engagement do more than hold a public hearing on the budget. For example, they create opportunities for dialogue with residents about community priorities in advance of preparing the budget. Some communities open up opportunities for community groups to make decisions when all stakeholders are at the table. Local governments that are leaders in ICMA's Center for Performance Measurement give feedback to the community on financial and performance results and benchmark their services with similar communities.

Enforcement trends and ethical questions

By joining the association, a member subscribes to the ICMA Code of Ethics. The code is enforced by the ICMA Executive Board and its Committee on Professional Conduct, which receives and investigates complaints, determines whether or not a violation has occurred, and levies or recommends sanctions. The ICMA Code of Ethics remains at the center of many of the debates that engage the profession.

The number of ethics cases ICMA receives each year is now 10-20, a somewhat lower figure than 10 years ago. In 2005 ICMA investigated complaints involving the endorsement of a commercial product, running for elected executive while serving as an appointed administrator, short job tenures, lying about credentials, steering business to a friend, and endorsing a political candidate. The most outrageous conduct that received a public censure and a membership bar involved a city manager who misused the city credit card, lied about his criminal background, and awarded himself 100 hours of overtime pay.

Perhaps one reason the number of cases has declined is because more members are seeking advice when they are unsure whether an action might be viewed as unethical. The majority of the calls are handled by ICMA's two ethics advisors in Washington, DC. In addition, members are encouraged to seek advice from ICMA's West Coast Director, senior advisors, range riders, state leadership, and Executive Board members.

The calls mirror situations that sometimes can lead to an ethics complaint. However, many callers seek advice on how to avoid any appearance of a conflict of interest. One town manager called to discuss his wife's work in advertising. She often donates her time to civic functions for the town. When the county government sought her professional services for a promotional activity, she said she would prefer to donate her services, rather than be paid. The town manager wondered if there could be complaints that she was volunteering her services only as a way to get future paid work. ICMA's ethics advice was that there was no problem with his wife's volunteer work. As long as the town manager is comfortable answering media questions about it, there probably will be no political issues, either.

ICMA members often ask for advice on political activity (e.g., running for office after retirement, which is allowed), investments (including home purchases), sensitive issues related to economic development, how to deal with personal attacks from an elected official, whether or not a social relationship might create the appearance of a conflict of interest, unusual procurement matters, and how to support ballot measures or other local causes in an ethical fashion.

The inquiries are often subtle. One chief administrative officer wanted to know if he had an ethical obligation to disclose his plans to leave the city when interviewing candidates for a department director vacancy. ICMA's ethics advice was that he was under no obligation to disclose his plans to a new hire since he was in the preliminary stages of his job search. If he were in the final negotiations for a position or had accepted a position, ICMA would advise him to disclose that.

ICMA members also grapple with dueling loyalties. One member called to say that a representative for Super Wal-Mart had told him confidentially of the store's plans to locate in his community. Ordinarily the city manager would inform everyone who serves on the economic development authority of such a possibility. However, one of the members of the authority has a business in the city that would be directly affected if a Super Wal-Mart were built. ICMA's advice was that the city manager should disclose this information to the appropriate governing authorities. By giving all of the appropriate officials this information, the manager puts them in a better position to guide the city in developing an appropriate strategy and response.

Sometimes an ethics question comes from an individual who is not an ICMA member. These individuals usually want to know if the facts as they describe them would be a violation of the ICMA Code of Ethics. ICMA explains how to file an ethics complaint, but does not offer an opinion about whether or not someone might have violated the ICMA Code of Ethics.

Each month ICMA publishes some of its ethics advice in *Public Management* magazine. The articles then are retained on ICMA's Web site, coded by topic. The questions, along with other ethical issues that come to ICMA's attention, help inform the ethics training that ICMA provides to members and to local governments.

City and county managers are more focused today on bringing ethical habits into their organizations. Because ICMA members have learned that there is value in asking others for advice when they are unsure, they can help create a climate in their organizations that encourages ethical conversations and behaviors.

Often the members who ask ICMA for ethics advice are not asking what they need to do to meet the letter of the law but rather how they can conduct themselves so that there will never be any question of even an appearance of wrongdoing.

The ICMA Code of Ethics is central to how city and county managers define their profession. They have become more comfortable in discussing ethical issues and in reaching out to others for advice. This profession, now almost 100 years old, carries its good government roots comfortably into the 21st Century.

Notes

1. Kellar, Elizabeth, "California Pushes the Envelope on Advocacy," *Public Management*, October 2005, p. 4.

2. Ibid, p. 7.

3. "Advice for ICMA Members on Involvement with Ballot Measure Campaigns," http://icma.org, 2003.

4. "ICMA Committee on Professional Conduct: Short Tenure Issues for the Profession," *ICMA Newsletter*, February 6, 2006, p. 11.

5. "Hitting the Interview Jackpot," *Public Management*, September 2005, p. 2.

6. "Guideline change for Tenet 11," *The Administrator*, North Carolina City and County Management Association, November 2004, Issue 9.

Appendix A: Ethics Cases

The following cases examine ethical dilemmas facing individuals in local government positions. In five of the six cases, the individual is a professional manager bound by the ICMA Code of Ethics. In the sixth, he is a county employee subject to county ethics laws. Each case includes a scenario, the various perspectives of the players involved in the case, a discussion of the ethical principles involved, and a series of questions for discussion. The cases are intended to help readers apply theoretical principles to real-world situations.

◼ Case 1: Go Along to Get Along

Elizabeth K. Kellar

Scenario

Unions are a fact of life in this city, and elected officials rarely win office without union support. Fortunately, the mayor in this council-manager government is a sophisticated business owner who offers good counsel to staff on a variety of issues. This is an election year and it coincides with the public safety union negotiations. The assistant city manager had responsibility for handling the negotiations and she feels good about the three-year deal, especially since the budget impact next year will be modest. While the unions had pressed for 5% wage increases for each of the next three years, she held them to a 3% increase in year one, 4% increase in year two, and 5% increase in year three. To get the wage concession, she went along with more generous pension terms than the city had wanted. The union won an additional 2% contribution to the city-funded pension plan beginning in the second year of the contract. In addition, the minimum years required to retire with a full pension will be reduced from 25 years of service to 20 years, a trend in the state.

The assistant city manager and city manager agree that this is a necessary concession to attract and retain quality law enforcement personnel, especially in the post-September 11 environment with strong public sentiment favoring generous compensation for first responders. They brief the mayor, requesting that she keep the terms confidential until the contract goes to the city council for approval. The mayor agrees that it is the best deal the city can expect to negotiate. To gain council support quickly, she suggests that staff play up the financial benefit in the first year, which guarantees no property tax increases for next year. Since most of the city council lacks business experience, she further advises staff not to go into too many details. She suggests that staff not provide a detailed analysis of the out-year costs since they are speculative: "We can't predict how many of our senior public safety personnel will opt for the early retirement."

As the mayor predicted, the city council approves the contract with little debate in early September. The council chambers are packed with uniformed police and fire personnel that night. With council elections in November, the union deal becomes a campaign issue in October. The mayor's opponent has charged that the mayor, city manager, and assistant city manager conspired to push through a contract that "mortgages the city's future."

Perspective: the city manager

"Staff disclosed the terms of the contract to the full city council and it was the council's decision to support those terms, knowing that there were more costs for the city in the out years. I don't like the fact that public safety unions are able to play hard ball in these times, but we can't afford to be out of step with other local government wage and benefit packages."

Perspective: the mayor's opponent

"This is a good example of why we should change the form of government in this city. Somebody has to be accountable for the fiscal fiascos. We will have to close libraries and recreation centers to pay for this sweetheart deal. It's not fair to our children or to the taxpayers who will have to foot the bill."

Perspective: the assistant city manager

"I'm trying my best to support the Administration's position and put the situation in the best light possible, but I am uncomfortable with the city manager's approach. If someone asks me a direct question about this deal I'll have to say I felt pressured to produce a council agenda communication that was weak on analysis."

Perspective: the editorial page writer

"I'm convinced that this is part of a pattern to 'hide and spin' information, and I think the city manager and top staff do this routinely for political purposes. I'm prepared to endorse the mayor's opponent in the election."

Ethical principles in this case: equity and transparency

Tenet 7 of the ICMA Code of Ethics reinforces the principle of equity—that professional administrators are required to serve all members of the governing body (and candidates for office) equally and impartially. Tenets 5 and 9 and a guideline for tenet 10 all speak to the principle of transparency—sharing information openly. Keep these principles in mind as you consider the following questions.

Discussion questions

1. Is there an appearance of political favoritism in the city manager's recommendation?
2. Are these top officials openly sharing information with the governing body and the public?
3. How might the city manager, the assistant city manager, and the mayor have handled their communications about the union agreement differently?
4. Is the public interest served by securing the union's agreement to the contract? Should that be a factor in deciding whether the actions of the top officials were ethical?

Case 2: Investing in Your Community

Elizabeth K. Kellar

Scenario

The city manager was born and raised near the city he now serves. He was appointed as manager 15 years ago and has played a key role in spearheading the redevelopment of the downtown district.

As in many U.S. communities, retirees in the city are the fastest growing sector of the population. The city manager is concerned because there are few facilities geared to this aging population in the vicinity. A few years ago, he decided to use some of his personal savings to join an investment partnership that specializes in assisted living facilities. He is one of three partners in this small venture. The partnership has built one attractive assisted living facility in a distant city.

Now the city manager wants to bring the same type of high-quality facility into the community he serves, and some people have raised complaints about his proposal.

Perspective: the owner of a nearby assisted living facility

"Our facility is conveniently located to serve city residents. There's no need for another one."

Perspective: the planning and zoning commission chair

"I agree with the city manager that another facility is needed, but I have to deny his request for a zoning change to accommodate his proposal. It may come back to haunt us later if somebody comes in and says that we did it for him because he's the city manager."

Perspective: a councilmember who voted against the project

"I believe the investment presents a conflict of interest. The city manager is also acting as a developer, and everybody in the review process works for him."

Perspective: the city attorney

"There's no legal problem here. The city manager fully disclosed his investment, and that is all that's required in this situation."

Perspective: the city manager

"I'm making a personal contribution to improving the quality of life in the city by building this facility, and the facility will comply fully with city building standards and laws. If I built a parts supply house and then contracted with the city to supply parts, that would be a conflict of interest. The city does not own assisted living facilities. (And privately, I believe the planning and zoning commissioner is retaliating against me because the city council didn't select his business for a competitive contract award.)"

Ethical principles in this case: equity, stewardship, honor, and integrity

Tenet 4 of the ICMA Code of Ethics requires members to "Recognize that the chief function of local government at all times is to serve the best interests of all the people"—in other words, to uphold the principles of equity and stewardship. The guideline for Tenet 5 reinforces the principles of honor and integrity, saying that a member who has multiple roles should avoid participating in matters that create the appearance of a conflict of interest, and that he or she should disclose a potential conflict of interest to the governing body "so that other opinions may be solicited." Similarly, a guideline for Tenet 12 says that a member should not make any personal investments that create a conflict with his or her official duties. Keep these principles in mind as you consider the following questions.

Discussion questions

1. Does the city manager's investment in the assisted living business create a conflict with his official duties?

2. Does the "greater good" to provide housing for an aging population outweigh any potential conflict of interest?

3. Because the city attorney has offered a legal opinion that the city manager's actions are in compliance with the law, should that outweigh any other objections?

4. Can the city manager ethically address the concern about his dual role as developer and supervisor of the city staff who do inspections and permits?

5. Is disclosure of the manager's investment sufficient to answer ethical concerns? Should that disclosure go beyond the completion of a financial disclosure form?

Case 3: Hurricane Season's Fast Track Procurement

Elizabeth K. Kellar

Scenario

The National Weather Service has warned that the hurricane season will be especially active this year. The county government realizes that its emergency operations center needs to replace its computer software, and it wants to move quickly before facing any emergencies. The Information Technology Department has recommended that the county sole-source the project to a technology firm that handled the last computer upgrade. The week that this comes to the county administrator to review, there is a media frenzy over the way the sheriff's department handled a student protest at a school board meeting. The sheriff's deputies physically ejected several students from a public meeting, and two of the students struggled and were slightly injured. The melee was captured on cable television and played over and over. Maybe that's why the county administrator doesn't pay more attention to the sole-source request. She initials the recommendation and it goes on the Board of Supervisors' consent agenda. Shortly after the recommendation is approved, two other vendors in the community cry, "Foul!"

Perspective: a losing technology vendor

"There wasn't any emergency that justified a sole-source contract, and the county could have fast-tracked this procurement without making it a sweetheart deal. All they had to do was advertise the opportunity on the Internet and figure out a way to get a list of qualified vendors who can move quickly on these projects. That doesn't take a genius! I suppose it's no coincidence that the county administrator's nephew recently went to work for the company that won the award."

Perspective: elected official who sympathizes with the losing vendor

"I'm furious that the county administrator put this item on the consent calendar. What was she thinking? A contract of this size needs to be given careful attention, especially if the administration is arguing that it should be awarded on a sole-source basis."

Perspective: the winning vendor

"It made perfect sense for the county to sole-source this project. I had no idea the county administrator's nephew was just hired by my company. How would we have known that? They don't even have the same last name."

Perspective: the county administrator

"I don't get it. Our residents expect us to be prepared in an emergency and would be ranting and raving if we had let this project lag due to lengthy procurement processes. We don't face a hurricane today, but the odds are that we could face one in a couple of months. We can't afford to wait. And that business about my nephew. He just got out of college! He's probably making only $30,000 a year. Our financial disclosure laws don't require us to report on where our nieces and nephews work. Geez!"

Ethical principles in this case: integrity and transparency

In addition to sharing information generously, it is important to ensure that there are transparent processes in sensitive areas like procurement. Tenet 3 of the ICMA Code of Ethics inspires members to be dedicated to the highest ideals of honor and integrity and to avoid any impression that they could be improperly influenced. Tenet 12 has a guideline that reminds members to disclose any personal relationship to the governing body where there could be the appearance of a conflict of interest. Keep these principles in mind as you consider the following questions.

Discussion questions

1. Would the administrator have been likely to handle this procurement differently if she had pondered the Code of Ethics and not been distracted by the incident involving the sheriff's department?

2. Does the nephew's employment with the winning vendor create an appearance of a conflict of interest?

3. Does the county's process for fast-track procurements add to the impression that this bid is "wired?"

4. Are the public safety issues compelling enough to justify the sole source recommendation?

Case 4: The Errant Elected Official

Elizabeth K. Kellar

Scenario

The city manager of this suburban community of 75,000 has held his position for 10 years and takes pride in his ability to establish a good working relationship with all of the elected officials he serves. As city manager, he serves at the pleasure of the seven-member city council, which includes a mayor who is selected each year by the city council. One of the newer council members comes from a family with historic ties in the community. He is a popular individual who ran on a platform to be a "neighborhood council member."

Soon after his election this council member began contacting staff at all levels of the organization, demanding that certain things be done or not done, and showing his temper freely. For example, he asked the public works staff to paint a "Do not stop" message on the street in front of his house. They refused. In a confrontation with a building official, he demanded that a multimillion-dollar private construction project be shut down because he thought the construction crane was unsafe and the developer was too influential in the community. He has attempted to influence code enforcement activities on properties near his home.

The pressures have grown since he was selected by the city council to serve as mayor for the next year. In the past month, the mayor has demanded that the police chief be fired for not giving the mayor advance warning of a search warrant that was to be served on his home as part of a criminal investigation of a family member. He also ordered the code enforcement staff to pursue action against a neighboring property owner (a property the mayor's family wants to buy). He refused to pay for the replacement of a fire hydrant destroyed by a family member and displayed his outrage to city staff when he received the bill. He has billed the city government for a number of expenses, including a request to be reimbursed for a tuxedo.

The city attorney has warned the mayor numerous times that his attempts to influence staff are violations of the law. In addition, the city manager has counseled the mayor on

This case is based on "Councilmanic Interference: When a Councilmember Crosses the Line," by Kevin Duggan, *Public Management*, November 2002.

more appropriate ways to raise issues and concerns with city staff. Last week the mayor made it clear to the city attorney that he expected the city staff to put pressure on the mayor's neighbor: "You got to do what you can to run this guy out of business because I need to buy the property." The financial stakes for the mayor are high. He could gain as much as $50 million if things go his way.

While the mayor's demands have been improper, the fact that city staff have refused to carry them out makes it difficult to bring criminal charges against the mayor. Furthermore, the mayor has a strong political base and knows how to present himself well. He belittles the city staff for being typical bureaucrats and frames his positions in a way that excites his supporters. The general public has no way of knowing what the facts are since the mayor's actions have escaped media attention so far.

The mayor's latest demand comes directly to the city manager. He insists that the city place conditions on the property he wishes to purchase. His aim is clear. He wants to discourage the present owner from proceeding with that owner's plans to improve the property so that the mayor will have a better chance of buying it at a reduced rate. This meeting took place just four hours before the city manager's scheduled annual performance evaluation. The implication is clear: how the city manager responds to his demands will influence the mayor's approach to the evaluation.

Perspective: the council member/mayor

"The city manager and staff are answerable to the council, and I have a right to tell them what to do. As mayor, I'm entitled to privileges above and beyond those given to other residents because I'm a member of the city family. And I need the staff's help to get that property."

Perspective: the city attorney

"I've tried to warn him that his conduct is illegal under our council-manager form of government. But since city staff haven't carried out his demands, it's hard to initiate any legal action against him."

Perspective: the media

"What misconduct? He's just a typical politician who always gives us an entertaining quote or two."

Ethical principles in this case: equity, honor, and stewardship

The ICMA Code of Ethics addresses the principles of equity, honor, and stewardship. A guideline for Tenet 7 says that members "should maintain a reputation for serving equally and impartially all members of the governing body." Tenet 10 urges them to "resist any encroachment on professional responsibilities," and Tenet 2 reminds members of their stewardship, urging "a deep sense of social responsibility as a trusted public servant." Keep these principles in mind as you consider the following questions.

Discussion questions

1. Is the city at risk because of the mayor's behavior with staff? What responsibility do the city manager and city attorney have to protect city staff from the mayor's outbursts and inappropriate conduct?

2. What responsibilities do they have to the community?

3. Do the city manager and city attorney have a responsibility to bring up their concerns in an open session with the city council or should they refer these matters confidentially to the district attorney?

4. If the mayor is indicted, what are the implications for the city staff, especially for the city manager and the city attorney? How should they handle inquiries from the media while the matter is under investigation, particularly when the mayor is holding regular news conferences to complain that he's the target of a political witch hunt?

Case 5: Let's Do Lunch

Stephen J. Bonczek

Scenario

The manager was really excited about his new career opportunity. He had just been hired as manager in a city in the Northeast with a population of 60,000 predominately moderate-income residents. While he was evaluating the advantages and disadvantages of the position before acceptance, however, he was concerned about two things:

- For the first time in his 25-year career as a manager, he would be dealing with partisan politics. In this jurisdiction, the local Republican and Democratic parties actively select and raise funds for candidates with the goal of electing a majority of the five-member council—in essence to control the government.

- In the last election about a year ago, after 20 years of Republican control, a new Democratic majority was elected on a platform of change to a more efficient and responsive government. Some of the early changes included preparing a lean budget (partially by not filling essential staff vacancies) and forcing out the previous manager, who had served for 15 years and had a positive relationship with the employees and the community. This action created resentment and morale issues with staff and concern among community leaders.

Despite these concerns, he told himself that the political environment would be no more difficult than the political turmoil he had experienced in other manager assignments. He had always been recognized as having excellent political skills and the ability to create coherency out of chaos. In terms of the ouster of the previous manager, he persuaded himself that turnover in the position of manager is expected and that the 15-year tenure was a good sign that he could expect a long tenure, too.

The manager spends his first two weeks on the job handling daily operations, dealing with disgruntled employees, analyzing staff effectiveness with an eye to reorganization, and getting to know the highly partisan council. He starts to wonder if this position is going to work out as expected. Then he gets a call from the council chairman inviting him to lunch at a restaurant in a nearby community with another council member (both Democrats) to discuss important issues facing the city.

Believing this would be a good opportunity to develop a working relationship with council leadership and to discuss strategies for addressing critical issues, he accepts. Open meeting requirements don't prohibit meeting with two council members, and the manager decides to avoid any appearance of a conflict by paying for his own lunch. He plans to arrange meetings with the other council members later to get their input on issues he and the council will be addressing.

A few days before the lunch meeting, the manager gets a call from the vice chair of the council (a Democrat active in the party) and mentions the upcoming meeting. The vice chair shares a rumor that others have been invited—primarily local Democratic party leaders—and that the alleged purpose of the meeting is to tell the manager what issues are priorities for the party and to make clear that they expect to exercise control over the hiring/firing of key positions (an authority granted to the manager under the form of government). The vice chair hints that if the manager doesn't attend there will be extreme pressure on council members who owe their election to the party's support to terminate him. Also, the restaurant where the lunch is to take place is a known Democratic "hang-out" owned by one of the party leaders.

The manager begins to realize that the partisan nature of local politics is becoming more serious and complicated than he had anticipated. If this lunch is a political party meeting with a perceived "shadow government" to determine and control the workings of the city, then he believes a professional manager should decline to attend. If it is simply a chance to meet with party/community leaders, then maybe he should attend and share his vision of an effective and responsive government. Perhaps he could reinforce the principles of council-manager government and educate the council members about the manager's role and his commitments under the Code of Ethics. The manager also considers the reaction of the Republican Party leaders—would they conclude that he's a party hack doing the bidding of the opposition and seek his removal from office? Lurking in the background is the manager's fear of termination, which would have severe career consequences.

The manager decides to discuss his concerns with the council chairman, who is somewhat evasive but denies the rumored purpose of the meeting and encourages the manager to attend. He also consults with several other players. The assistant city manager, who has been with the local government for 10 years, urges him not to attend the lunch, saying that the majority of the staff and the community will perceive it as a political meeting and raise concerns about his ethical leadership. On the other hand, the chair of the Economic Development Board, an active Democrat whose support the manager needs, recommends that he attend.

After wrestling with the question overnight, the manager decides not to attend the meeting, concluding that the risk of appearing to favor certain council members or appearing to engage in partisan political activity outweighs the potential benefits of attending.

Perspective: the city manager

"I have to establish good working relationships with local political leaders, and I've been invited to a forum where I'll have that opportunity. Still, I don't like the fact that the restaurant is associated with the Democratic Party, and there's a rumor about the presence of a 'shadow government' at the lunch. Even though I'm confident that I understand my authority to hire and fire under the council-manager plan, and that I can stand up to the political forces, I think it's wiser not to attend."

Perspective: the assistant city manager

"The new manager almost walked into a hornet's nest. If he went to this meeting, the community would perceive him as being 'in the pocket' of the Democrats."

Perspective: the chair of the Economic Development Board

"The new manager needs to develop a base of support with community leaders who can make things happen, or he's not going to be able to achieve the transformation the government needs. This lunch is just a way of doing business, and he doesn't want to start off appearing difficult to get along with."

Perspective: the council chairman

"This guy sounds like he's going to use his professional credentials as a way to avoid open communication with us. I wonder if he's going to be a control freak who resists our guidance."

Ethical principles in the case: equity and integrity

A guideline to Tenet 7 of the ICMA Code of Ethics requires members to "maintain a reputation for serving equally and impartially all members of the governing body they serve, regardless of party," and the tenet itself states that the professional manager should refrain from all political activities that undermine public confidence in professional administrators. A guideline to Tenet 3 reminds members to avoid the impression that they can be improperly influenced in performing their duties. Tenet 10 requires the member to "resist any encroachment on professional responsibilities." Yet Tenet 10 also has a guideline that tells members that they should openly share information with the governing body. Keep these principles in mind as you consider the following questions.

Discussion questions

1. Would attending the lunch have put the manager in a position of undermining public confidence?

2. Would meeting with political party leaders have facilitated earning "the respect and confidence of the elected officials, of other officials and employees, and of the public," as required by Tenet 3?

3. Would attending the lunch have put the manager in a position of treating council members inequitably?

4. Should the venue of the meeting have been a factor in the manager's decision? Would it have been appropriate for him to attend if the meeting had occurred at a city facility instead of at the restaurant?

5. Did the manager have an obligation to educate these council members about the authority of the manager under the council-manager plan?

6. Based on your answers to the previous questions, did the manager make the right decision in declining to attend the lunch?

Case 6: Private Gain or Public Victim?

Carol W. Lewis and Stuart C. Gilman

> The Law Enforcement Oath of Honor of the International Association of Chiefs of Police (undated) states, "On my honor, I will never betray my badge, my integrity, my character, or the public trust. I will always have the courage to hold myself and others accountable for our actions. I will always uphold the constitution, my community and the agency I serve." According to the Montgomery County Police Department (undated), Charles A. Moose is a member.

In the fall of 2002, an unknown sniper or snipers terrorized the Washington D.C. area, randomly killing people no matter their age, race, or gender. A person was killed mowing the lawn, a child shot on the way to school, a bus driver gunned down in the door of his bus, a woman shot through the head as she put packages in the trunk of her car, and an elderly man shot dead as he pumped gas into his car. The investigations drew in police from two states, over a dozen counties, the District of Columbia, and several federal police authorities. After the first week, police officials determined that they had to co-ordinate their own activities and needed a single voice to speak for the investigation. This would help squelch rumors and implement a strategy to use the media to help track down leads and provide accurate information. The decision was made to make Montgomery County Police Chief Charles A. Moose the spokesperson for the investigation. His calm persona and professionalism captured the national media, and Chief Moose became a common feature on national and international television for more than a month.

Chief Moose was hailed for his steady hand with the media and the public; he was viewed as the one individual responsible for coordinating the massive and successful law enforcement effort. John Lee Malvo and John Allen Mohammed were captured in the early morning of October 24, 2002, after remarkable police work that linked events in the states of Washington and Alabama to the horror that was occurring in the D.C. area. The men were accused of killing ten people and critically injuring three others, and were subsequently tried and found guilty.

Moose signed a deal with Dutton Publishing Company of New York in January 2003 to write a book about the manhunt. The chief also received more than $4,000 for an open movie contract about his experiences. Moose said money was a motivating factor in the decision to sign the deals. "If it helps me and my family with the law school bills my wife has…it's my good fortune" (Mosk, May 23, 2003, B1). The chief negotiated the book and movie deals before he sought permission from his supervisor or from the ethics commission for any of the outside employment work he had pursued (and for which he was compensated), as required by law and specifically referenced in his employment agreement.

Montgomery County ethics officials soon began questioning whether it was appropriate for the nationally known lawman to profit personally from the investigation he helped

From Carol W. Lewis and Stuart C. Gilman, *The Ethics Challenge in Public Service: A Problem-Solving Guide,* 2d ed., copyright © 2005 by Jossey-Bass. Reprinted with permission of John Wiley & Sons, Inc.

lead. The ethics commission met on March 3 to hear Moose's requests for outside employment, including a possible waiver from stringent ethics laws that restrict county employees from profiting from their public work. The panel also was asked to consider whether it was proper for Moose to sell his story to a Hollywood television production company and to launch a consulting firm with his wife to market the chief's skills as a motivational speaker and his expertise in team-building, crisis management, and conflict resolution. The chief described the book as a "once-in-a-lifetime" chance to taste the rewards of fame.

The commission scheduled another meeting to decide the issues. According to the commission's chairperson, Elizabeth K. Kellar, "All of this would have been kept confidential (required by law), except for Chief Moose's decision to talk about it with the media."

Hired after the chief requested a waiver, the chief's attorney argued that forbidding people to write books raises serious constitutional issues, and public officials do not give up the right to free speech when they enter public service. In addition, hearing about Chief Moose's experience would provide a real public benefit. The attorney also argued that the ethics rules were designed to prevent bribery or undue influence over legislation, which is not the case with Moose's book.

With the limelight comes opportunity, as well as the spotlight of increased public scrutiny. Capitalizing on new-found fame "'can easily overwhelm a person,' said Vivian Weil, head of the Illinois Institute of Technology's Center for the Study of Ethics in the Professions. 'You can understand someone being unsettled by it and even failing to pass it by the ethics board,' Weil said. 'To have clouded judgment—you can easily imagine that'" (Associated Press, 2003, unpaginated). According to John Kleinig, director of the Institute for Criminal Justice Ethics, Chief Moose is not the first police chief to write books on major crimes or their memoirs. "But that can lead to conflicts of interest. Those can include too much outside work that distracts a chief from his police job, a book or speech that reveals confidential information, or the appearance that a chief is cashing in on a tragedy.... He must be aware that others have had problems and that he could find himself in a bit of difficulty.... It's probably in his interest that it is reviewed." Kleinig notes, "It's like the guy who wins the lottery and suddenly finds he's the subject of enormous amounts of attention and pressures" (Associated Press, 2003).

The powerful, popular, and elected Montgomery County Executive, Doug Duncan, weighed in on behalf of permitting Moose to write his book. Duncan vowed to ask the county council to grant the chief a special exemption from the ethics rules, should the commission attempt to derail his book. Duncan argued that, if Chief Moose were turned down, he would only resign and find a job elsewhere. Duncan urged the members to grant Moose a waiver so that the county could retain this exemplary public servant.

On March 20, just before Moose was called to active duty in the Air National Guard, the five-member ethics commission issued a six-page ruling arguing that Moose's for-profit ventures would violate "bedrock principles" of county ethics law. The commission ruled:

> It is not in the best interest of the County to allow its employees to "trade on" their government activities for private gain in such a direct and immediate fashion. Such conduct leads citizens to question whether public employees are discharging their duties in the public interest or in furtherance of some private interest. This diminishes citizens' faith in their public servants and erodes their trust in [c]ounty government.

In the commission members' view, "These principles are at the core of the prohibition against using the prestige of one's office for private gain." The ruling added that neither Moose nor Duncan, who had asked the commission to make an exception for the chief, "has convinced the commission that this situation is a good platform to begin waiving those principles." A waiver now "could lead to undesirable behavior" in the future, the panel said, such as employees "jockeying for position" during high-profile incidents in hopes of winning fame and fortune.

His attorney protested the "flawed" decision and said he was astonished. "They concede that the county executive has decided that this is in the best interest of the county. But these five unelected members of this commission say, 'No, we know better'" (Mosk, Mar. 21, 2003, B1).

In late April, in a significant turnaround from its past positions, the *Washington Post*'s editors argued that in this balancing test they would come down on "the side of more speech in this case." But, they continued, he should not be allowed to write for the "wrong reasons," namely his poor salary as compared to other police chiefs. This created a double standard when it came to other police officers on the force. The solution, according to the newspaper's editors, was for the commission to "reexamine its earlier ruling barring police officers from accepting honorariums to speak about the sniper case." In October 2003, the *Washington Post* printed five long excerpts from Moose's book.

Charles Moose resigned as Chief of the Montgomery County Police on June 18, 2003, rather than comply with the ethics commission's ruling. The settlement agreement that he negotiated with Montgomery County when he resigned required that he return movie compensation to the county that he had accepted prior to seeking permission or a waiver and that he dismiss his lawsuit against the commission. The commission agreed that (absent any breach of confidentiality) it would not take any action to restrain Moose's book, movie, or speaking opportunities after he resigned.

Discussion questions

1. Most public codes forbid using public office for private gain. Is this the core problem here? What do you consider in arriving at your answer?

2. Should the value of free speech override ethics rules for public officials? Why? There is a long history of government employees' freedom of speech being restricted for reasons of "compelling government interest." Federal employees' participation in partisan activities has been restricted since 1939 under the Federal Hatch Act (5 U.S.C. §§ 7321-7326), amended to expand employees' rights in 1993. See the U.S. Office of Special Counsel at http://www.osc.gov. For some important court cases on limitations and liberties of government employees, see *Wild* v. *United States Dep't of Housing & Urban Dev.*, 692 F.2d 1129, 1132-34 (7th Cir. 1982) and *Van Ee* v. *EPA*, 202 F.3d 296 (D.C. Cir. 2000).

3. Did Chief Moose do anything unethical by pursuing the book and movie contracts before seeking a waiver of the county's standards? Why?

4. Did Chief Moose do anything unethical by seeking a waiver of the county's standards? Why?

5. Did Chief Moose do anything unethical by resigning in order to fulfill the book contract? Why?

6. As a member of the ethics commission, would you have granted Chief Moose a waiver? Why?

References

Associated Press. "Charles Moose Faces Ethics Probe." CNN, Mar. 3, 2003. Internet [http://www.cnn.com] (accessed Mar. 8, 2003).

International Association of Chiefs of Police. Law Enforcement Oath of Honor. Internet [http://www.theiacp.org/profassist/ethics/presentation_of_oath.htm] (accessed Feb.29, 2004).

Montgomery County Department of Police. "Career History of Charles Alexander Moose." Internet [http://www.montgomerycountymd.ws/MooseEthicsTranscript.PDF] (accessed Jan. 24, 2004).

Mosk, M. "Moose Feared Losing His Job." *Washington Post*, May 23, 2003, p. B1.

Mosk, M. "Panel Forbids Moose's Book and Movie: Montgomery Chief Had Boss's Backing for Deals from Sniper Case." *Washington Post*, Mar. 21, 2003, p. B1.

Appendix B: Techno Quiz
Ethics in the Age of Cybertechnology

This age of cybertechnology brings with it a host of new ethical and management challenges. Here's a quiz to help you think about some of the problems you may encounter and how to respond to them.

▧ Situation 1

Many of your employees have Internet access on their computers to help them do research on pressing issues. You are concerned about Dan, however. Once one of the department's most productive employees, Dan now asks for more time than you think should be necessary to complete his work. You suspect he's using the Internet for a lot of personal business. What do you do?

a. Install an Internet filter on every employee's computer so you can find out if anyone is accessing inappropriate sites.

b. Take away Dan's Internet access, and assign his research work to another employee.

c. Establish an Internet policy to make it clear that employees may not use the local government's Internet service for personal business.

d. Set up a meeting with Dan to discuss your concerns about his difficulty in meeting deadlines.

▧ Situation 2

You've heard rumors that two of your department heads are accessing pornographic sites on their city computers. Fred, the head of the information services department, has admitted that he has been surfing the Web to look at various pornographic sites. His explanation was that he wanted to see how easy it would be for city employees to access illicit material without detection. Sam, the other department director, has said that he accidentally stumbled across a couple of sites with pornography and that he did show them

Reprinted with permission from *Public Management* magazine, May 2000. Copyright © 2000 by the International City/County Management Association, Suite 500, 777 N. Capitol St., N.E., Washington, DC 20002.

to some of the staff, who thought they were pretty funny. How do you handle these two situations?

a. Relieved that the explanations sound innocent, you move on to other matters.

b. While you find both of the explanations plausible, you realize that these department heads have put the city in an embarrassing situation that could lead to legal liability if strong steps are not taken. You warn Fred that he should not undertake the sensitive task of testing the city's safeguards against accessing pornographic sites without openly communicating with his employees and his supervisor. Sam's brush with pornography concerns you even more because he showed it to other staff, who might view such actions as part of a hostile work environment.

c. You conclude that you should increase the city's human resources training to make sure that the city's values and policies are clear to all employees.

d. You put both department heads on probation for violating the city's Internet policies.

■ Situation 3

Angela has complained to you that her colleague Mary has made disparaging remarks about her and other Hispanics in the office. Mary made these remarks via e-mail to Bill, another employee in the same workgroup. You've long suspected that Mary was racist, and now you have evidence of it. Mary denied making the comments until you showed her a copy of one of her messages, which had been retrieved by the network administrator. Mary then became angry and accused you of violating her right to privacy. How do you react?

a. You remind Mary that county e-mail is not private and that all employees receive a copy of the county's e-mail policy when they join the workforce. You give Mary a verbal warning and review the county's policy on diversity with her.

b. Mary has been a problem employee, and this gives you a golden opportunity to push her out of her job. Because you work in a state where e-mails are subject to disclosure under the state's public disclosure statutes, you decide to encourage one of the local reporters to request copies of some of these embarrassing e-mails. It's about time some of this racism got exposed!

c. You report the incident to the county manager because you remember the manager's talking about a similar problem in another part of the organization.

d. You forward Mary's e-mail to five of your colleagues, who you think would share your views about Mary's offensive comments. You plan to talk with them about their views of the comments at lunch.

■ Situation 4

Several of your colleagues in other communities have created a "share the humor" e-mail list. It often brightens your day to read one of the jokes that they send. Today, when you turn on your computer, you see there's a file waiting for you to open. When you open the file, you are stunned to see a photograph of a naked woman in a parody of a popular advertisement. What do you do?

a. You delete the file and pray that you will never see a message like that one again.

b. You contact the sender, making it clear that you do not want to receive mail like that again and that it is a violation of your city's policy to use the Internet to access this kind of material.

Commentary

Situation 1 All of the options have some merit, but the place to begin is with (d). Until you meet with Dan, you have no way of knowing why his productivity has slipped; his problem may have nothing to do with his work on the Internet. Of course, if your local government does not have a policy on Internet use, you should develop one right away for the good of the entire organization. (To read a detailed discussion of how to set up an Internet policy, or to find examples of policies, see ICMA's Special Report, "Local Government On-Line: Putting the Internet to Work." For information, visit ICMA's online bookstore at bookstore.icma.org.)

Situation 2 Both of these situations require management action, and a good place to begin is with (b), a warning to both employees about their actions. If there has been a pattern of misconduct, you might look at more serious personnel actions. An ongoing training program is valuable in any organization to make sure that your employees understand the local government's values and policies.

Situation 3 Here, there are two good answers, (a) and (c), and two bad answers, (b) and (d). It's important that local governments have a clear policy on e-mail. Windsor, Connecticut's policy states that "any message sent or received by e-mail in the conduct of public business is by law a 'public record,' and that . . . all messages sent or received by e-mail are considered discoverable (not private) communications. . . ." The policy includes some great advice: "The content of any message sent should consist of information that the sender would not object to reading in a newspaper headline." It's also helpful to provide this feedback to top management so that any organization-wide problems can be addressed.

Situation 4 In these cases, you will do your colleagues a favor by contacting them (b) and letting them know that their e-mail is inappropriate. Most local government Internet policies prohibit the transmission of any "harassing" or "offensive" messages, and courts have upheld the employer's interest in preventing such messages.

Appendix C: ICMA Code of Ethics with Guidelines

*T*he ICMA Code of Ethics was adopted by the ICMA membership in 1924, and most recently amended by the membership in May 1998. The Guidelines for the Code were adopted by the ICMA Executive Board in 1972, and most recently revised in July 2004.

The mission of ICMA is to create excellence in local governance by developing and fostering professional local government management worldwide. To further this mission, certain principles, as enforced by the Rules of Procedure, shall govern the conduct of every member of ICMA, who shall:

Tenet 1

Be dedicated to the concepts of effective and democratic local government by responsible elected officials and believe that professional general management is essential to the achievement of this objective.

Tenet 2

Affirm the dignity and worth of the services rendered by government and maintain a constructive, creative, and practical attitude toward local government affairs and a deep sense of social responsibility as a trusted public servant.

Guideline

Advice to officials of other local governments   When members advise and respond to inquiries from elected or appointed officials of other local governments, they should inform the administrators of those communities.

Tenet 3

Be dedicated to the highest ideals of honor and integrity in all public and personal relationships in order that the member may merit the respect and confidence of the elected officials, of other officials and employees, and of the public.

Guidelines

Public confidence   Members should conduct themselves so as to maintain public confidence in their profession, their local government, and in their performance of the public trust.

Impression of influence   Members should conduct their official and personal affairs in such a manner as to give the clear impression that they cannot be improperly influenced in the performance of their official duties.

Appointment commitment   Members who accept an appointment to a position should not fail to report for that position. This does not preclude the possibility of a member considering several offers or seeking several positions at the same time, but once a *bona fide* offer of a position has been accepted, that commitment should be honored. Oral acceptance of an employment offer is considered binding unless the employer makes fundamental changes in terms of employment.

Credentials   An application for employment or for ICMA's Voluntary Credentialing Program should be complete and accurate as to all pertinent details of education, experience, and personal history. Members should recognize that both omissions and inaccuracies must be avoided.

Professional respect   Members seeking a management position should show professional respect for persons formerly holding the position or for others who might be applying for the same position. Professional respect does not preclude honest differences of opinion; it does preclude attacking a person's motives or integrity in order to be appointed to a position.

Reporting ethics violation   When becoming aware of a possible violation of the ICMA Code of Ethics, members are encouraged to report the matter to ICMA. In reporting the matter, members may choose to go on record as the complainant or report the matter on a confidential basis.

Confidentiality   Members should not discuss or divulge information with anyone about pending or completed ethics cases, except as specifically authorized by the Rules of Procedure for Enforcement of the Code of Ethics.

Seeking employment   Members should not seek employment for a position having an incumbent administrator who has not resigned or been officially informed that his or her services are to be terminated.

Tenet 4

Recognize that the chief function of local government at all times is to serve the best interests of all of the people.

Guideline

Length of service   A minimum of two years generally is considered necessary in order to render a professional service to the local government. A short tenure should be the exception rather than a recurring experience. However, under special circumstances, it may be in the best interests of the local government and the member to separate in a shorter time. Examples of such circumstances would include refusal of the appointing authority to honor commitments concerning conditions of employment, a vote of no confidence in the member, or severe personal problems. It is the responsibility of an applicant for a position to ascertain conditions of employment. Inadequately determining terms of employment prior to arrival does not justify premature termination.

Tenet 5

Submit policy proposals to elected officials; provide them with facts and advice on matters of policy as a basis for making decisions and setting community goals; and uphold and implement local government policies adopted by elected officials.

Guideline

Conflicting roles   Members who serve multiple roles—working as both city attorney and city manager for the same community, for example—should avoid participating in matters that create the appearance of a conflict of interest. They should disclose the potential conflict to the governing body so that other opinions may be solicited.

Tenet 6

Recognize that elected representatives of the people are entitled to the credit for the establishment of local government policies; responsibility for policy execution rests with the members.

Tenet 7

Refrain from all political activities which undermine public confidence in professional administrators. Refrain from participation in the election of the members of the employing legislative body.

Guidelines

Elections of the governing body   Members should maintain a reputation for serving equally and impartially all members of the governing body of the local government they serve, regardless of party. To this end, they should not engage in active participation in the election campaign on behalf of or in opposition to candidates for the governing body.

Elections of elected executives   Members should not engage in the election campaign of any candidate for mayor or elected county executive.

Running for office   Members shall not run for elected office or become involved in political activities related to running for elected office. They shall not seek political endorsements, financial contributions or engage in other campaign activities.

Elections   Members share with their fellow citizens the right and responsibility to vote and to voice their opinion on public issues. However, in order not to impair their effectiveness on behalf of the local governments they serve, they shall not participate in political activities to support the candidacy of individuals running for any city, county, special district, school, state or federal offices. Specifically, they shall not endorse candidates, make financial contributions, sign or circulate petitions, or participate in fund-raising activities for individuals seeking or holding elected office.

Elections on the council-manager plan   Members may assist in preparing and presenting materials that explain the council-manager form of government to the public prior to an election on the use of the plan. If assistance is required by another community, members may respond. All activities regarding ballot issues should be conducted within local regulations and in a professional manner.

Presentation of issues   Members may assist the governing body in presenting issues involved in referenda such as bond issues, annexations, and similar matters.

Tenet 8

Make it a duty continually to improve the member's professional ability and to develop the competence of associates in the use of management techniques.

Guidelines

Self-assessment   Each member should assess his or her professional skills and abilities on a periodic basis.

Professional development   Each member should commit at least 40 hours per year to professional development activities that are based on the practices identified by the members of ICMA.

Tenet 9

Keep the community informed on local government affairs; encourage communication between the citizens and all local government officers; emphasize friendly and courteous service to the public; and seek to improve the quality and image of public service.

Tenet 10

Resist any encroachment on professional responsibilities, believing the member should be free to carry out official policies without interference, and handle each problem without discrimination on the basis of principle and justice.

Guideline

Information sharing   The member should openly share information with the governing body while diligently carrying out the member's responsibilities as set forth in the charter or enabling legislation.

Tenet 11

Handle all matters of personnel on the basis of merit so that fairness and impartiality govern a member's decisions pertaining to appointments, pay adjustments, promotions, and discipline.

Guideline

Equal opportunity   All decisions pertaining to appointments, pay adjustments, promotions, and discipline should prohibit discrimination because of race, color, religion, sex, national origin, sexual orientation, political affiliation, disability, age, or marital status.

It should be the members' personal and professional responsibility to actively recruit and hire a diverse staff throughout their organizations.

Tenet 12

Seek no favor; believe that personal aggrandizement or profit secured by confidential information or by misuse of public time is dishonest.

Guidelines

Gifts   Members should not directly or indirectly solicit any gift or accept or receive any gift—whether it be money, services, loan, travel, entertainment, hospitality, promise, or any other form—under the following circumstances: (1) it could be reasonably inferred or expected that the gift was intended to influence them in the performance of their official duties; or (2) the gift was intended to serve as a reward for any official action on their part.

It is important that the prohibition of unsolicited gifts be limited to circumstances related to improper influence. In *de minimus* situations, such as meal checks, some modest maximum dollar value should be determined by the member as a guideline. The guideline is not intended to isolate members from normal social practices where gifts among friends, associates, and relatives are appropriate for certain occasions.

Investments in conflict with official duties   Member should not invest or hold any investment, directly or indirectly, in any financial business, commercial, or other private transaction that creates a conflict with their official duties.

In the case of real estate, the potential use of confidential information and knowledge to further a member's personal interest requires special consideration. This guideline recognizes that members' official actions and decisions can be influenced if there is a conflict with personal investments. Purchases and sales which might be interpreted as speculation for quick profit ought to be avoided (see the guideline on "Confidential information").

Because personal investments may prejudice or may appear to influence official actions and decisions, members may, in concert with their governing body, provide for disclosure of such investments prior to accepting their position as local government administrator or prior to any official action by the governing body that may affect such investments.

Personal relationships   Members should disclose any personal relationship to the governing body in any instance where there could be the appearance of a conflict of interest. For example, if the manager's spouse works for a developer doing business with the local government, that fact should be disclosed.

Confidential information   Members should not disclose to others, or use to further their personal interest, confidential information acquired by them in the course of their official duties.

Private employment   Members should not engage in, solicit, negotiate for, or promise to accept private employment, nor should they render services for private interests or conduct a private business when such employment, service, or business creates a conflict with or impairs the proper discharge of their official duties.

Teaching, lecturing, writing, or consulting are typical activities that may not involve conflict of interest, or impair the proper discharge of their official duties. Prior notification of the appointing authority is appropriate in all cases of outside employment.

Representation   Members should not represent any outside interest before any agency, whether public or private, except with the authorization of or at the direction of the appointing authority they serve.

Endorsements   Members should not endorse commercial products or services by agreeing to use their photograph, endorsement, or quotation in paid or other commercial advertisements, whether or not for compensation. Members may, however, agree to endorse the following, provided they do not receive any compensation: (1) books or other publications; (2) professional development or educational services provided by nonprofit membership organizations or recognized educational institutions; (3) products and/or services in which the local government has a direct economic interest.

Members' observations, opinions, and analyses of commercial products used or tested by their local governments are appropriate and useful to the profession when included as part of professional articles and reports.

Appendix D: For Further Reading

Anechiarico, Frank. The Cure for a Public Disease: The Foibles and Future of Corruption Control. In *Ethics in Public Management*, ed. H. G. Frederickson and R. K. Ghere. Armonk, NY: M. E. Sharpe, 2005: 243-58.

Balogun, M. J. Causative and Enabling Factors in Public Integrity: A Focus on Leadership, Institutions, and Character Formation. *Public Integrity* 5, 2, 2003: 122-47.

Bell, A. Fleming. *Ethics, Conflicts, and Offices: A Guide for Local Officials*. Chapel Hill, NC: Institute of Government, University of North Carolina, 1997.

Berman, Evan M. Ethics in Organizations, Implementation of. In *Encyclopedia of Public Administration and Public Policy*, ed. J. Rabin. New York: Marcel Dekker, 2002: 461-64.

Bonczek, Stephen J., and Jane G. Kazman. *Ethics in Action: Leader's Guide and Participant's Handbook* (2 volumes). Washington, DC: International City/County Management Association, 1999.

Bowman, James S. Virtue Ethics. In *Encyclopedia of Public Administration and Public Policy*, ed. J. Rabin. New York: Marcel Dekker, 2003: 1259-63.

Bowman, James S., Jonathan P. West, Evan M. Berman, and Montgomery Van Wart. *The Professional Edge: Competencies in Public Service*. Armonk, NY: M. E. Sharpe, 2004.

Brattebo, Douglas M., and Eloise F. Malone, eds. *The Lanahan Cases in Leadership, Ethics & Decision Making*. Baltimore, MD: Lanahan, 2002.

Brown, Marvin T. *The Ethical Process*. Upper Saddle River, NJ: Prentice Hall, 1999.

Caiden, Gerald E. The Anatomy of Official Corruption. In *Ethics in Public Management*, ed. H. G. Frederickson and R. K. Ghere. Armonk, NY: M. E. Sharpe, 2005: 277-96.

Carter, Stephen L. *Integrity*. New York: Harper Perennial, 1996.

Cooper, Terry L. The Emergence of Administrative Ethics as a Field of Study in the United States. In *Handbook of Administrative Ethics*, ed. T. L. Cooper, 2d ed. New York: Marcel Dekker, 2001.

Day, Carla. Balancing Organizational Priorities: A Two-Factor Values Model of Integrity and Conformity. *Public Integrity* 1, 2, 1999: 149-66.

Denhardt, Kathryn G., and Stuart C. Gilman. Extremism in the Search for Virtue: Why Zero Gift Policies Spawn Unintended Consequences. *Public Integrity* 4, 1, 2002: 75-80.

Dobel, J. Patrick. Can Public Leaders Have Friends? *Public Integrity* 3, 2, 2001: 145-58.

Dobel, J. Patrick. *Public Integrity*. Baltimore, MD: Johns Hopkins University Press, 1999.

Driscoll, Dawn-Marie, and W. Michael Hoffman. Spot the Red Flags in Your Organization. *Workforce* 76, 6, 1997: 1325-26.

Fain, Herbert. The Case for a Zero Gift Policy. *Public Integrity* 4, 1, 2002: 61-74.

Feldheim, Mary Ann, and Xiaohu Wang. Ethics and Public Trust: Results from a National Survey. *Public Integrity* 6, 1, 2004: 63-75.

Folks, Susan R. A Potential Whistleblower: To Tell or Not to Tell, That Is the Question. *Public Integrity* 2, 1, 2000: 61-74.

Frederickson, H. George. Public Ethics and the New Managerialism: An Axiomatic Theory. In *Ethics in Public Management*, ed. H. G. Frederickson and R. K. Ghere. Armonk, NY: M. E. Sharpe, 2005: 165-83.

Frederickson, H. George, and Richard K. Ghere, eds. *Ethics in Public Management*. Armonk, NY: M. E. Sharpe, 2005.

Frederickson, H. George, and Meredith A. Newman. The Patriotism of Exit and Voice: The Case of Gloria Flora. *Public Integrity* 3, 4, 2001: 347-62.

Garofalo, Charles, and Dean Geuras. *Ethics in the Public Service.* Washington, DC: Georgetown University Press, 1999.

Geuras, Dean, and Charles Garofalo. *Practical Ethics in Public Administration.* Vienna, VA: Management Concepts, 2002.

Ghere, Richard K. Public Integrity, Privatization, and Partnership: Where Do Ethics Fit? *Public Integrity* 1, 2, 1999: 135-48.

Guttman, Amy, and Dennis Thompson, eds. *Ethics and Politics.* Belmont, CA: Thompson/Wadsworth, 2006.

Heichelbech, James R. Deontology. *Encyclopedia of Public Administration and Public Policy.* New York: Marcel Dekker, 2003.

Heichelbech, James R. Teleology and Utilitarianism. *Encyclopedia of Public Administration and Public Policy.* New York: Marcel Dekker, 2003.

Jensen, Laura S., and Sheila Suess Kennedy. Public Ethics, Legal Accountability, and the New Governance. In *Ethics in Public Management*, ed. H. G. Frederickson and R. K. Ghere. Armonk, NY: M. E. Sharpe, 2005: 220-40.

Johnson, Craig E. *Meeting the Ethical Challenges of Leadership.* Thousand Oaks, CA: Sage, 2005.

Johnson, Terrance A., and Raymond W. Cox III. Police Ethics: Organizational Implications. *Public Integrity* 7, 1, 2004: 67-79.

Josephson, Michael. *Preserving the Public Trust: The Five Principles of Public Service Ethics.* Los Angeles, CA: Josephson Institute of Ethics, 1997-2005.

Jurkiewicz, Carole L., and Roger G. Brown. Power Does Not Corrupt Absolutely: An Empirical Study. *Public Integrity* 2, 3, 2000: 195-210.

Lewis, Carol W., and Stuart Gilman. *The Ethics Challenges in Public Service.* San Francisco, CA: Jossey-Bass, 2005.

Mackenzie, G. Calvin. *Scandal Proof: Do Ethics Laws Make Government Ethical?* Washington, DC: Brookings, 2002.

Meine, Manfred F., Charles A. Watson, and C. W. Cowles. Ethics Training in Local Police Agencies: The Virginia Example. *Public Integrity* 2, 1, 2000: 75-83.

Menzel, Donald C. Ethics Management for Public Administrators: Building Organizations of Integrity. Armonk, NY: M. E. Sharpe, forthcoming 2007.

Menzel, Donald C. Research on Ethics and Integrity in Governance: A Review and Assessment. *Public Integrity* 7, 2, 2005: 147-68.

Menzel, Donald C. A Review and Assessment of Empirical Research on Public Administration Ethics: Implications for Scholars and Managers. *Public Integrity* 1, 3, 1999: 239-64.

Morgan, Peter W., and Glenn H. Reynolds. *The Appearance of Impropriety.* New York: The Free Press, 1997.

Nieuwenburg, Paul. Can Administrative Virtue be Taught? Educating the Virtuous Administrator. *Public Integrity* 3, 5, 2003: 25-38.

Pasquerella, Lynn, and Alfred G. Killilea. The Ethics of Lying in the Public Interest: Reflections on the "Just Lie." *Public Integrity* 7, 3, 2005: 261-73.

Petrick, Joseph A., and John F. Quinn. *Management Ethics: Integrity at Work.* Thousand Oaks, CA: Sage, 1997.

Petter, John. Responsible Behavior in Bureaucrats: An Expanded Conceptual Framework. *Public Integrity* 7, 3, 2005: 197-217.

Plant, Jeremy. Standards of Conduct. *Encyclopedia of Public Administration and Public Policy.* New York: Marcel Dekker, 2003.

Pritchard, Michael S. *Professional Integrity: Thinking Ethically.* Lawrence, KS: University Press of Kansas, 2006.

Richter, William L., and Francis Burke, eds. *Combating Corruption, Encouraging Ethics.* 2d ed. Blue Ridge Summit, PA: Rowman & Littlefield, forthcoming, 2007.

Rohr, John. The Ethical Aftermath of Privatization and Contracting Out: A Constitutional Analysis. *Public Integrity* 4, 1, 2002: 1-12.

Roth, William F. *Ethics in the Workplace: A Systems Perspective.* Upper Saddle River, NJ: Pearson/Prentice Hall, 2005.

Shalala, Donna. The Buck Starts Here: Managing Large Organizations with Honesty and Integrity. *Public Integrity* 6, 4, 2004: 349-56.

Stark, A. *Conflict of Interest in American Public Life.* Cambridge, MA: Harvard University Press, 2000.

Strait, Patricia Bellin. The Voyeur Trilogy, Part Three: Anecdotal Evidence of the Ethical Behavior of Public Employees. *Public Integrity* 1, 2, 1999: 167-74.

Svara, James H. The Ethics Primer for Public Administrators in Government and Nonprofit Organizations. Sudbury, MA: Jones and Bartlett Publishers, forthcoming 2007.

Swisher, Laura Lee, Ann-Marie Rizzo, and Marsha Ann Marley. Moral Reasoning Among Public Administrators: Does One Size Fit All? *Public Integrity* 3, 1, 2001: 53-68.

Thompson, John. *Political Scandal.* Cambridge, UK: Polity Press, 2000.

Tranter, R. A. F. Ethical Problems Today. *Public Management* 69, 1987: 25.

Trevino, L., L. Hartman, and M. Brown. A Qualitative Investigation of Perceived Executive Ethical Leadership: Perceptions from Inside and Outside the Executive Suite. *Human Relations* 1, 2003: 5-38.

Van Wart, Montgomery. *Changing Public Sector Values.* New York: Garland. 1998.

Van Wart, Montgomery. Codes of Ethics as Living Documents. The Case of the American Society for Public Administration. *Public Integrity* 5, 4, 2003: 331-46.

Van Wart, Montgomery. *Dynamics of Leadership in Public Service.* Armonk, NY: M. E. Sharpe, 2005.

West, Jonathan P. Ethics and Human Resource Management. In *Public Personnel Administration*, ed. S. W. Hays and R. C. Kearney. Upper Saddle River, NJ: Prentice Hall, 2003: 301-15.

West, Jonathan P, Evan M. Berman, Stephan Bonczek, and Elizabeth Kellar. Frontiers in Ethics Training. *Public Management* 80, 6, 1998: 4-9.

White, Richard D., Jr. Moral Development Theory. *Encyclopedia of Public Administration and Public Policy.* New York: Marcel Dekker, 2003.

White, Richard D., Jr. Public Ethics, Moral Development, and the Enduring Legacy of Lawrence Kohlberg: Implications for Public Officials. *Public Integrity* 1, 2, 1999: 121-34.

Williams, Russell L. Conflict of Interest. *Encyclopedia of Public Administration and Public Policy.* New York: Marcel Dekker, 2003.

Williams, Russell L. and Mary E. Guy. The Archer's Conundrum: Why Don't More Arrows Add More Virtue? *Public Integrity* 2, 4, 2000: 217-28.

Witmer, Dennis. Developing a Behavioral Model for Ethical Decision Making in Organizations: Conceptual and Empirical Research. In *Ethics in Public Management*, ed. H. G. Frederickson and R. K. Ghere. Armonk, NY: M. E. Sharpe, 2005: 49-69.

Witmer, Dennis. Individual Moral Development: An Empirical Exploration of Public- and Private-Sector Differences. *Public Integrity* 2, 3, 2000: 181-94.

The Ethics Edge
Second Edition

Design and layout: Will Kemp
Text type: Slimbach, Interstate

Printer: HBP, Inc., Hagerstown, MD